Philip Bounds is a historian, journa
Politics from the University of Wales and is the author of a number of books, including *British Communism and the Politics of Literature, Notes from the End of History* and *Cultural Studies.* He has recently co-edited *British Marxism and Cultural Studies.*

'First and foremost, this study can be warmly recommended to Orwell scholars and to those wanting a well-balanced and detailed survey of communist thought that informed Orwell and his period. Dr Bounds negotiates the minefield that is communist influence with a delicacy that would have impressed Agag and he writes with a direct simplicity that is particularly engaging. I was far better informed having read this book than when I began... this is an excellent study, balanced and well considered, and can be warmly recommended to readers.'
Professor Peter Davison, *American Communist History*

'Bounds's book is wide-ranging, stimulating and well written.'
Professor Richard Vinen, *Times Literary Supplement*

'A really impressive piece of work. This is one of the best books on Orwell I have read recently. An important contribution that points the direction Orwell studies should take.'
John Newsinger, Professor of History, Bath Spa University

Philip Bounds

Orwell & Marxism

The Political and Cultural Thinking of George Orwell

I.B. TAURIS
LONDON · NEW YORK

New paperback edition published in 2016 by
I.B.Tauris & Co. Ltd
London • New York
www.ibtauris.com

First published in hardback in 2009 by I.B.Tauris & Co. Ltd

ISBN: 978 1 78453 704 3
eISBN: 978 0 85773 282 8
ePDF: 978 0 85771 535 7

A full CIP record for this book is available from the British Library
A full CIP record is available from the Library of Congress

Library of Congress Catalog Card Number: available

Printed and bound by CPI Group (UK) Ltd, Croydon, CR0 4YY
from camera-ready copy edited and supplied by the author

FSC www.fsc.org MIX Paper from responsible sources FSC® C013604

FOR MY PARENTS,
AND FOR DAISY

CONTENTS

ACKNOWLEDGEMENTS

I am especially grateful to Noorul Hasan for his comments on an earlier draft of this book. I have also benefited greatly from the encouragement, help and support of the late Margaret Bounds, Andy Croft, Alan Finlayson, Liz Friend-Smith, Vincent Geoghegan, Aftab Hamid, Jayne Hill, Mala Jagmohan, Heather Jordan, Alan Mauro, Ian and Tania Morgan, Edward Parr, Jonathan Smith, Richard Taylor and Ieuan Williams. My parents were as supportive as ever – I thank them for everything. I owe a similar debt to Daisy Hasan, whose selfless generosity ensured that I persevered to the end.

Orwell…is and probably always will be a critic of literature who, while not a communist, has nevertheless corresponding preoccupations.

Q.D. Leavis, *The Literary Life Respectable: Mr George Orwell* (1940)

…the most lively criticism [of the last ten years] has nearly all of it been the work of Marxist writers, people like Christopher Caudwell and Philip Henderson and Edward Upward, who look on every book virtually as a political pamphlet and are far more interested in digging out its political and social implications than in its literary qualities in the narrow sense.

George Orwell, *The Frontiers of Art and Propaganda* (1941)

…Marxism is seen in the middle of the intellectual conflict. Bourgeois thought is shown to be dominated by Marxism: whether it steals from it, or distorts it, or abuses it, Marxism is the intellectual power from which there is no escape.

Alick West, *Marxism and Modern Thought* (1935)

I personally would agree with Professor Macmurray that humanity must move in the direction of Communism or perish…

George Orwell, Review of *The Clue of History* by John Macmurray (1939)

INTRODUCTION

George Orwell is at once the most widely read and curiously neglected of all modern cultural critics. Although he is still primarily known as the author of *Animal Farm* and *Nineteen Eighty-Four*, there is a thriving market for his prolific writings on literary and cultural themes. Yet his record as a cultural thinker is often entirely overlooked in modern universities (at least in Britain and the USA), where students are rarely asked to assess his contribution to Literary and Cultural Studies. The most influential historians of these subjects seem similarly uninterested in his work. There is no reference of any kind to Orwell in the relevant volume of René Wellek's magisterial *History of Modern Criticism 1750–1950*, nor in the lengthy surveys of the development of Cultural Studies which now appear with increasing frequency. Orwell's omission from the history of Cultural Studies is especially puzzling, since (as was once widely acknowledged) his pioneering essays on popular culture made a decisive contribution to getting the subject started. He has effectively been made an unperson by his own literary heirs.

There are several reasons for the academic neglect from which Orwell's work currently suffers. One of the most important is that Orwell is extremely difficult to integrate into the historical narrative. At a time when historians of Cultural Studies are still preoccupied with identifying different 'schools' and the relationship between them, he is widely regarded as an out-and-out maverick whose writings had nothing in common with those of other cultural critics. The perception of Orwell as an intellectual outsider has a lot to do with his legendary political independence. In spite of being one of the greatest socialist teachers of the age, his most salient characteristic was his deep unease with his own side. Uncomfortably aware of the totalitarian perversions to which socialism is susceptible (and determined to write about them at every possible opportunity), he loathed his fellow intellectuals on the left, recoiled instinctively from all forms of party discipline and generally took great pleasure in what his biographer Bernard Crick has called 'rub[bing] his own cat's fur the wrong way'.[1] He was the ultimate outsider in politics – insecure, scornful of orthodoxies, cussedly independent. It is hardly surprising that intellectual historians should treat him with such suspicion. The most persuasive scholarly attack on his non-joining individualism occurs in Raymond Williams's brief book *Orwell* (1971), written at the point when Williams was first formulating the principles of what he came to call his 'cultural materialism'. According to Williams, Orwell's life and work illustrate the inherent weaknesses of upper-class radicalism. Having conceived a bitter hatred of his own class, Orwell gravitated to the left and made a genuine attempt to turn himself into a socialist, only to discover that he was incapable of forging meaningful ties with working people and his new political associates. The inevitable result was that he slowly drifted back to the public-school prejudices of his youth, ending his career with what Williams regarded as unconscionable attacks on socialism in *Animal Farm* and *Nineteen Eighty-Four*.[2] Indeed, some years after *Orwell* was published, Williams pronounced himself so disillusioned with its subject that he now found his work 'unreadable'.[3]

The purpose of this book is to show that academic suspicion of Orwell is misplaced and that his cultural writings have been neglected for too long. It seeks to make its case in two ways. On the one hand it provides a lengthy introduction to Orwell's cultural thinking, showing that his ideas about literature, class, popular culture and a range of other subjects were simultaneously tough-minded and informed by a solidly political purpose. On the other hand, even at the risk of seeming deeply counterintuitive, it seeks to qualify the assumption that Orwell's political eccentricities made his critical project a wholly idiosyncratic one. While Orwell was indeed a lifelong outsider and a persistent critic of his own side (and deserves to be honoured for it), it is simply not true that his writings about culture bore no resemblance to those of his socialist contemporaries. It could even be argued that he owed a special intellectual debt to the very people on the left to whom he was most opposed politically. More precisely, I argue throughout this book that there are some striking parallels between Orwell's cultural writings and those of the young literary intellectuals who were either members of, or closely associated with, the Communist Party of Great Britain (CPGB) in the 1930s and 1940s. These writers had a major influence on English literary culture in the ten years or so after 1935 and were studied extensively by Orwell. The most famous were probably Alick West, Ralph Fox, Christopher Caudwell, Edgell Rickword, Jack Lindsay, and T.A. Jackson, though there were perhaps twenty others who also made an important contribution to English Marxist cultural theory.[4] My argument is that their influence on Orwell was so profound that his cultural writings can in one sense be interpreted as a sort of a dialogue with them. Aware that the communists had achieved what turned out to be a temporary dominance of English cultural life, Orwell produced a body of critical writings which implicitly addressed their main concerns and provided a fresh perspective on their main ideas. In practice he tended to respond to their writings in one of three ways. Surprisingly often he seemed to agree with what they said and tried to rework or extend their main arguments, nearly always achieving a much higher level of critical insight in the process. By contrast, there were other occasions on which he violently *disagreed* with the communists and developed a critical position which directly contradicted them. More rarely, in a manner which perhaps betrayed a certain carelessness in his reading habits, he misunderstood the communist perspective and used what were effectively non-existent arguments as the basis of his own position.[5] I am not suggesting that Orwell was any less anti-communist than he is usually regarded as being, nor that the British communists were the only important influences on his cultural thinking. I am certainly not claiming that the communists were the only Marxist or *Marxisant* thinkers whose ideas he found valuable.[6] What I *am* suggesting is that English cultural Marxism provides an essential context (perhaps even the most important context of all) in which his work must be read.[7]

How can we be sure that Orwell was familiar with the work of the British communists? One of the many virtues of the twenty-volume edition of *The Complete Works of George Orwell*, edited by Peter Davison and published by Secker and Warburg in 1998, is that it proves beyond any doubt that Orwell took a steady interest in communist literature from the early 1930s onwards. A list of the communist and semi-communist authors whom he either discussed, reviewed or in some other way referred to would include Christopher Caudwell, Alec Brown, Christopher Hill, T.A. Jackson, John Strachey, Jack Lindsay, Wal Hannington, Mulk Raj Anand, Claud Cockburn, Philip Henderson, D.S. Mirsky, Edgell Rickword, Edward Upward, D.N. Pritt, Charles Madge, Arthur Calder-Marshall, Joseph Needham, V. Gordon Childe, J.D. Bernal and R. Palme Dutt. He also made frequent references to communist newspapers and journals such as *Left Review*, *Labour Monthly*, the

Daily Worker and *The Modern Quarterly*. In a radio broadcast in 1941 he even claimed that the 'most lively criticism' of the previous decade had 'nearly all of it been the work of Marxist writers', taking Caudwell, Henderson and Upward as his examples.[8] On most of the occasions when I relate Orwell's writings on culture to the broader Marxist tradition, I will thus be invoking authors whom we know for certain that Orwell read. However, as Jonathan Rose has pointed out in a fine essay on the sources of *Nineteen Eighty-Four*, anyone who tries to speculate about Orwell's intellectual influences will also have to refer from time to time to 'invisible' sources – that is, sources which we cannot be sure that Orwell read but which nevertheless bear marked similarities to his work.[9] Where sources of this type are concerned, I have confined myself to citing works whose thematic correspondences to Orwell's writings are too dramatic to overlook. It is not necessary to assume that Orwell had first-hand knowledge of all these works, simply that he had learned about their contents through one channel or another. As anyone who has participated in it will be able to confirm, the hard left in Britain (as in most other countries) is largely made up of intensely cerebral people who take a deep interest in their rivals' perspectives. Even in the 1930s, when the relevant literature was less readily available than it is today, socialists closely monitored the work of their counterparts in other organisations and ideas circulated freely across boundaries of party and doctrine. Since Orwell had a very large number of left-wing acquaintances, some of whom were close friends and some of whom were card-carrying communists, it seems probable that he often absorbed communist ideas simply by being told about them in conversation. It should also be remembered that Marxism enjoyed a position of considerable intellectual pre-eminence in the Western world in the fifty or so years after 1917. As a result of the October Revolution, which rescued it from the obscurity in which it had begun to sink, it came to be regarded by many thinkers as what Alick West once called 'the intellectual power from which there is no escape.'[10] Even people who deeply disagreed with it often found it necessary to define their own ideas against it – and sometimes (as West pointed out) to appropriate its insights without acknowledgement and in a distorted form. This makes it all the more likely that a young intellectual like Orwell would have tried to acquire a full understanding of communist doctrine.

There is one obvious question which needs to be answered before we move on. If the British communists had such a profound influence on Orwell's cultural writings, why has it been overlooked? The answer is that it has not been overlooked – or at least not entirely. Significantly enough, several of Orwell's contemporaries noted his debt to the communists in early reviews of his work. It was Q.D. Leavis, of all people, who argued in an admiring review of *Inside the Whale* in *Scrutiny* (September 1940) that Orwell '…is and probably always will be a critic of literature who, while not a communist, has nevertheless corresponding preoccupations'.[11] By contrast, in a much less complimentary piece in the *New English Weekly* (14 March 1940), Philip Mairet observed that 'He [i.e. Orwell] is really a sociological writer, but the only traces of sociological theory that his work exhibits are remains of a Marxism which he has almost outgrown and which it is doubtful if he ever more than half accepted.'[12] There have also been several references to Orwell's relationship to the communists in post-war academic literature, though most of them take the form of unsupported assertions. For example, Jon Wain observed in 1963 that 'Orwell was, in fact, very close in spirit to the other writers of his generation, though the closeness has been obscured by the different turn he took after 1945'.[13] Alok Rai endorsed Wain's argument in *Orwell and the Politics of Despair* (1988), noting that Orwell's account of middle-class unemployment in the *New English Weekly* was very similar to that of Edgell Rickword in a 1934 article in *Left Review*.[14] Even Maurice Cowling, one of Orwell's sternest conservative critics, recently pointed out that 'his [i.e. Orwell's] life even more than his writings was a theatrical enactment of the intelligentsia preoccupations he despised in others…'[15] More importantly, John Newsinger has written at some length about Orwell's polemical exchanges with J.D. Bernal and Randall Swingler in 1945 and 1946.[16] However, the only real attempt to gauge Orwell's borrowings from the communists is Andy Croft's remarkable essay 'Worlds Without End Foisted Upon the Future – Some Antecedents of *Nineteen Eighty-Four*' (1984), which meticulously describes a wealth of Marxist and *Marxisant* novels (most of them from the 1930s and now completely forgotten) which clearly anticipated the world of Big Brother, O'Brien and the Thought Police.[17] Apart from that there is nothing.[18]

The failure of more than a handful of writers to explore the links between Orwell and the communists is not difficult to explain. The most obvious reason is that Orwell's political identity prevents us from appreciating the full scope of his intellectual interests. Because he was a passionate anti-Stalinist, one of the doughtiest opponents not merely of the USSR but of the world communist movement as a whole, we tend to believe that he cannot have been influenced – except negatively – by the things which communists said or wrote. There is also the fact that he often launched vicious attacks not merely on British Marxists in general but on the very writers and critics to whom he actually owed a substantial debt.[19] Quite apart from his hilarious onslaught on sandal wearers, fruit-juice drinkers and nudists in *The Road To Wigan Pier* (1937), there were also his withering observations in *The Lion and the Unicorn* about English intellectuals who 'take their cookery from Paris and their opinions from Moscow.'[20] By the same token, British communists have cheerfully resorted to libelling Orwell on various occasions over the last seventy years. The attacks began with Harry Pollitt's notoriously bad-tempered review of *The Road to Wigan Pier* in the *Daily Worker* (March 17 1937), which described Orwell as a 'disillusioned little middle-class boy' who would have to 'try to learn himself before he takes on the role of new up-to-date Socialist mentor and professor.'[21] They continued with R. Palme Dutt's uncomprehending denunciation of *Nineteen Eighty-Four* in the *Guardian* (January 5 1955), A.L. Morton's similarly misconceived remarks on the novel in *The English Utopia* (1952), James Walsh's apoplectic survey of the Orwellian oeuvre in *The Marxist Quarterly* (1956) and Christopher Norris's venomous symposium *Inside the Myth* (1984).[22] Even as late as 2003, on the occasion of Orwell's centenary, there was an article in the *Morning Star* which strongly implied that Orwell co-operated with the fascists during the Spanish Civil War. The British communists have done more than anyone else to portray Orwell as a sort of Tory fifth-columnist in the camp of the working class. The aim of this book is to show that they were also one of his biggest influences.

British Communism and the Politics of Culture

There are two things which need to be done before we can examine Orwell's debt to the communists in detail. The first is to provide a brief sketch of the particular tradition of Marxist criticism to which his work is being related. Although there was nothing systematic about Orwell's engagement with this tradition, the ideas he chose to invoke (and the work of the writers who developed them) cannot be fully understood except in this broader context. It is also necessary to say something about the development of Orwell's political ideas, since his writings on literature and culture were always underpinned by what he famously termed his 'political purpose'. Moreover, an account of Orwell's politics will serve to remind us that his intellectual debt to the communists was never translated into political sympathy – except perhaps for a brief period in 1936.

An identifiable group of communist writers, critics and cultural theorists began to emerge in Britain in the early 1920s, though it was not until the 1930s that it achieved real distinction. The single biggest influence on the work of this group was the CPGB's relationship to the world communist movement in general and the USSR in particular – a relationship which briefly needs placing in its historical context. The CPGB was established in 1920, nearly three years after the October Revolution.[23] Most of its members were initially drawn from existing hard-left organisations such as the British Socialist Party (BSP), the Socialist Labour Party (SLP) and the Workers' Socialist Federation (WSF). The Party's political identity was determined for much of its first 25 years by its membership of the Communist International or 'Comintern'. Established in 1919 to co-ordinate the work of the new wave of pro-Soviet communist parties, the Comintern was based in Moscow and dominated by Soviet politicians. Its main function was to determine the political strategies which its member parties should follow in their respective national contexts. (The 16th of its 21 conditions of membership famously stipulated that 'All decisions of the Communist International are binding on member parties.')[24] Although there is no truth in the assumption that British communists were merely 'Moscow stooges' (a point which has been proven beyond all doubt by the relatively new school of what some writers have called 'revisionist' CPGB historiography),[25] it is nevertheless the case that all the CPGB's early 'lines' were ultimately decided outside Britain. It was only with the dissolution of the Comintern in 1943 that the British communists acquired genuine political autonomy.

The influence of the Comintern extended not merely to the CPGB's political activities but to its cultural work as well.[26] This was largely for two reasons. On the one hand, either implicitly or explicitly, the political strategies which the Comintern imposed on its member parties always had a cultural dimension – that is, it was always assumed that the strategy of the day would not be successful unless communists intervened at the level of culture as well as at the levels of economics and politics. On the other hand, especially from the late 1920s onwards, the Soviet government went out of its way to develop an arts policy which communists throughout the world were expected to follow. As far as cultural criticism was concerned, the first really distinctive period in the development of the CPGB's approach to culture (and the first to significantly influence Orwell) occurred between 1928 and 1933. The defining characteristic of this period was the attempt to adapt cultural work to the needs of the Comintern's notoriously sectarian 'Class Against Class' policy.[27] For much of the period between 1920 and 1928, British communists had followed a 'united front' strategy which obliged them to co-operate with the established institutions of the Labour Movement – the Labour Party, the trade unions and so on. The Class-Against-Class years brought all this to an end. On the assumption that world capitalism had entered a deep crisis from which recovery was simply impossible, British communists were now instructed to (1) cease their efforts to co-operate with and affiliate to the Labour Party (which it now dismissed as a 'social fascist' organisation), (2) establish 'revolutionary' trade unions in opposition to the existing 'reformist' unions, and (3) prepare to assume the leadership of the working class in what was regarded as an imminent socialist revolution. The consequence of this descent into ultra-leftism was a disastrous reduction in influence which saw the Party's membership dwindle to 2555 by November 1930. However, in the sphere of cultural politics, the Class-Against-Class period was one of limited but real advance. Intent on creating a 'proletarian culture' that was independent from mainstream leisure institutions and the wider Labour Movement, the CPGB either established or assumed control of the British Workers' Sports Federation (BWSF), the Workers' Theatre Movement (WTM) and a whole host of workers' film societies in the years between 1928 and 1933. Its intellectuals also began to produce literary and cultural criticism in large quantities. From the point of view of Orwell scholarship, the most important aspect of this body of work was its emphasis on the idea of cultural crisis. Anxious to show that capitalism's terminal decline extended not merely to economics but to all other levels of society (and therefore to prove that the age was 'rotten ripe' for socialism), many communists began to argue that culture in all its forms had become so degraded that only a revolution could set it on the road to recovery. Although the idea of cultural crisis was central to the work of such Class-Against-Class critics as P.R. Stephensen,[28] John Cornford[29] and Montagu Slater,[30] its most distinguished exponent was probably the 'fellow traveller' John Strachey, whose classic book *The Coming Struggle for Power* (1932) achieved a very large readership. In Part Three of the book, entitled 'The Decay of Capitalist Culture', Strachey cast a gloomy eye over the state of modern religion, science and literature, insisting that religion had fallen into decline because its role in reinforcing the status quo had now become too readily apparent, that the fruits of scientific knowledge were no longer receiving practical expression (in consequence of the slump) and that modernist writers such as Proust, Lawrence and Huxley had lost the ability to convey a 'tragic view of life'. His attack on modern literature continued in *Literature and Dialectical Materialism* (1932), where he argued that the work of many contemporary writers displayed alarming fascist or *fascisant* tendencies. As we shall see, one of Strachey's remarks in *The Coming Struggle for Power* was approvingly invoked by Orwell in *The Road to Wigan Pier* and arguably did a great deal to shape the argument of *Nineteen Eighty-Four*.[31]

There were two factors which brought about a fundamental change in communist attitudes towards culture from 1934 onwards. The first was the development of a new arts policy by the Soviet government. The outlines of the new policy were announced at the famous Soviet Writers' Congress in Moscow in August 1934, primarily in the keynote speeches by A.A. Zhdanov, Maxim Gorky, Nikolai Bukharin and Karl Radek. (An English translation of the conference proceedings was published in London in 1935 under the title *Problems of Soviet Literature*. It proved to be the single biggest influence on British communist critics until at least the end of the decade.)[32] At the core of the new policy was the demand that all communist artists should adopt the conventions of 'Socialist Realism'.[33] Defined by Zhdanov as a wholly new form which aimed to 'depict reality in its revolutionary development',[34] Socialist Realism was characterised by the use of traditional techniques to express a 'Marxist-Leninist' message. The basic assumption of the Soviet theorists was that the masses could only be drawn into political activity by an ambitiously *synoptic* form of art – that is, one which provided an overview of the 'dialectical' relationship between the various levels of the existing social system. It therefore followed that writers and artists should illuminate the struggle for socialism by producing work which (1) interpreted reality from a Marxist perspective (the principle of *ideinost*), (2) illustrated the leading role of the working class in the creation of a socialist society (the principle of *klassovost*), (3) took its broad political line from the Communist Party (the principle of *partiinost*), and (4) strove to be as accessible as possible to ordinary working people (the principle of *narodnost*). Moreover, at the level of form, Soviet artists were expected to ignore the technical innovations of modernism and employ established techniques such as rhyme and rhythm, linear narrative and renaissance perspective. The result was the well-nigh worthless parade of genres which disfigured Soviet culture for so long – reverential portraits of Lenin or Stalin, sentimental novels about life on collective farms, improbable evocations of muscular 'positive heroes' in state-of-the-art factories.

If the main purpose of the Writers' Congress was to prescribe the characteristics of Socialist Realism, there was also a sustained effort to identify the sort of *philosophical*, *historical* and *comparative* arguments which could justify the new form. At the level of philosophy, Nikolai Bukharin tried to formulate an 'official' understanding of art by combining several important concepts from the history of aesthetic thought. His first move was to affirm that all art is essentially a 'reflection' of the real world – in the process implying that nothing could be more appropriate than for the artist to engage with politics. Rejecting the Kantian assumption that aesthetic experience is largely 'disinterested' (that is, devoid of 'desire or will' – the phrase is Hegel's), he went on to argue that the artist's main purpose is to express his feelings about the world around him. More precisely, in defining art as an expression of 'active militant force', he implied that the most exalted function of art is to stir up discontent with existing circumstances and stimulate the desire for social change. Finally, shifting his attention to more technical matters, Bukharin also endorsed the old Hegelian assumption that a work of art depends for its success on a unified relationship between form and content. By insisting that an artist's chosen techniques are only appropriate if they allow him to convey his message swiftly and clearly, he obviously intended to justify the technical conservatism of the new Soviet art in the face of modernist demands for formal experimentation.[35]

The purpose of the historical element in Soviet thinking was to portray Socialist Realism as the latest instalment in a rich tradition of oppositional art. Making good use of their immense knowledge of the history of Russian culture, Maxim Gorky and others argued that the new generation of Soviet artists had inherited the mantle of such distinguished artistic dissidents as Tolstoy, Chernyshevsky, Repin and Yaroshenko. More surprisingly, Gorky also tried to legitimise Socialist Realism by speculating about the role of art in primitive societies. His special interest was in the nature of myths. Rejecting the idea that primitive man was essentially a sort of 'philosophising idealist and mystic' (that is, someone wholly preoccupied with the influence of supernatural forces), Gorky argued that the primary function of myth was to express a plebeian yearning for the domination of nature. Myths, he pointed out, were full of scenes in which human beings employed fantastical methods in order to overcome the elements – some wore 'seven-league boots' and strode across vast distances in a matter of seconds, others made magic carpets and learned how to fly. The effect of these scenes was at once psychological and practical. Apart from providing temporary respite from the uncomfortable realities of primitive labour, they also stimulated real improvements to the forces of production. Since art clearly fulfilled an economic function at the very moment of its origin, or so Gorky implied, it follows that Socialist Realism is less a distortion of the aesthetic ideal than its ultimate realisation.[36] These arguments were supplemented by the comparative element in Soviet criticism, which essentially carried forward the emphasis on cultural crisis which had characterised the Class-Against-Class period. According to the Soviet critics, whose argument probably alienated thousands of potential supporters, Soviet culture was taking the arts to dizzy new heights while capitalist culture was reducing them to barbarism. The deadliest symptom of capitalism's decline was the emergence of modernism, which Karl Radek famously dismissed (in the course of some notorious remarks about Joyce's *Ulysses*) as a despicably lavatorial form whose main purpose was to induce a mood of 'neutrality' in the face of political and economic crisis.[37] The message was clear. If artists in all countries wished to produce meaningful work, they had no choice but to embrace the new Soviet vision of progressive art. They had to become Socialist Realists.

The publication of *Problems of Soviet Literature* launched an entirely new phase in the development of British communist criticism. For much of the period between 1935 and the end of the 1930s (and arguably for much longer), British communists aspired to deepen the insights of Soviet theory by combining them with ideas drawn from their own cultural traditions. (This willingness to combine Marxist and non-Marxist perspectives was a further sign that the British communists were never merely slavish in their attitude to the USSR.) The birth of British Marxist literary theory is generally traced to 1937, which saw the publication of three pioneering texts: Christopher Caudwell's *Illusion and Reality*, Alick West's *Crisis and Criticism* and Ralph Fox's *The Novel and the People*. Fox's book was the most straightforwardly pro-Soviet of the three, making the case for Socialist Realism and arguing (or at least implying) that the novel is better suited than any other form to the expression of socialist beliefs.[38] West's *Crisis and Criticism* was altogether more impressive, not least because of its startling variation on Bukharin's theory of the unity of form and content. (Its argument was that literature is ultimately inspired by the majesty of economic production. Since literary form is always modelled on the prevailing techniques of production, or so West insisted, it follows that the only successful works are those which seek to evoke the progressive elements in the existing economic system.)[39] More impressive still was Caudwell's *Illusion and Reality*, which (in line with the Soviet attack on 'disinterested' theories of art) portrayed poetry as a form which adapts our unruly instincts to the limits of the environment.[40] Other attempts to develop Soviet theory occurred in a series of less important books, notably Philip Henderson's *The Novel Today* (1936), Jack Lindsay's *A Short History of Culture* (1939) and C. Day Lewis's symposium *The Mind in Chains* (1937). There was also a flurry of important articles in the journal *Left Review*, which had been founded in 1934 as the official publication of the British Section of the Writers' International.[41] Cultural matters even received regular attention in the pages of the *Daily Worker*, whose books section was described by Raphael Samuel as late as 1985 as 'quite excellent'.[42]

The second major influence on British communist criticism in the years before the War was the Comintern's introduction of its so-called 'People's Front' strategy. One of the many baleful consequences of the Class-Against-Class line was that it divided the European left at a time when fascism was beginning to win mass support. These divisions proved especially disastrous in Germany, where the German Communist Party (KPD) responded to Hitler's bid for power by rejecting all calls for an anti-fascist alliance with other forces on the left. First formulated at the Seventh Congress of the Comintern in 1935 (specifically in a keynote address by the Bulgarian communist Georgi Dimitrov), the new People's Front strategy aimed to bring this sort of sectarianism to an end. It was rooted in two simple propositions. The first was that the main immediate goal of the communist movement was to resist the advance of fascism, not least by defending democratic institutions in the countries where they still existed. The second was that fascism could only be successfully resisted by the widest possible alliance of all the 'democratic' forces ranged against it, including those on the centre and centre-right which communists normally regarded as their natural political enemies. As we shall see in Chapter One, this emphasis on the building of alliances was supplemented by a far-reaching programme of cultural radicalism.[43] According to Dimitrov, fascist organisations had sunk deep roots among sections of the masses by disseminating a perverted form of patriotism. The only viable response was for communists to embrace a new form of democratic patriotism, primarily by drawing attention to the rich traditions of popular radicalism in their respective countries. The result in Britain was an outpouring of work on the 'English radical tradition', some of it concerned with the history of plebeian movements (e.g. the Levellers, the Diggers and the Chartists) and some of it with the radical instincts of leading British writers.[44] Among the several important books and pamphlets which addressed these themes, the most widely read were probably A.L. Morton's *A People's History of England* (1938), Jack Lindsay's *John Bunyan: Maker of Myths* (1937), T.A. Jackson's *Charles Dickens: The Progress of a Radical* (1937) and Lindsay's pamphlet *England my England* (1937). There was also a series of articles on radical writers in *Left Review* and the *Daily Worker*, those in the latter being published under the title 'The Past is Ours'.[45] Although much of this work tended to blur the distinction between history and propaganda, we know that it greatly inspired the generation of Marxist historians who put the study of English radicalism on the academic map in the twenty or so years after the war – Eric Hobsbawm, E.P. Thompson and Christopher Hill among them. This makes the obscurity into which it has fallen all the more bewildering.

The history of communist criticism in the period between 1939 and 1950 (that is, between the outbreak of the Second World War and Orwell's premature death) was one of steadily increasing influence followed by a precipitous decline. In Britain generally, the early years of the War witnessed an extraordinary and largely successful attempt to nourish public interest in high culture. Under the auspices of state-funded organisations such as the Council for the Encouragement of Music and the Arts (CEMA) and the Entertainments National Service Association (ENSA), professional actors and musicians gave scores of well-attended performances in factories, army barracks and other provincial locations. Exhibitions of painting and sculpture were held throughout the country, while a number of daily newspapers (including the *Evening Standard* and the *Daily Mirror*) carried popularising articles on history, literature and the other arts. Members and supporters of the CPGB played a well-documented role in this brief cultural renaissance. One of their most important initiatives was the launch of the monthly magazine *Our Time* (February 1941 – July/August 1949), which for some years succeeded in bringing Marxist criticism to a paying readership of at least 15,000 people. The critical articles which appeared in the magazine were broadly of two kinds. On the one hand, seeking to extend the pioneering work of the People's Front years, Edgell Rickword, Jack Lindsay, T.A. Jackson and others contributed important studies of radical writers such as Blake, Bunyan and Dickens. By contrast, and altogether more surprisingly, there was also a concerted effort to transcend the aesthetic sectarianism of the previous decade. Abandoning the opposition between

Socialist Realism and modernism which had defined Marxist criticism in the wake of the Soviet Writers' Congress, several British communists began to argue that a radical culture in Britain could only be built along pluralist lines. The most surprising sign of the new mood of tolerance was the reverence which *Our Time* now showed to Pablo Picasso, whose great work *Guernica* had famously been dismissed by Anthony Blunt in 1937 as a symptom of bourgeois decadence.[46]

The vigour and energy of *Our Time* helped to attract a new generation of literary intellectuals to the CPGB. Prominent among them were such important figures as E.P. Thompson, Arnold Rattenbury, Jack Beeching and Charles Hobday. Immediately after the War, in the mood of optimism engendered by the Labour Party's victory in the 1945 General Election, several of the new recruits joined with a core of older members to form the so-called 'Salisbury Group' of Party writers, which seems to have exercised considerable influence in the literary London of the day. Moreover, the Party's reputation as a haven for talented critics was reinforced throughout the 1940s by the publication of a number of pioneering books and pamphlets, including George Thomson's *Aeschylus and Athens* (1940), A.L. Lloyd's *The Singing Englishman* (1943), Jack Lindsay's *A Perspective for Poetry* (1944) and A.L. Morton's *Language of Men* (1945). However, as Andy Croft has pointed out, the CPGB's thriving artistic and critical subculture had been all but destroyed by the end of the decade. The root cause of its sudden implosion was a hardening of cultural attitudes in the USSR. Early in 1947, in his capacity as Stalin's Minister of Culture, A.A. Zhdanov gave a series of brutally intolerant speeches in which he reaffirmed the USSR's commitment to Socialist Realism, attacked all forms of modernism and called for a 'battle of ideas' against bourgeois influences in culture. The CPGB responded by establishing a National Cultural Committee (there had been no similar body in the 1930s) and manning it with machine politicians whose expertise in cultural matters was severely limited. This immediately resulted in a sort of artistic civil war in the Party, with the new breed of NCC apparatchiks (e.g. Emile Burns, Sam Aaronovitch and Maurice Cornforth) trying to bully the cultural workers into wholesale acceptance of the Soviet line. The inevitable consequence was a mass evacuation of talent.[47] Although the CPGB would make further important contributions to British culture in the forty years which remained to it, its hopes of installing itself in the literary and cultural mainstream effectively came to an end at about the same time that George Orwell died.

Orwell and Socialism: A Biographical Sketch

Although the internal culture of the CPGB was never as authoritarian as its detractors tended to claim, there is no doubt that British communists placed a premium on such things as collective loyalty, discipline and unity. George Orwell's approach to politics could scarcely have been more different. The story of his engagement with the left is essentially the story of what John Carey has called a 'misfit by vocation.'[48] Orwell's conversion to socialism had its roots in his feelings of being excluded from his own class, combined with a deep romantic attachment to the culture of working people. Having grappled with his own quietist instincts in order to transform himself into a political writer, he could always be relied upon to embrace minority opinions, excoriate the mainstream left and act as a one-man opposition in whichever organisation he happened to sympathise with. Far from confining himself to making a positive case for socialism, he spent much of his time describing the totalitarian impulses which threatened to corrupt the left from within. Whatever else he might have been, the author of *Animal Farm* and *Nineteen Eighty-Four* was never a 'good party man'.

Escaping from the Middle Class

George Orwell was born Eric Arthur Blair on June 25 1903 in Motihari, India, though he spent most of his first eighteen years in the South of England.[49] As he famously observed in the autobiographical sections of *The Road to Wigan Pier* (1937), his family belonged to what he called the 'lower-upper-middle class'.[50] Although his father Richard enjoyed a certain amount of prestige as a result of working for the Indian Civil Service (specifically as an official in the Opium Department), his income was always comparatively meagre. Since his wife Ida did not go out to work (and since there were two children other than Eric to bring up), there was always a sense in which the Blairs were struggling against the odds to project the requisite air of gentility. The disparity between the family's status and its income became cruelly apparent to the young Orwell when he was sent away at the age of eight to St Cyprian's, an intensely snobbish preparatory school in Eastbourne. Run on profit-making lines by Mr and Mrs Vaughan Wilkes, St Cyprian's was largely attended by the sons of genuinely wealthy families. The Wilkeses only accepted Orwell because they thought he might enhance the school's reputation by winning a place at a top public school – even then he had to be admitted at reduced fees. In 'Such, Such Were the Joys' (published posthumously in 1952), one of his greatest and certainly most bitter essays, Orwell made it clear that his time at St Cyprian's had been marked by endless petty humiliations over his family's lack of wealth. Whenever he seemed not to be working hard enough, Mrs Wilkes would remind him that a boy with indigent parents could ill afford to 'slack off'. He never received as much pocket money as his contemporaries (even though his parents had 'not given instructions to this effect'),[51] nor did he ever receive a special cake on his birthday – a privilege that was accorded to most of the other boys as a matter of course. Worst of all were the tauntings of his wealthier classmates, who were already 'intimately, intelligently snobbish' about gradations in middle-class income:

> I recall a conversation that must have taken place about a year before I left St. Cyprian's. A Russian boy, large and fair-haired, a year older than myself, was questioning me:
>
> 'How much a year has your father got?'
>
> I told him what I thought it was, adding a few hundreds to make it sound better. The Russian boy, neat in his habits, produced a pencil and a small notebook and made a calculation.
>
> 'My father has over two hundred times as much money as yours,' he announced with a sort of amused contempt.[52]

Orwell's status as a boy on 'reduced fees' was only one of the things which made him feel like an outsider. He was also deeply affected by an early lesson in how the powerful exercise their rule. In a searingly candid passage at the start of 'Such, Such Were the Joys', he famously recalled being punished for wetting the bed in his first few weeks at St Cyprian's. Although he was clearly not responsible for the act which led to his being beaten with a riding crop ('There was no volition about it, no consciousness'),[53] the whole premise of the punishment was that he had somehow behaved wilfully. Whereas other small boys might have shrugged off the unfairness of it all, Orwell seems to have been traumatised by it. His immediate conclusion was that his bed-wetting marked him out as someone of exceptional moral depravity: 'It was possible, therefore, to commit a sin without knowing that you committed it, without wanting to commit it, and without being able to avoid it. Sin was not necessarily something that you did: it might be something that happened to you.'[54] By holding him responsible for something he never wanted to do in the first place, the Wilkeses had reinforced their power over him by inducing a deep conviction of 'sin and folly and weakness'.[55] What else could he conclude but that he was deeply unworthy of his school, his fellow pupils and his class? It was probably his first major intimation that power and virtue are not necessarily synonymous.

The Wilkeses were right to predict that Orwell would make it to a good public school. In 1915 he won a place at Eton and was a less-than-conscientious King's Scholar there between 1917 and 1921. His time at Eton was a lot less unhappy than his time at St Cyprian's, not least because he played a minor role in the pupils' successful attempt to liberalise the school in the years after the First World War. At this stage he might well have become a more or less conventional member of his class, seeing out his days in the sort of solid but uninspiring job to which his father had devoted nearly forty years. What transformed him into one of the most virulent anti-bourgeois voices of the age were his extraordinary experiences in the five years after leaving Eton. Having passed up the chance to go to university (his parents could not afford the fees and his academic performance at Eton had been mediocre), Orwell spent the years between 1922 and 1927 as a member of the Indian Imperial Police in Burma. It was a job he came to hate. Called upon to enforce a manifestly unjust system and exposed to the worst excesses of English racism, he began to regard his fellow imperialists as a blight on Asian civilisation. All his latent contempt for the middle- and upper classes was brought back to the surface. His mature understanding of imperialism was eventually embodied in an early newspaper article in *Le Progrès Civique* (1929), his first novel *Burmese Days* (1934) and his two great essays 'A Hanging' (1931) and 'Shooting an Elephant' (1936). At one level the message of these writings was very similar to that of other English radicals. Far from being the selfless expression of the 'White Man's Burden' (as Orwell's one-time hero Rudyard Kipling had famously put it), the British empire was actually a vast mechanism for depriving the colonial peoples of their economic resources. As such, it could only be run on the basis of racism and physical brutality – there was no such thing as progressive or enlightened imperialism. The distinctive feature of Orwell's analysis was his belief that imperialism nearly always ends up dehumanising the colonisers themselves. Since one nation can only colonise another by ceaselessly projecting an air of high authoritarian menace, or so the argument went, it follows that the colonisers will often feel obliged to behave brutally even when there is no good reason to do so. The humanity of the colonising nation seeps away simply because certain impressions have to be maintained. Orwell dramatised the point with great delicacy in 'Shooting an Elephant', which recorded one of his most painful memories from his period in the Moulmein region of Burma. After being summoned one morning to deal with an elephant which had been rampaging through the local bazaar, Orwell discovered that its 'attack of "must" was already passing off' and that it posed no further threat. There was no reasonable justification for shooting it, save for the fact that a large crowd of Burmese were urging him on. A harmless elephant was duly dispatched to its maker because the imperial mask could not be allowed to slip:

> ...it was at this moment, as I stood there with the rifle in my hands, that I first grasped the hollowness, the futility of the white man's dominion in the East. Here was I, the white man with his gun, standing in front of the unarmed native crowd – seemingly the leading actor of the piece; but in reality I was only an absurd puppet pushed to and fro by the will of those yellow faces behind. I perceived in this moment that when the white man turns tyrant it is his own freedom that he destroys.[56]

Orwell's resignation from the Imperial Police took effect on the first day of 1928, though he had returned to England on leave in the Summer of the previous year. He had two immediate priorities. The first was to set about launching his career as a writer. The second was to acquire a first-hand knowledge of the lives of the dispossessed. At various times between the Autumn of 1927 and the Spring of 1932 he spent lengthy periods posing as a member of the 'down and out' and mixing with what we might now call the 'underclass' – tramps, the homeless and the long-term unemployed. Although he always knew that he could escape the world of absolute poverty if he wanted to (except for a period in the Autumn of 1929 when he seems to have hit rock bottom while living in Paris),[57] he was careful not to shirk the worst aspects of the underclass experience. Dressed in the filthiest clothes he could muster he trudged the roads with tramps, begged for food, slept rough in Trafalgar Square, worked as a hop-picker in Kent and a dishwasher in Paris, endured long hours in filthy common lodging houses and even spent a night in police custody for public drunkenness. He later claimed that his main motivation for this extraordinary experiment in downward mobility was a profound sense of guilt.[58] After serving the interests of a corrupt ruling class in Burma, he felt that he could only atone for his crimes by sinking to the bottom of society and steeling himself against its horrors. What he tended to leave unsaid was that his behaviour was also that of a classic romantic outsider. Feeling rejected by his own class (as well as morally outraged by it), Orwell was clearly looking to working people to provide him with a new and more humane way of life. Nor was he disappointed. While he never lost sight of the truly awful deprivation which existed in the lower reaches of society, he seems rapidly to have concluded that his friends in the underclass were more compassionate, more libertarian and even more creative than their social superiors. It was the single most important moment in his personal history. Although he never became authentically *declassé* (not least because the majority of his friends had similar backgrounds to his own), he had now acquired the streak of populism which shaped the whole of the rest of his life. From now on his basic theme was the decency of the common man and the untrustworthiness of the elite.

Orwell gave full expression to his populist instincts in the four books which he published between 1933 and 1936. *Down and Out in Paris and London* (1933) was a deeply evocative account of his experiences among the underclass, truthful enough to be categorised as non-fiction. By contrast, *Burmese Days* (1934), *A Clergyman's Daughter* (1935) and *Keep the Aspidistra Flying* (1936) were lengthy naturalistic novels whose central theme was the banality of middle-class life. The conventional wisdom is that Orwell's outlook at this time was essentially pre-political, in the sense that his respect for working people had not yet translated into a commitment to the left. However, as Peter Sedgwick has pointed out in a seminal article, there is evidence that the Marxist left was affecting his thinking long before he reinvented himself as a political writer.[59] In the first half of the 1930s he was a frequent contributor to John Middleton Murry's journal *The Adelphi*, one of whose priorities was to win support for Murry's unstable combination of humanist Christianity and anti-Soviet Marxism. Unlike most other factions on the left, Murry and his followers were preoccupied with the basic Orwellian issue of how relationships could successfully be established across class lines, insisting (in Murry's characteristically earnest words) that 'Real identification with the proletariat demands real incorporation with it.'[60] Conceiving of socialism more in ethical than in economic terms, they regarded working-class culture as the potential source of a new form of anti-bourgeois morality. Implicit in their work was the assumption that the great virtue of socialism is that it allows working-class values to seep outwards and form the basis of a genuinely common culture. This was precisely the theme which Orwell would make his own once he decided to make the leap from cultural radical to fully fledged socialist.

Becoming a Socialist

It was early in 1936 that Orwell's admiration for working people hardened into a genuine commitment to socialism. The cause of his renewed interest in politics was a trip to the North of England which he undertook at the behest of the publisher Victor Gollancz, who had commissioned him to write a book on the effects of the slump on industrial communities. Orwell spent the better part of two months in towns such as Wigan, Leeds and Sheffield, living predominantly in working-class households and being shown around by a variety of left-wing activists – many of them communists. His experiences in the North were of a curiously contradictory kind. On the one hand, ill-prepared for Northern poverty by his comparatively affluent lifestyle in the South, he was clearly appalled by the evidence of economic decay which he witnessed all around him – the industrial dereliction, the misery of the unemployed, the ghastly housing conditions and the pervasive atmosphere of quiet despair. This alone was enough to convince him that capitalist society had now run its course. Yet at the same time, even as he longed to see the existing order swept aside, he thrilled to the recognition that working-class culture retained all the qualities of humanity, tolerance and courage which he had experienced in the past. Often addressed as 'comrade' by the people who put him up, he revelled in the 'peculiar easy completeness' and 'perfect symmetry' which governed relationships in the proletarian family.[61] For the first time he also acquired a sense of exactly what it takes to do a working-class job. Early in February he accompanied the miners at Crippen's colliery in Wigan on their day's work. Having exhausted himself on the mile-long walk to the coalface ('For a week afterwards your thighs are so stiff that coming downstairs is quite a difficult feat'),[62] he looked on with a mixture of awe and humiliation as the miners slaved for eight hours in intolerably insanitary conditions. His enduring conclusion was that it was the efforts of working people, not the vaunted leadership of cosseted toffs like himself, which provided industrial civilisation with its true foundation:

> More than anyone else, perhaps, the miner can stand as the type of the manual worker, not only because his work is so exaggeratedly awful, but also because it is so vitally necessary and yet so remote from our experience, so invisible, as it were, that we are capable of forgetting it as we forget the blood in our veins. In a way it is even humiliating to watch coal-miners working. It raises in you a momentary doubt about your own status as an 'intel-

> lectual' and a superior person generally. For it is brought home to you, at least while you are watching, that it is only because miners sweat their guts out that superior persons can remain superior. You and I and the editor of the *Times Lit. Supp.*, and the Nancy poets and the Archbishop of Canterbury and Comrade X, author of *Marxism for Infants* – all of us *really* owe the comparative decency of our lives to poor drudges underground, blackened to the eyes, with their throats full of coal dust, driving their shovels forward with arms and belly muscles of steel.[63]

The immediate result of Orwell's trip to the North was *The Road to Wigan Pier*, the first of his books to be written from an avowedly socialist perspective. The early chapters contained some searing descriptions of what Orwell had seen on his travels, including a famous account of his experiences underground. By contrast, the later chapters consisted of a preliminary statement of his approach to socialism. It was already clear that Orwell's radicalism was anything but orthodox. His technique was to define his understanding of socialism *against* that of other left-wing intellectuals, whom he usually condemned in the most hilariously unrestrained terms. (At one point he famously announced that 'One sometimes gets the impression that the mere words "Socialism" and "Communism" draw towards them with magnetic force every fruit-juice drinker, nudist, sandal-wearer, sex-maniac, Quaker, "Nature Cure" quack, pacifist and feminist in England.')[64] In opposition to what he regarded as the *étatisme* of the Stalinist and Fabian traditions, Orwell's fundamental point was that the essence of socialism is a belief in 'justice and liberty' – it is only in a fully democratic, fully decentralised society that ordinary people's innate creativity and decency can come to the fore. Orwell also launched a highly unusual attack on the left's obsession with science and technology. While recognising that a socialist society would be based on heavy industry, he insisted that 'machine civilisation' has a tendency to create a culture in which heroism is impossible, everyday life becomes sedentary and all forms of work are stripped of their aesthetic significance. The role of the left is not to deify technology but to guard against its dangers. By the same token, Orwell upbraided his fellow socialists for their chauvinism towards the middle class. If the left were to stand any chance of success, he argued, it would need to recruit plentifully among people like himself – that is, socially conscious members of the 'shabby genteel' classes whose security had been destroyed by the crisis of capitalism. However, while these and other arguments were to remain central to Orwell's work for the rest of his life, there was one aspect of *The Road to Wigan Pier* which sharply distinguished it from his later writings. This was its comparative warmth towards the communists. In spite of his evident suspicion of the CPGB, which he already regarded as an excessively centralised and pro-Soviet organisation, Orwell studded his book with guarded statements of praise for its role in the working-class movement.[65] He also made an impassioned call for socialist unity which made it clear that he regarded the communists as natural allies in the struggle against fascism and poverty: 'We are at a moment when it is desperately necessary for left-wingers of all complexions to drop their differences and hang together…As for minor differences – and the profoundest philosophical difference is unimportant compared with saving the twenty million Englishmen whose bones are rotting from malnutrition – the time to argue about them is afterwards.'[66] No one who read these lines in March 1937 (the month in which *The Road to Wigan Pier* was published) would have realised that their author was already becoming an implacable opponent of communism. The transformation was largely the result of his experiences during the Spanish Civil War.

The Spanish Civil War began in July 1936 when senior figures in the armed forces launched a military coup against the elected left-wing government of Manuel Azana.[67] Their leader was General Francisco Franco, who was generally regarded as a man of fascist or semi-fascist sympathies. Supporters of the government immediately took up arms against the coup, with the result that Spain was plunged into three years of intense conflict. In the areas which remained under government control (initially they made up about two-thirds of Spanish territory), there were significant disagreements among the left as to how the anti-fascist struggle should be prosecuted. The overall view of the Socialist Party, which began the war as the most important organisation in the government, was that Franco's forces could best be resisted by a broad anti-fascist alliance. According to socialist leaders such as Largo Caballero, there should be no question of proceeding with radical reforms until the threat to democracy had been seen off. This People's Front strategy was supported by the Spanish Communist Party (PCS), which based its approach on the advice of the Comintern. By contrast, there were some powerful forces on the ultra-left which believed that fascism would only be defeated if the people immediately staged an anti-capitalist revolution. The most influential advocates of the revolutionary line were undoubtedly the anarchists, who were organised throughout Spain in the Federación Anarquista Ibérica (FAI) and the Confederación Nacional del Trabajo

(CNT). Also prominent in the revolutionary camp was Andrés Nin's Partido Obrero de Unificación Marxista (POUM), which retained a broadly Trotskyist outlook in spite of falling out with Trotsky over issues of day-to-day politics. One of the curious features of the early months of the War was that the two strategies were effectively implemented at the same time. Areas under socialist or communist control focused primarily on the struggle against Franco, while the more radical regions (Catalonia is the most famous example) immediately began abolishing private property and establishing a revolutionary culture. It was only the growing strength of the Communist Party which eventually tilted the balance of forces in favour of the People's Front strategy. Although the communists had been comparatively weak at the start of the war, their influence grew rapidly in the ensuing months as a result of Soviet aid to the Spanish government. By the early months of 1937, when the war had entered a period of stalemate, they were using their influence to bring the nascent revolutions in Catalonia and elsewhere to an end. This process reached its bloody climax in May 1937, when government assault guards moved into Barcelona and took scores of anarchists, Trotskyists and radical leftists into custody. Whether or not these developments were justified (and no one can defend the torture to which many of the revolutionaries were exposed while still in prison), John Newsinger is surely right in saying that the communists had carried out an 'effective counter-revolution…behind the Republican lines.'[68]

Orwell experienced these events at first hand and they had a decisive influence on his mature understanding of socialism. At first, arriving in Barcelona (the most revolutionary of all the Spanish cities) in December 1936, his response to the Civil War was almost wholly positive. Barcelona's revolution seemed to confirm his belief that a society run by the workers would be more civilised than any other. The first chapter of *Homage to Catalonia* (1938), the great memoir of the Civil War which he wrote after returning to England, contains a breathtaking description of all the things which marked the city out as a sort of oasis of proletarian virtue – the air of rude comradeship, the burning belief in liberty and equality, the emphasis on public ownership ('…even the bootblacks had been collectivised'),[69] the contempt for the established Catholic culture, the prohibition on tipping, the hammers and sickle painted on every wall. Having immediately decided that this was 'a state of affairs worth fighting for',[70] Orwell enrolled in the local POUM militia and was sent to the Aragón Front in January 1937. At this stage he knew next to nothing about the divisions on the left and aspired only to kill as many fascists as possible. In this he was unsuccessful. The months he spent at a variety of fronts and in a variety of militias were largely uneventful, though he managed to get himself shot through the throat on the Huesca Front towards the end of May. The battles which defined his Spanish experience were not with the fascists but with the communists. On leave in Barcelona in the first two weeks of May and the first few weeks of June, he was in a good position to observe the decisive communist onslaught on the city's revolutionary forces. After helping to defend the POUM headquarters on the Ramblas against the Catalan Civil Guard, he looked on in horror as former comrades such as Andrés Nin, Georges Kopp and Bob Smillie were arrested and imprisoned without charge. By the time he left Spain in the last week of June, scarcely recovered from the wound to his throat, he had been identified by Soviet intelligence as a 'rabid Trotskyist' and there was a warrant out for his arrest. Had he not been informed in advance about a police raid on the Hotel Continental, where he was staying with his wife Eileen, he would probably have been murdered in a Stalinist prison.

Orwell's experiences in Spain affected his political outlook in two ways. In the first place they turned his vague suspicions of the world communist movement into outright hostility. From the moment he arrived back in Britain in July 1937, intent on describing the suppression of the Spanish revolution to a largely indifferent left-wing intelligentsia, one of his main political goals was to expose orthodox communism as a terrible perversion of the socialist ideal – though (as this book seeks to prove) the fact that he embarked on a long-term attack on the communists also obliged him to read their work more carefully than ever before. The tentative note of left-wing ecumenicism which characterised *The Road to Wigan Pier* was never to reappear in his work. The less predictable consequence of his trip to Spain was that he briefly threw himself into the politics of the extreme left. In the couple of years leading up to the outbreak of the Second World War, Orwell fell under the influence of the Independent Labour Party (ILP) – the only political party to which he ever belonged. Having enjoyed considerable influence in the 1920s under the leadership of such figures as James Maxton, A.J. Cook and Oswald Mosley, the ILP had entered a period of decline after disaffiliating from the mainstream Labour Party in 1932 and following a quasi-Trotskyist path. The most salient aspect of its programme in Orwell's day was its wholesale opposition to the CPGB's People's Front strategy. Since fascism was an inevitable consequence of the decline of capitalism, or so the argument went, it followed that the only way to guard against it was to establish a socialist society. There was simply no point in seeking a temporary alliance with social democrats, liberals and progressive conservatives, since these were the very people who wished to sustain the system that had created fascism in the first place. An important corollary of this ultra-sectarian position was that socialists should oppose the forthcoming 'imperialist' war against the fascist powers, on the grounds that ostensibly democratic governments in Britain, France and elsewhere would simply use the conflict as an excuse to introduce 'home grown' varieties of fascism. Orwell loyally rehearsed the ILP's line in a series of articles and reviews between February 1938 and September 1939, notably 'Why I Join the I.L.P.' (June 1938), 'Political Reflections on the Crisis' (December 1938) and the truly venomous 'Not Counting Niggers' (July 1939). The politics of the ILP also informed the outlook of his fine novel *Coming Up for Air* (1939), which described the doomed efforts of a middle-aged salesman to relive the pastoral pleasures of his Edwardian youth. If the book betrayed a definite note of despair, it was probably because its author's health had begun to break down. After falling seriously ill with tuberculosis in early 1938 (he probably acquired the illness in the 1920s though it was not formally diagnosed until 1947), Orwell was forced to recuperate for over a year – first in a sanatorium in Kent, then on a six-month holiday in Morocco. He would never be entirely well again.

Orwell's flirtation with the extreme left took an increasingly unusual form as the Second World War drew nearer. At about the time of the Nazi–Soviet pact in August 1939 he abandoned his opposition to British preparations for war and affirmed that Hitler would indeed have to be met by force. By his own admission he had rediscovered the 'instinctive' sense of patriotism which his education had instilled in him. Yet his conversion to the war party did nothing to moderate his militant leftism. Insisting that Britain had been condemned to military inefficiency by its ailing capitalist economy and its antediluvian ruling class, he now began to argue that the war could only be won if the country immediately underwent a socialist revolution. It was an obvious attempt to adapt the POUM's strategy in Spain to the very different conditions which prevailed in England in 1939.[71] Orwell gave his fullest account of this new perspective in his astonishing short book *The Lion and the Unicorn: Socialism and the English Genius* (1941), written at the height of the Blitz in the Autumn of 1940. At the heart of the book was an audacious attempt to reclaim the concept of patriotism for the left. Since the English people already possess a set of characteristics which make them sympathetic to socialism, Orwell argued, it follows that the left has everything to gain from celebrating the virtues of Englishness – indeed, there will be no revolution of any kind in Britain unless left-wingers take patriotism to their hearts. For much of the period between 1939 and 1943 he clearly believed that capitalist Britain was on its last legs. Exasperated by the series of humiliations which Britain endured in the early stages of the war (notably the evacuation from Dunkirk in 1940 and the various losses in the Middle East in 1942), he thought it only a matter of time until Churchill and his allies were turfed out of office and replaced by an authentically socialist administration. His commitment to the war effort was also reflected in his personal and professional circumstances. In 1940 he moved to London after living for a number of years in the remote village of Wallington, apparently on the grounds that he wished to share in the sufferings of ordinary Londoners. And between 1941 and 1943 he worked as a Talks Producer for the Indian Service of the BBC, preparing political and literary programmes for a comparatively small audience of English-speaking Asians in the subcontinent. Although he came to despise his work, not least because it left him with no time for proper writing, he never doubted that the role of anti-fascist propagandist was an honourable one.

Orwell left the BBC in November 1943 and immediately replaced John Atkins as Literary Editor of *Tribune* – a post he retained until the early months of 1945. His change of job heralded a major shift in his political outlook. Founded by Stafford Cripps in 1937, *Tribune* was essentially an outlet for the views of the Labour Left – or at least that part of it associated with the likes of Aneurin Bevan, Michael Foot, Richard Crossman and Harold Laski. Although Orwell had been extremely critical of the Labour Party since becoming a political writer, it was the ideology of what later became known as 'Bevanism' to which he now chose to subscribe. Rejecting the various forms of ultra-leftism which he had preached over the previous few years, he 'came to see [in the words of his biographer Bernard Crick] that "the revolution" in Britain...could not be an event like 1917 or 1789, only at best a long revolution, a process through time.'[72] His support for the Labour Left was especially apparent during the first three years of Clement Attlee's 1945 administration, whose election he described as a 'great victory' for the British people. Broadly supportive of the government, he nevertheless followed the *Tribune* line in calling on Attlee and his colleagues to show a greater degree of socialist resolve. His special complaint (and a characteristically eccentric one) was that the government had done nothing to abolish such potent symbols of class privilege as the House of Lords, the public schools and titles. He also sympathised with *Tribune*'s controversial approach to foreign affairs, insisting in the essay 'Toward European Unity' (1947) that the left should campaign for the establishment of a 'Socialist United States of Europe' as an alternative to Soviet communism and American imperialism. This argument was very similar to that of Labour left-wingers such as Foot, Crossman and Ian Mikardo (whose famous pamphlet *Keep Left* appeared a mere three months before Orwell's essay),[73] though some writers have also detected the influence of the group of American Trotskyists around the journal *Politics* – an important reminder that Orwell never sold his soul to a single faction.[74]

The thing which most obviously distinguished Orwell from other members of the Labour Left was his deep loathing of Soviet communism. In the period between his departure from the BBC and his death from tuberculosis in 1950, Orwell's overriding concern was to provide a rounded understanding of totalitarianism – something he had not succeeded in doing before. The most famous results of his efforts were *Animal Farm* (1945) and *Nineteen Eighty-Four* (1949), the two novels which propelled him to international fame. His obsession with totalitarianism at this time was closely related to his interpretation of contemporary events. Having long since sloughed off the optimism of his ultra-left phase (and in spite of his cautious support for the Attlee administration), Orwell became convinced in the mid- to late 1940s that democracy was increasingly under threat. Taking it for granted that capitalism would soon be abolished across the planet, he feared that the system which replaced it would not be socialism so much as an extreme form of Stalinism. In his darker moments he foresaw the emergence of three enormous power blocs (one dominated by the USSR, one dominated by the USA and the other dominated by China or Japan), each of them characterised by an unwieldy command economy and outright political dictatorship. Moreover, while recognising that nuclear weapons posed an enormous threat to world peace, he thought it entirely possible that the three blocs would tacitly agree not to use them and resort instead to an endless series of 'phoney wars' – their real purpose being political control rather than military conquest. What is sometimes overlooked is that Orwell's later works were written in a spirit of satire rather than prophecy. In spite of his deep pessimism (some of it prompted by the onset of serious illness), he believed until the end of his life that a totalitarian future could still be averted by the concerted action of libertarian socialists. Shortly before his death, asked to comment on the political assumptions of *Nineteen Eighty-Four*, he made it clear that the novel's chief message was '*Don't let it happen. It depends on you.*'[75] Far from being a 'sick counter-revolutionary' (to use the scornful phrase employed by an adolescent Marxist in Saul Bellow's *Mr Sammler's Planet*),[76] he remained an unabashed radical who simply believed that worst-case scenarios should always be faced. If the thing he feared most was the exponential expansion of Stalinism, it was nevertheless the case that the culture of international communism had influenced him deeply.

This book proposes that Orwell's writings on literature and culture can broadly be divided into five categories. Since Orwell's socialism was rooted in his respect for working-class culture, Chapter One assesses his portrayal of the 'common people' in his early writings on the underclass and his later books on Englishness. Its central argument is that Orwell's interest in the English character was not a personal idiosyncrasy but something he shared in common with many other people on the left, notably the variety of communist writers who excavated the history of the 'English radical tradition' at the time of the People's Front. Chapter Two continues the focus on working-class culture by examining Orwell's writings on mass communication. Surveying the great essays on boys' comics, popular fiction and seaside postcards, I argue that Orwell's interpretation of mass culture was deeply influenced by contemporary Marxist writings on the relationship between fascism and conservatism. Chapter Three shifts the focus to Orwell's interest in high culture, seeking to demonstrate that his most important essays on literature took their lead from (1) communist writings on English literary radicalism, and (2) the communist critique of modernism. The purpose of Chapter Four is to examine the small number of essays in which Orwell made positive proposals for cultural reform. While acknowledging that Orwell was always contemptuous of the idea of Socialist Realism, I suggest that his prescriptive writings on language and broadcasting owed a substantial debt to some of the more philosophical passages in the work of Christopher Caudwell, Jack Lindsay and other communist critics. The book concludes with a chapter on Orwell's theory of totalitarianism. Its particular focus is his account of the cultural methods by which the USSR and other totalitarian states enforced their rule. Although the book is primarily concerned with Orwell's non-fiction rather than his novels, I have also included a brief Appendix which examines his approach to cultural issues in his four novels of the 1930s.

1

THE COMMON PEOPLE

George Orwell's writings on what he sometimes called the 'common people' are at the heart of his cultural criticism, since they go a long way towards explaining his reasons for becoming a socialist. As we saw in the Introduction, Orwell was a disaffected member of the 'lower-upper-middle class' who believed that working people possess a 'common decency' which is often lacking in their social superiors. His conversion to socialism stemmed from the belief that these reserves of decency can only spread outwards and permeate the whole of society if power is somehow devolved to the workers themselves. The great interest of the writings on the common people is that they show why Orwell was attracted to working-class culture in the first place. They can broadly be divided into two categories: (1) the early writings in which Orwell explored his experiences as a member of the 'down and out', and (2) the later work in which he defined his understanding of Englishness. The first category largely consists of a full-length work of reportage (*Down and Out in Paris and London*) and three major essays ('The Spike', 'Clink' and How the Poor Die'), though it is also worth looking at the so-called 'Hop-Picking Diary' from 1931 and the handful of letters and magazine articles which Orwell wrote at about the same time. The major works in the second category are two remarkable short books which a number of editors have downgraded to mere pamphlets: *The Lion and the Unicorn* (1941) and *The English People* (1947). This chapter provides a brief account of both these bodies of work, though it also glances at certain other writings in which Orwell evoked working-class culture in less detail – notably *The Road to Wigan Pier* (1937) and *Homage to Catalonia* (1938). In line with my thesis that Orwell's cultural and literary criticism was often deeply influenced by the work of British communists, I will try to relate his ideas about the common people to those of Marxist contemporaries such as Edgell Rickword, A.L. Morton and Jack Lindsay. Although Orwell's work on the down and out has relatively few parallels in communist criticism (though not, as we shall see, in communist fiction), I will argue that his account of Englishness can reasonably be seen as a response to the emphasis on 'radical patriotism' which defined Marxist criticism in the years of the People's Front.

Orwell and the Underclass

When Orwell tried to explain his decision to explore the world of what we might now call the 'underclass', he gave the impression that his main desire was to cleanse himself of moral and political impurities by pursuing a strict programme of self-mortification. Having been corrupted by his work as an Imperial Policeman in Burma, the only way he could restore his humanity was to experience the worst conditions which the people at the bottom of society had to endure: 'I was conscious of an immense weight of guilt that I had got to expiate…I wanted to submerge myself, to get right down among the oppressed, to be one of them and on their side against their tyrants.'[1] However, if the element of guilt in Orwell's decision to go 'on the toby' (i.e. tramping) should not be underestimated, it is nevertheless clear that other and perhaps more fundamental impulses were also at work. The sheer obsessiveness with which he donned shabby clothes and roamed through a twilight world of spikes, dirty cafés and common lodging houses suggests that at some level he actually *enjoyed* what he was doing. His descent into the underclass was as much a consequence of his deep romanticism as of any desire for moral improvement. Like many another sensitive public schoolboy who feels that he has been rejected by his own class, Orwell suspected that the wretched of the earth possessed a broader humanity than the people at the top of the 'system', and believed (obscurely at least) that he could somehow achieve redemption by immersing himself in their rambunctious, unlettered but deeply egalitarian culture. Indeed, some two or three pages after insisting that guilt was his main motive for going down and out, Orwell made a startling admission about his experiences among the tramps of London:

> I was very happy. Here I was, among 'the lowest of the low', at the bedrock of the Western world! The class-bar was down, or seemed to be down. And down there in the squalid and, as a matter of fact, horribly boring sub-world of the tramp I had a feeling

> of release, of adventure, which seems absurd when I look back, but which was sufficiently vivid at the time.[2]

There is no doubt that Orwell's adventures in the badlands of London, Paris and Kent played a crucial role in his later conversion to socialism. Although he recognised that tramps and criminals were hardly representative of the working class as a whole, it was his experience of the rough comradeship of life on the road which first convinced him that socialism provided a real solution to the moral crisis of capitalist civilisation. As such, this section explores the political significance of Orwell's writings on the underclass by examining their three most important features: first, their barely concealed admiration for the antinomianism of the dispossessed; second, their account of the more constructive elements of tramp culture (especially its comradeship, its curious aesthetic intensities and its instinctive libertarianism); and third, their critical response to the various institutions with which the underclass most frequently comes into contact.

Outsiders are often deeply attracted to the spectacle of moral anarchy. Alienated from a society which has failed to accept them (or which has not accorded them the respect they feel they deserve), they tend to react with disproportionate enthusiasm when its most cherished values are openly defied. Although Orwell is often portrayed as the most morally incorruptible of men, he clearly took a mischievous delight in the behaviour of what we might call the underclass antinomians – those cheerfully amoral men and women who fend for themselves in difficult circumstances by resorting to all kinds of larceny, dishonesty and petty crime.[3] The most memorable example of this sort of character in Orwell's writings is probably Ginger, the 'strong, athletic youth of twenty-six, almost illiterate and quite brainless' who befriended Orwell when they both tramped into the Kent countryside to seek temporary employment as hop pickers.[4] Ginger featured prominently in the 'Hop-Picking Diary' of 1931 and later formed the basis of the character Nobby in *A Clergyman's Daughter*. Since all his efforts to lead a respectable life had ended in disaster (his wife died young and he had been forced to leave the army after injuring an eye) his only means of eking out a living was to 'steal anything that is not tied down.'[5] Orwell portrayed him as a sort of roguish force of nature whose thieving could only be brought under control with the greatest difficulty: 'On several nights Ginger tried to persuade me to come and rob the church with him, and he would have done it alone if I had not managed to get it into his head that suspicion was bound to fall on him, as a known criminal.'[6] What Orwell seemed to find especially amusing was Ginger's extreme fecklessness, the way he invariably blew any sum of money within hours of receiving it. There was perhaps a sense in which he regarded this sort of behaviour as a salutary contrast to the penny-pinching of the dominant culture, which (as he was rapidly coming to understand) sought to reconcile the poor to their poverty by preaching the virtues of thrift. Orwell also admired the way that the underclass's immorality was accompanied by a supreme indifference to the disdain of other people. Observing a group of prostitutes in a slummy café in St Martin's Lane in 1931, he found it remarkable that they should be so roundly abused by the other customers and yet remain unruffled: '...the prostitutes did not mind much.'[7] Like several other characters in the writings on the underclass, they had insulated themselves against society's contempt by nurturing a state of near egolessness – theirs was the enlightenment of the gutter. It is easy to see why the young Orwell, still smarting from the humiliations of his youth and early manhood, should have been so deeply attracted to the sort of self-forgetfulness which more confident people might merely have found abject.

Orwell was obviously not suggesting that a taste for larceny and a contempt for public opinion could somehow form the basis of a new society. He knew perfectly well that all societies have 'to demand faultless discipline and self-sacrifice' from their members, even though absolute virtue is an ideal which no single individual can ever live up to.[8] Yet his account of underclass antinomianism was not without its political significance. As he showed in *Nineteen Eighty-Four* and in some of his literary essays, especially the marvellous brief essays on Mark Twain and Tobias Smollett (to which we will return in Chapter Three), Orwell tended to regard people who challenge the prevailing morality as a specific against totalitarianism. By ordering their lives according to so uncompromising a vision of personal liberty, they serve to remind the rest of us that mindless conformity can never be justified. It is true that Orwell was not yet preoccupied with totalitarianism when he wrote about the underclass; but even in the 'Hop Picking Diary' (one of his least self-conscious pieces of writing) the sense of Ginger and the prostitutes in St Martin's Lane as exemplars of English liberty still comes through strongly.

When Orwell turned his attention to the more constructive aspects of tramp culture, he began by emphasising the spirit of mutual aid which animated the lower reaches of society. While recognising that tramps could frequently be mean, selfish and narrow minded (qualities which are focused to high comic effect in the portrait of Paddy in *Down and Out in Paris and London*), he often portrayed their culture as a sort of miniature welfare system in which people behaved compassionately to others through choice rather than compulsion. There were two simple principles to which tramps invariably seemed to adhere. The first was that favours must always be returned. As he walked away one morning from an awful spike in Lower Binfield, Orwell was surprised to discover that 'little Scotty', a tramp from Glasgow to whom he had given a small amount of tobacco, insisted on repaying him with four pitifully decrepit cigarette ends:

> 'Here y'are mate,' he said cordially. 'I owe you some fag-ends. You stood me a smoke yesterday. The Tramp Major give me back my box of fag-ends when we come out this morning. One good turn deserves another – here y'are.'[9]

More importantly, Orwell also made it clear that the underclass instinctively refused to distinguish between the deserving and undeserving poor. If someone had fallen on especially hard times, he or she deserved help *as of right*. Describing the men who congregated in the communal kitchen of a cheap lodging house in Pennyfields, Orwell noted that 'There was a general sharing of food, and it was taken for granted to feed men who were out of work.'[10] By focusing on the unwillingness of the tramps to make pompous moral judgements, Orwell was perhaps implying that a ruthless capacity to be honest about one's own faults is an essential feature of the good society. Because most of the tramps in Orwell's writings were prepared to admit their own weaknesses, their approach to the destitute was shaped by an inescapable sense of 'There but for the grace of God go I'. They were largely innocent of the sort of cruel high-mindedness which denies assistance to anyone whose difficulties are 'self-inflicted' – a feature of the British welfare system in Orwell's day as well as in ours. Since Orwell was notoriously prone to brooding on his own 'sins both real and imagined' (the phrase is Gordon Bowker's),[11] he probably took a lot of comfort from the thought that feelings of personal inadequacy can sometimes result in greater social solidarity.

If the first principle of the tradition of literary populism to which Orwell belonged is that the common people are more compassionate than anyone else, the second is that they are often more fully alive as well. Orwell's writings on the underclass teem with characters whose aesthetic capacities seem far greater than those of their social superiors. There is the 'pale and consumptive-looking' youth who gives impassioned recitals of poetry in the kitchen of a common lodging house on the Southwark Bridge Road, dropping every 'h' and modulating nearly every 'a' into an 'i': 'A voice so thrilling ne'er was 'eard/In Ipril from the cuckoo bird'.[12] There is the self-obsessed young Parisian called Charlie who entertains his drinking partners with highly improbable Gothic reminiscences, most of them about the tragic consequences of love: 'Alas, *messieurs et dames*, women have been my ruin, beyond all hope my ruin.'[13] And, most remarkably of all, there is the disabled pavement artist called Bozo whose story is told in detail in the second part of *Down and Out in Paris and London*.[14] Bozo had an extraordinary ability to pursue his cultural and artistic interests in the most difficult circumstances imaginable. He had been obliged to take up pavement artistry or 'screeving' on London's Embankment at some point in the early 1920s, shortly after sustaining a horrific injury to his foot while working as a housepainter (he had gone to work drunk and fallen over forty feet from a stage). He lived in terrible poverty for most of the year but his pictures were always meticulously drawn. He invariably used 'proper colours' rather than ordinary chalks and specialised in topical cartoons. (Interestingly enough, some of these cartoons expressed a subversive message by depicting social forces in symbolic form: 'Once I did a cartoon of a boa constrictor marked Capital swallowing a rabbit marked Labour.')[15] If Orwell was impressed by his commitment to art, he seemed positively awestruck by his deep knowledge of astronomy. One night, resting in the alcove of a bridge in Lambeth, he listened in astonishment as Bozo rhapsodised about the stars and constellations above them: 'From the way he spoke he might have been an art critic in a picture gallery.'[16] He found it especially noteworthy that this down-at-heel aestheticism seemed to be the expression of a deep need for personal liberty. Whereas many destitutes had effectively sunk to the level of their surroundings, leading miserable lives which revolved around begging for food and cigarette ends, Bozo was determined to create an inner space in which he could be temporarily free from the brute realities of his everyday circumstances. There are few more moving passages in *Down and Out* than the one in which Bozo tells Orwell that: 'You can still keep on with your books and your ideas. You just got to say to yourself, "I'm a free man in *here*" – he tapped his forehead – "and you're all right."'[17] This is another area in which Orwell's work on the underclass clearly anticipates his later concern with totalitarianism. As we shall see in Chapter Five, Orwell came to believe that the thing which most obviously distinguished Stalin's Russia or Hitler's Germany from earlier authoritarian regimes was their ability to invade the inner lives of the people they governed. Instead of compelling obedience through the threat of force (though this was obviously important) they exercised the sort of mind control which made it almost literally impossible for anyone to question the official ideology. By erecting an aesthetic barrier between himself and his miserable surroundings, Bozo was displaying precisely the sort of resistance to hostile external influences which Orwell thought increasingly rare in the age of the dictators. In this sense he was a distant relative of Winston and Julia in *Nineteen Eighty-Four*, though one trusts that his rebellion proved longer lasting and more successful than theirs.[18]

Why exactly were men like Bozo able to sustain an aesthetic approach to life while living in such squalor? Orwell did not give a clear answer to this question, though at times he implied that they had been forced to turn inwards by their obvious inability to pursue the holy grail of wealth. In an industrial society which usually subordinates spiritual well-being to the accumulation of material goods, Orwell seemed to be saying, Bozo and his friends were at least spared the indignity of scurrying around in search of the latest consumer durables. Their greater sensitivity to the 'surface of the earth' was a direct consequence of their complete exclusion from the rituals of the market.[19] Orwell also implied that the underclass enjoyed an advantage over everyone else by being forced to create a culture for themselves. In a remarkable passage towards the end of *Down and Out*, he described the way that tramps would often while away the time by telling each other long and elaborate stories – stories about ghosts, gruesome deaths and rebellions against the existing order. He found it especially striking that the tramps would often go to great lengths to rewrite historical anecdotes so that criminals, rebels and other misfits seemed more successful than they actually were. This was nothing if not an *active* approach to storytelling. One tramp insisted that the Scottish robber Gilderoy had not been put to death but had actually 'captured the judge who had sentenced him, and (splendid fellow!) hanged him.'[20] Another seemed to believe that the Great Rebellion had been an insurrection of the common people against the ruling class. The information which the tramps used in their stories had not been derived from the media but had been handed down by word of mouth from one generation to another. At a time when most people relied on the culture industry for their entertainment, the tramps were sustaining an oral (and oppositional) tradition which perhaps went back as far as the Middle Ages. Orwell's brief comments on this tradition would not have been out of place in the later work of the great communist writer A.L. Lloyd, who provided the British Folk Revival with its guiding ideology in the first 15 years after the War.[21] If the thesis of this book is that the British communists often exercised a deep influence on Orwell, this is arguably a case of Orwell's work anticipating the later concerns of the communists.

There is one other theme in Orwell's writings on the underclass which needs to be examined before we move on. This is the attitude of the destitute towards the prevailing forms of social organisation. Orwell was often inclined to portray the underclass as if they were wholly isolated from the rest of society, wandering aimlessly from street to street and area to area in search of food, warmth and shelter. Yet his work was usually at its most politically effective when it recorded the impact on the poor of the various *institutions* with which they came into contact – the charities which purported to care for them, the medical organisations which treated them when they were ill, the businesses which made use of their labour and so on. The behaviour of the people who ran these institutions seemed especially significant to Orwell, since – in its sheer callousness – it revealed a great deal about what capitalist society is really like when the veil of decency which conceals its workings is finally stripped away. The writings on the underclass are full of employers who exploit their workers in the most blatant ways imaginable, slum landlords who never lift a finger to ensure that their tenants live in humane conditions, medical professionals who treat the poor as if they were already corpses on a mortuary slab. Especially memorable is Orwell's account of the treatment he received while working as a *plongeur* or dishwasher in a top Paris hotel, not least because the physical layout of the building allowed him to characterise the nature of class inequality in vividly spatial terms – a favourite trick of radical writers. While Orwell and his fellow workers slaved away in the near darkness of 'labyrinthine passages',[22] forced by apoplectic managers to work for eleven hours at a time in conditions of indescribable filth, the Parisian bourgeoisie sat many feet above them enjoying their meals in the well-lit splendour of the hotel restaurant. Orwell was nevertheless cheered by the quiet determination with which the underclass resisted this sort of treatment. The tramps he mixed with in London seemed particularly prone to displays of rudeness and defiance. They were natural libertarians. What invariably roused them to anger was any interference with their personal freedoms (such as the demand that they surrender their tobacco when entering a spike) and any hint of paternalism. They were happy to receive a free cup of tea from a church or charity, or even to spend the night in one of the Salvation Army's notoriously cheerless hostels; but this did not mean that they recognised the right of cloistered middle-class philanthropes to lecture them about morality. The funniest moment in the writings on the underclass, specifically in *Down and Out*, comes when a group of tramps are forced to attend a church service in King's Cross in return for a free meal:

> The tramps treated the service as a purely comic spectacle... There was one old fellow in the congregation – Brother Bootle or some such name – who was often called on to lead us in prayer, and whenever he stood up the tramps would begin stamping as though in a theatre...It was not long before we were making far more noise than the minister...What could a few women and old men do against a hundred hostile tramps? They were afraid of us, and we were frankly bullying them. It was our revenge upon them for having humiliated us by feeding us.[23]

The institutions which Orwell encountered when he was down and out clearly hardened his mind against the oppression of the poor – so much is obvious. But there is also evidence, specifically in the essay 'How the Poor Die' (first published in *Now* in 1946 but perhaps written as early as 1931),[24] that they also played a major role in shaping his approach to social reform. 'How the Poor Die' describes Orwell's grim experiences while receiving treatment for influenza at the 'Hôpital X' (actually the Hôpital Cochin in Paris) in March 1929. After vividly evoking the horribly inhumane treatments to which Orwell and his fellow patients were routinely subjected, it ends with a fascinating account of the emergence of hospitals in the Middle Ages. Orwell argued that the original purpose of hospitals was not to provide humane care for the sick but rather to segregate lepers and enable medical students to practise their craft 'on the bodies of the poor.'[25] While accepting that the invention of anaesthetics and disinfectants had brought us a long way from the 'reeking, pain-filled hospitals of the nineteenth century',[26] he also argued that there is at least a residual element of cruelty and inhumanity in all modern hospitals. This is because 'every institution will always bear upon it some lingering memory of its past.'[27] If the staff at the Hôpital Cochin were still administering needlessly invasive treatments and allowing patients to die in squalor, they had clearly fallen victim to a sort of impersonal historical law which ensured that no institution can ever be reformed beyond a certain point. It is easy to see how Orwell might have taken this lesson and applied it to capitalist institutions as a whole. Shocked by the way that the indignities he experienced in his sick bed were in one sense determined by the cruelties of the past, he might well have concluded that the only way to deal with poverty was not to reform the capitalist system but to abolish it altogether. It is one of the more unlikely links between his period as a tramp and his later conversion to democratic socialism.

There were no obvious parallels between Orwell's writings on the underclass and the Marxist criticism of the 1930s. With the exception of Wilfred Macartney, whose prison memoir *Walls have Mouths* was reviewed admiringly by Orwell in November 1936,[28] there were practically no communist intellectuals who wrote sympathetically about the 'lumpenproletariat'. This was probably because the genuinely dispossessed were often regarded as politically unreliable, usually on the grounds that their desperate circumstances made them susceptible to the appeal of fascism. Yet none of this means that Orwell's interest in the underclass was entirely foreign to the communist and socialist subcultures with which he was beginning to make contact in the early 1930s. The book which most critics regard as the biggest influence on Orwell's investigations into the underclass, namely Jack London's *The People of the Abyss* (a lugubrious account of London's journeys into the worst areas of the East End in 1902), seems to have been staple reading for working-class communists throught the inter-war period. No doubt it was partly London's prestige among communists which later prompted Orwell to seek out his dystopian novel *The Iron Heel* (1908), which (as is well known) exercised a major influence on *Nineteen Eighty-Four*. Moreover, as H. Gustav Klaus has pointed out, there was an entire group of working-class writers in the Twenties and early Thirties who portrayed the tramp as a sort of walking protest against the dull conformity of the capitalist workplace: 'Perhaps at a time when the factory system, and its concomitant discipline and routine, has at last come to regulate the lives of the majority of the working population, the man who eschews work and rambles through the country acquires an aura of freedom and a touch of romanticism which serves as an antidote to the treadmill and dead-end prospects of factory life.'[29] Many of these writers, including Liam O'Flaherty, R.M. Fox and James Hanley, sympathised deeply with either the CPGB or the Independent Labour Party (ILP) and wrote most of their work for radical publications such as the *Sunday Worker*, the *Worker* and *Forward*. Even if Orwell was unfamiliar with this lively sub-genre of Marxist and *Marxisant* fiction, it had undoubtedly come to the attention of at least some of the socialist intellectuals who befriended him when he was experimenting with the down-and-out lifestyle in the early Thirties. Indeed, the most important of Orwell's early socialist friends were all associated in one way or another with John Middleton Murry's journal *The Adelphi*, which had itself made a token effort to publish working-class writers. Since we know that Orwell often discussed his experiences of tramping while visiting the *Adelphi* offices on Bloomsbury Street in London, it seems entirely possible that he indirectly absorbed the ethos of the tramp stories through his conversations with such men as Richard Rees, Jack Common and Max Plowman. For instance, it is interesting to note that Common, a proletarian author from Newcastle who worked as *The Adelphi*'s Circulation Manager, took a special interest in Orwell's tramping and encouraged him to regard the destitute as 'kickers[s] against authority'.[30] Whether or not this had an influence on Orwell's conception of the underclass is not something we can know for sure – but it is a hypothesis that is surely worth bearing in mind. The influence of the communists on Orwell's conception of Englishness is altogether easier to establish.

The Idea of Englishness

Although he began his exploration of working-class culture with a descent into the underclass, Orwell knew perfectly well that the people he met were 'no more typical of the working class as a whole than, say, the literary intelligentsia are typical of the bourgeoisie.'[31] His main goal after the publication of *Down and Out in Paris and London* was to increase his knowledge of what he once called the 'normal working class'.[32] In the two full-length works of non-fiction which he wrote in the second half of the 1930s, Orwell recorded his travels through some very different proletarian landscapes. Written after a two-month research trip in the 'distressed areas' of Northern England, *The Road to Wigan Pier* (1937) evoked the horrific plight of the industrial workers in the face of a deep and and unyielding slump. By contrast, *Homage to Catalonia* (1938) chronicled Orwell's perilous experiences while fighting on the Republican side in the Spanish Civil War. While both these books reflected their author's deep commitment to working-class culture, neither of them had very much to say about actual workers – a contradiction which has often been commented on. *The Road to Wigan Pier* contained some hair-raising descriptions of slum housing, poor working conditions and environmental despoliation; but it said practically nothing about the efforts of working people to resist the capitalist crisis. And with the exception of a deeply inspiring chapter set in revolutionary Barcelona ('It was the first time that I had ever been in a town where the working class was in the saddle'),[33] *Homage to Catalonia* was primarily concerned with the 'evil atmosphere' of war and the political divisions on the Spanish left. It was not until he turned his attention to the issue of 'Englishness' that Orwell wrote about the 'normal working class' in any detail.

As we have seen in the Introduction, Orwell's decision to write about English identity was a direct consequence of the outbreak of the Second World War. After opposing the 'drive to war' in the late 1930s, Orwell concluded in August 1939 (allegedly as the result of a dream) that Hitler's Germany would have to be met by force in the event of it attacking England.[34] Yet his attitude towards the war was different from that of practically everyone else on the British left. Unlike the communists (who opposed the war between 1939 and 1941 and supported it enthusiastically thereafter) and his former comrades in the ILP (who opposed the war outright), Orwell argued that Hitler could not be defeated unless Britain immediately took the path of socialist revolution: 'A capitalist Britain cannot defeat Hitler; its potential resources and its potential allies cannot be mobilised. Hitler can only be defeated by an England which can bring to its aid the progressive forces of the world – an England, therefore, which is fighting against the sins of its own past.'[35] It was this highly idiosyncratic perspective (pro-war and pro-revolution at the same time) which accounted for the basic themes of *The Lion and the Unicorn* (1941), Orwell's first major statement of English patriotism. On the one hand, as a supporter of the war, Orwell wished to make a straightforward case for the importance of loving one's country: 'One cannot see the modern world as it is unless one recognizes the overwhelming strength of patriotism, national loyalty...as a *positive* force there is nothing to set beside it.'[36] On the other hand, as an advocate of immediate revolution, Orwell also wished to prove that a distinctively left-wing form of patriotism had now become possible. This explains why so many of his patriotic writings were given over to a lyrical tribute to the qualities of the working-class. At bottom, Orwell's implied argument was extremely simple. Since the common people *already* possess an outlook which inclines them towards socialism (or at least to a muscular form of populist libertarianism) it is perfectly rational for the left to forge a new form of patriotism around its support for the working class. Instead of insisting that 'workers have no country', socialists should realise that it is precisely because of the workers that England is worth loving in the first place.

If the political background to Orwell's writings on Englishness is comparatively well known, the same cannot be said for the cultural and intellectual circumstances in which they took shape. The consensus among Orwell scholars is that the shift towards patriotism was something wholly exceptional, a sort of intellectual quirk which distinguished Orwell from an inter-war left that was somehow more 'internationalist' in perspective. But the consensus is wrong. As Orwell knew perfectly well, an attempt to transfigure socialist politics with an infusion of English patriotism had been absolutely central to the left-wing culture of the 1930s. The most distinguished exponents of the new form of 'radical patriotism' were a group of intellectuals in and around the Communist Party, all of whom linked their concern with Englishness to the CPGB's attempt to build a 'People's Front' against fascism. The purpose of the rest of this section is not merely to show that Orwell's writings on Englishness were often strikingly similar to those of the communists; but also to suggest (though no absolute proof is possible) that texts such as *The Lion and the Unicorn* can reasonably be interpreted as a critical response to the communist orthodoxy. After briefly surveying the most important communist writings on Englishness, I will concentrate on three themes which bind the two bodies of work together: (1) the idea that there was a complex mixture of liberal and socialist elements in the political outlook of the English workers, (2) the assumption that the English workers were instinctively suspicious of theory, and (3) the idea that sections of the middle class were now ripe for conversion to the left. Although I will mainly refer to *The Lion and the Unicorn* and *The English People*, Orwell's most sustained expressions of radical patriotism, I will also bring in other writings which help to clarify their themes.

British Communism and the 'English Radical Tradition'

The idea of Englishness became an obsession for British communists after the Seventh Congress of the Communist International in 1935. (As we have seen in the Introduction, the Communist International or 'Comintern' had been established in Moscow in 1919. Its function was to determine the policies of the various pro-Soviet Communist Parties which came into existence in the wake of the October Revolution.)

Meeting at a time when Hitler's Germany and Mussolini's Italy posed an increasingly obvious threat to international order, the Seventh Congress was primarily important for determining communist strategy towards the growth of fascism. The most important speech was delivered by the Bulgarian communist Georgi Dimitrov, newly appointed President of the Comintern, who had become a hero throughout the world movement after being acquitted by a Nazi court on charges of burning down the Reichstag (Germany's parliament) in 1933. After defining fascism as 'the open, terrorist dictatorship of the most reactionary, most chauvinistic and most imperialist elements of finance capital',[37] Dimitrov insisted that communists should now give priority to defending established democratic institutions against the fascist attempt to overthrow them. This could best be done by uniting all anti-fascists, including those whom the communists had previously dismissed as 'bourgeois' (e.g. liberals and even progressive conservatives), into nationally based 'People's Fronts'. By insisting that fascism could only be rolled back by the disciplined co-operation of virtually everyone who opposed it, Dimitrov inaugurated a period in which the defence of 'bourgeois democracy' proved far more important to communist politics than the pursuit of socialist revolution. The Comintern had come a long way since the terrible sectarianism of the early 1930s. The point we need to understand here is that the CPGB's interest in Englishness was a sort of secondary consequence of the strategy which Dimitrov had outlined. In a passage of his speech devoted to cultural matters, Dimitrov argued that fascist parties had gained an advantage over the left by seeming to embody the most powerful characteristics of the national traditions to which they happened to belong. One of the reasons for this was that they had consistently posed as the natural inheritors of the great heroes of their respective national pasts. Mussolini's fascists had come to seem quintessentially Italian by invoking the example of Garibaldi; French fascism had been ingenious enough to link itself to the tradition of Joan of Arc; while even the British fascists (in an example which Dimitrov did not mention) had claimed to be resurrecting the glorious traditions of the Tudor state under Queen Elizabeth.[38] Dimitrov's point was that Communist Parties could only outflank the fascists by launching a sort of parallel project from the left. Instead of acquiescing in the idea that fascist values had deep roots in the history of every country, member parties of the Comintern had to persuade people of the precise opposite – that national traditions were actually continuous with the politics of communism. More precisely, Dimitrov called on the communists to draw people's attention to the existence of rich traditions of popular revolt in their respective countries – traditions which had gone a long way towards shaping the established forms of national identity:

> Communists who do nothing to enlighten the masses on the past of their people...in a genuinely Marxist spirit, who do nothing to link up the present struggle with the people's revolutionary traditions and past...voluntarily hand over to the fascist falsifiers all that is valuable in the historical past of the nation.[39]

The CPGB only had limited success in its efforts to build a People's Front in Britain. Although the Party played a central and honourable role in the struggle against Oswald Mosley's British Union of Fascists (and although many British communists made a heroic contribution to the Republican side in the Spanish Civil War), it never persuaded the majority of democratic forces in Britain that a united movement against fascism was indeed urgently required. Limited co-operation from the leading figures on the Labour Left (Stafford Cripps, Harold Laski, Aneurin Bevan), maverick liberals (Richard Acland) and even Tory members of the landed aristocracy (the Duchess of Atholl) scarcely compensated for the resounding indifference of the major democratic parties. But what was not in doubt was the Party's extraordinary success in taking up Dimitrov's challenge to redefine the idea of Englishness along radical lines. From 1935 onwards, in a flurry of intellectual activity, many of the CPGB's leading writers made a sustained effort to excavate the history of what was usually called the 'English radical tradition'. The body of work which they produced can broadly be divided into two categories. On the one hand there was a series of writings which traced the history of plebeian revolt in Britain since the Peasants' Rising of 1381. These were supplemented by a more extensive (though perhaps not so influential) group of works which explored the influence of radical ideas on a selection of Britain's most famous writers – Shakespeare, Milton and Dickens among them. Our concern in this chapter is with the assumptions about the nature of the English character which underpinned the writings on popular revolt. We will return to the work on literature in Chapter Three.

Although the communist historians of the 1930s wrote a series of monographs on particular aspects of English radicalism, their first priority was to survey the entire history of popular revolt since the close of the Middle Ages. The most influential works were probably A.L. Morton's

A People's History of England (1938) and Jack Lindsay's pamphlet *England My England* (1939), each of which assumed that the tradition of popular radicalism had begun in 1381 with the Peasants' Rising, renewed itself with the various early rebellions against enclosure (e.g. the Midlands Rising of 1609) and then extended forwards through the English Civil War, Chartism and the birth of modern socialism. These works were supplemented by an anthology of extracts from English radical literature which Lindsay co-edited with Edgell Rickword and which appeared in the space of less than a year under two different titles: *Volunteers for Liberty* (1939) and *A Handbook of English Freedom* (1940). It was the latter volume which contained the most succinct summary of the communist understanding of popular radicalism, specifically in Rickword's important Introduction entitled 'On English Freedom'. Rickword's starting point was the implied argument that the English people had always been the *real* custodians of liberal values by virtue of their unswerving commitment to communism. Whenever the masses had risen up against their rulers, or so it was argued, they had invariably been motivated by the dream of a communist society. The immediate causes of popular rebellion had varied from century to century, ranging from exasperation with feudal hierarchies to a hatred of enclosure, low pay and factory discipline, but the ultimate goal of the people had always been the establishment of a classless society based on common ownership: '...[the people have basically been asserting] a common human right which can only find satisfaction in social equality, the demand so to modify the state system that the way will be clear for free and equal collaboration in the productive life of the community.'[40] The twist in Rickword's argument was a startling assertion about the *political* consequences of popular radicalism. Although the people had not yet succeeded in establishing a communist society in Britain, their struggles against the ruling class had been almost wholly responsible for the emergence of democratic institutions and liberal values. Because they realised that the ultimate purpose of the state was to defend the property owners against pressures from below, the people had no choice but to supplement their fight for economic justice with a demand for such things as parliamentary government, trial by jury and freedom of speech. The strategic importance of this argument was clear. By insisting that 'English liberty' was essentially the by-product of a broader struggle for a communist society, Rickword was trying to prove that the modern communists could be relied upon to defend 'bourgeois democracy' against fascist attack – not something which everyone took for granted.

At a time when the CPGB was having considerable success in attracting middle-class intellectuals into its ranks, Rickword was quick to point out that the people's struggle for communism had always won the support of a large number of writers, philosophers and other cultural workers. If these 'gifted individuals' had never achieved a position of genuine leadership in the popular movement (in the sense that popular struggles had always been started by the people themselves), they had nevertheless played an important role in clarifying the people's objectives and imbuing them with a sort of visionary lustre: '…we recognise in the combinations of recalcitrant journeymen, in the staunch bearing of farm-labourers in the felon's dock, the seed of all the formulations of the rights of man and the rhapsodies of the poets on the theme of liberty.'[41] Rickword even came close to suggesting that the alliance between the intellectuals and the people had been a decisive influence on the development of modern rationalism. Whenever the intellectuals had given their support to the people, they had tended to articulate an optimistic world-view which emphasised the ability of human beings both to understand the world around them and to impose their will on it. It was only during periods of intellectual elitism that modern thought had been plunged into irrationalist gloom. The obvious problem with Rickword's vigorous brand of radical patriotism was that it raised difficult questions about the origins of national character. Anxious to avoid the taint of biological determinism, Rickword tried to show that the people's communist sympathies resulted from their historical experience and not from some mysterious genetic inheritance. The origins of popular radicalism lay in the 'communal nature of labour' under both feudalism and capitalism – the fact that ordinary people had worked so closely together that they naturally regarded each other as comrades and equals.[42] Moreover, radical movements had been sustained over centuries by powerful political myths which held that a communist society had already existed in England, specifically in the period between the departure of the Romans and the arrival of the Normans. And if the common people's 'independent turn of mind' had now been raised to the level of an instinct, it was surely because their 'innate' responses had been conditioned by centuries of class struggle: 'The plain necessity of having to work and fight through long centuries for every advantage has fixed the strain, and has ingrained that deep suspicion of the bosses which Froissart noted as making us a nation very awkward to rule'.[43] Yet it was not always possible for Rickword to avoid a suggestion of English exceptionalism. In an extremely important passage whose significance I will return to later, he argued that the English idea of freedom had always been marked by a salutary suspicion of unworldly theorising. The people had always campaigned for 'some specific form' of freedom and been relatively unconcerned with 'freedom in the abstract'.[44] As we shall see, this insistence on portraying the English people as radical particularists concealed a highly unorthodox impulse which gave Rickword's socialism more than a passing resemblance to Orwell's.

Liberals into Socialists

Books and pamphlets such as *A People's History of England*, *England My England* and *Volunteers for Liberty* sold an enormous number of copies in the years before the war, though there is no direct evidence that Orwell read them. What we do know is that Orwell reviewed a number of communist writings on the radical tradition in the period after he returned from Spain, including Neil Stewart's *The Fight for the Charter* (1937) and Christopher Hill's *The English Revolution 1640* (1940).[45] He also referred on a number of occasions to C. Day Lewis's symposium *The Mind in Chains* (1937), which contained Rickword's important essay 'Culture, Progress, and English Tradition'.[46] It is therefore unsurprising that there were so many similarities between the communist interpretation of Englishness and the one which Orwell advanced in books such as *The Lion and the Unicorn* and *The English People*. Let us begin with the crucial issue of the relative balance of liberal and socialist elements in the political outlook of the common people. Whereas Rickword had effectively claimed that the English people were good liberals because they were also good communists, Orwell took a more historically nuanced view. Instead of claiming that the people had somehow been socialists since the late Middle Ages, he insisted (at least implicitly) that the characteristics which had previously inclined them towards liberalism now made them sympathetic to the idea of socialist revolution. More precisely, he believed that the peculiarities of the English temperament had prompted ordinary Englishmen to embrace a number of relatively vague political principles, each of which could be bent to either liberal or socialist purposes. Writing in 'England Your England', the first and most compelling part of *The Lion and the Unicorn*, he famously argued that the two most essential features of English culture were its 'gentleness' and its 'privateness'.[47] The people who thronged the streets of the big English cities, marked out by their 'mild knobby faces, their bad teeth and gentle manners',[48] were undoubtedly the most pacific in the industrial world: 'In no country inhabited by white men is it easier to shove people off the pavement.'[49] Their instinct was always to shy away from 'official' spaces and activities and to organise their culture around 'the pub, the football match, the back garden, the fireside and the "nice cup of tea".'[50] Their passion for privacy had even given them a shameless and decidedly un-European taste for life's lower pleasures, exemplified by their frequent drunkenness, their obscene jokes and their prodigious swearing. When these temperamental traits expressed themselves in political terms, they primarily did so through an overwhelming belief that 'might is not right'.[51] The English people invariably took the side of the downtrodden and oppressed, even if their detachment from current affairs (a symptom of what Orwell had earlier called the 'deep, deep sleep of England')[52] often meant that they were blissfully ignorant of gross abuses of power perpetrated by their own country – the obvious example being the treatment of the colonial peoples throughout the British Empire. A related aspect of the English suspicion of power was a deep hatred of militarism. Writing at a time when Winston Churchill was famously trying to rally the nation with his talk of 'blood, toil, tears and sweat', Orwell insisted that nearly everyone in England 'loathe[d] from the bottom of their hearts...the swaggering officer type, the jingle of spurs and the crash of boots'.[53] If the British Army ever decided to adopt the goose-step, which Orwell regarded as a horrific symbol of untrammelled power, they would probably find that the common people laughed at them in the streets. Just as important was the people's deep respect for the idea of constitutional government. While recognising with one part of his mind that the legal system is skewed in favour of the rich, the ordinary Englishman nevertheless 'takes it for granted that the law, such as it is, will be respected, and feels a sense of outrage when it is not.'[54] In a barely concealed dig at the great communist lawyer D.N. Pritt, Orwell wryly observed that the English respect for constitutional proprieties even extended to those 'eminent Marxist professors' who protested so frequently against miscarriages of 'British justice'.[55]

Support for the underdog, hatred of militarism and the strong state, respect for due constitutional process – these were the political principles to which the English people tended to adhere. Orwell's point was that none of these principles could realistically be pursued within the confines of bourgeois democracy. If the English people wanted to live in a society which fully reflected their identity, they had no choice but to abolish capitalism and opt for socialism instead: 'By revolution we become more ourselves, not less.'[56] However, despite the fact that *The*

Lion and the Unicorn and *The English People* shared this emphasis on the Englishness of the socialist ideal, Orwell's understanding of the political situation in Britain changed significantly in the three years which separated the one book from the other.[57] As we have already seen, Orwell's argument in *The Lion and the Unicorn* was that the war against Hitler could not be won unless Britain took the socialist path. The country's dismal performance in the early months of the war showed that the free market could not produce weapons efficiently enough. It also showed that capitalism tended to concentrate political power in the hands of the wealthy and the old (ineffably complacent 'lords of property' like Lord Halifax) who were simply too set in their ways to provide effective leadership. If the English people were to be spared the indignity of seeing German troops washing their boots in the Thames, they had to take matters into their own hands and implement a full-blooded socialist programme including nationalisation of all basic industries, reduction of income inequality and democratic reform of education. As surprising as it may seem in retrospect, Orwell was convinced for much of the period between 1940 and 1942 that this sort of revolution was not merely necessary but also imminent. Whenever Britain experienced some especially grave military setback, such as the evacuation from France in 1940 or the defeats in the Far East in 1942, he thought it almost inevitable that the people would rise up and turn out their rulers. His optimism on this score increased markedly when Sir Stafford Cripps emerged as the possible leader of an independent left in 1942. Moreover, Orwell seemed perfectly comfortable with the idea that the people might have to resort to violence in order to achieve power ('I dare say the London gutters will have to run with blood. All right, let them, if it is necessary.')[58] and even argued that the Home Guard (to whose St John's Wood section he belonged) might soon be transformed into a sort of citizen's militia. Not much of this revolutionary bravado survived into *The English People.* Having accepted at some time in late 1942 that his predictions of imminent revolution were wrong, Orwell was now anxious to point out that Britain was not a country in which political violence was at all likely: '…civil war is not *morally* possible in England. In any circumstances that we can foresee, the proletariat of Hammersmith will not arise and massacre the *bourgeoisie* of Kensington: they are not different enough.'[59] What was new about *The English People* was Orwell's implied argument (later spelled out more explicitly in essays such as 'Towards European Unity') that England's ultimate political destiny was to exercise a civilising influence on socialist revolutions throughout the rest of the world. Since the 'outstanding and...highly original quality of the English is their habit of *not killing one another*' (Orwell's emphasis),[60] it followed that the socialist movement in Britain had at least a sporting chance of building a planned economy without surrendering to the totalitarian temptations which go with it. This might well lead to a situation (or so Orwell implied) in which the example of a socialist Britain would serve to stimulate change elsewhere in the world, not least by puncturing the myth that any attempt to overthrow capitalism leads necessarily to the sort of Stalinist 'deformations' seen in the USSR.

Perhaps because most of his readers were likely to be culturally ambitious members of the lower middle-class, Orwell made no reference in either of the books on Englishness to the 'radical tradition' whose history the communists had uncovered. There were no stirring references to the Peasants' Revolt or even to the Lollards, the Levellers and the Diggers. However, in a number of his other writings, Orwell made it clear that he was familiar with communist research on the radical tradition and that he agreed with much of what it had to say. At the same time (and unsurprisingly) he also took a great delight in holding some of its more tendentious assumptions up to criticism. There is an amusing example of this dual attitude in Orwell's Introduction to Volume One of *British Pamphleteers* (1948), the anthology of extracts from British political pamphlets which he co-edited with his friend Reginald Reynolds. In the context of a stimulating discussion of the role of the pamphlet in British life, Orwell pointed to the fact that 'revolutionary' and 'visionary' pamphlets by the likes of Gerrard Winstanley had appeared time and again in the course of British history. Much of what he said about this revolutionary tradition would not have been out of place in a pamphlet by Lindsay or an essay by Rickword. For instance, he noted that Winstanley's writings were authentically socialist in spite of being written in a pre-industrial society (the communists had often been fiercely criticised for arguing that socialism had pre-existed the industrial age), and also that British revolutionaries frequently tried to bolster their support by claiming that a communist society had already existed in Britain. Yet many of his other comments might have been specifically designed to stick in the communist gullet. Most obviously, Orwell disagreed spectacularly with the communists over the relevance of the radical tradition to contemporary politics. Whereas writers like Morton, Lindsay and Rickword clearly believed that the vision of human brotherhood which the radical tradition had passed down through the centuries (and which formed the core of its appeal) would at last be realised in the communist society of the future, Orwell seemed to regard it as profoundly inspiring but also deeply quixotic, a sort of necessary myth to leaven the harsh realities of practical politics: 'The most encouraging fact about revolutionary activity is that, although it always fails, it always continues. The vision of a world of free and equal beings, living together in a state of brotherhood…never materialises, but the belief in it never seems to die out.'[61] There was also an interesting difference of opinion over whom should be regarded as the radical tradition's modern heirs. On most of the occasions when the communists wrote about the history of English revolt, they were careful to emphasise that the only modern organisation that could claim the mantle of Wat Tyler, Robert Owen or William Morris was the CPGB itself – the 'party of a new type' that would finally allow the English people to achieve their dream of a classless society. Orwell saw things rather differently: 'The English Diggers and Levellers…are links in a chain of thought which stretches from the slave revolts of antiquity, through various peasant risings and heretical sects of the Middle Ages, down to the Socialists of the nineteenth century and the Trotskyists and Anarchists of our own day.'[62] Of all Orwell's barbs against the communists, this might well have been the one that hurt the most.

Science and the Suspicion of Theory

If Orwell agreed with the communists that the English people had conflated socialist and liberal concerns in a very distinctive way, he also echoed Rickword's point about their distrust of theory. One of his first observations in 'England Your England' was that '…the English are not intellectual' and that they '…have a horror of abstract thought, they feel no need for any philosophy or systematic "world-view".'[63] Moreover, in spite of belonging to one of the most emphatically doctrinal movements in the history of world politics, he not only recognised the strain of anti-intellectualism in the English sensibility but actually seemed to endorse it.[64] One of the reasons for this was his paradoxical belief that indifference to intellectual achievement can often be of great help in keeping liberal values alive. Since the English people cared so little about ideas, Orwell appeared to argue, they were unlikely to call for restrictions on anyone's right to express them. Orwell also took great pleasure in the sheer inconsistency to which his fellow countrymen were prone, even predicting on one occasion that an element of scatterbrained illogicality would be absolutely typical of the socialist future. For instance, while a revolutionary government in Britain would undoubtedly take steps to abolish capitalism and reduce social inequalities, it might also decide to keep the monarchy in place – not least (or so Orwell implied) because of the historical myth which stated that kings and queens had frequently taken the poor's side against the ruling class of the day. Yet his real reason for endorsing the English suspicion of theory went much deeper than any of this. One of the most salient characteristics of English socialism in Orwell's period was its reverence for the physical sciences. Convinced that the capitalist system was incapable of exploiting the latest advances in technology, many of the left's most powerful advocates argued that socialism's chief mission was to liberate scientific science from the distortions of the free market. By celebrating the common people's instinctive preference for concrete particulars over the scientist's drab abstractions, Orwell was therefore implicitly distancing himself from what he called the left's habit of 'machine worship'. Like Rickword before him (though much more explicitly) he was setting himself up as a 'diagnostician of the Left's ills' whose purpose was more to bury science than to praise it.[65]

Orwell's attitude to science reminds us once again of how deeply he was influenced by his communist contemporaries.[66] The close association between science and socialism in the 1930s was largely brought about by a very distinguished group of scientists, including J.D. Bernal, J.B.S. Haldane, Hyman Levy, Joseph Needham and Lancelot Hogben, who either joined or became actively sympathetic to the CPGB at about this time. Apart from pursuing research in their respective areas of expertise, these and other writers exercised a major influence on the public debate about science through their membership of the so-called 'Social Relations of Science' movement (SRS).[67] The SRS movement was an informal grouping of Marxist and *Marxisant* intellectuals which set out to understand the relationship between scientific activity and broader forms of social organisation. Its guiding assumption was that scientific research could not be expected to prosper if capitalism remained in existence. The most powerful version of this argument was put forward by Bernal in a flurry of books, essays and articles, notably 'Science and Civilisation' (1938) and *The Social Function of Science* (1939). Bernal's point was that capitalism tends to undermine scientific research by doing two things: (1) creating an intellectual climate in which 'pure' science is better regarded than 'applied' science', and (2) preventing individual scientists from fully co-operating with other experts in their respective fields. The root of both problems was what Marxists often called the 'anarchy' of capitalist production. Because there is no guarantee in a free market that goods and services will necessarily find a buyer, there is a natural tendency for companies greatly to delay investing (and sometimes not to invest at all) in the most expensive forms of new technology. This creates a mood of profound disillusionment among scientists which causes them to devalue the idea of applied research (that is, research carried out for explicitly practical ends) and to retreat instead into compensatory fantasies about the 'disinterested' pursuit of knowedge. However, since scientists are usually at their most creative when seeking to solve practical problems, this means that the finest scientific minds are effectively robbed of one of their most powerful intellectual stimulants. Matters are compounded by the sheer isolation which market societies impose on their scientific workers. Scientists employed by private companies are usually forbidden from sharing their knowledge with their peers in other organisations (on the obvious grounds that to do so might be to lose a competitive advantage), while state-employed scientists have no record of meaningful collaboration with their foreign colleagues. The consequence is an immense loss of intellectual power, since (or so Bernal argued) scientific research can only proceed efficiently if knowledge is firstly pooled and then rigorously assessed by all the relevant experts. The only solution to the crisis of scientific research is the creation of a socialist society, since it is only in a planned economy that technological advances can immediately be applied to practical problems. The advent of socialism also allows the entire population to receive an extensive scientific education, thereby creating a situation in which scientific workers can be held to account by ordinary working people. Bernal insisted that these benevolent developments were already underway in the Soviet Union.[68]

Orwell's attitude to the work of the SRS movement was deeply ambiguous. On the one hand, as we shall see in a moment, there were passages in his work in which he reproduced the tenets of 'Bernalism' almost exactly. But there were many other passages (infinitely more heartfelt ones) in which he implicitly defined his attitude to science *against* the SRS orthodoxy. The most interesting example of the anti-scientific strain in Orwell's thinking can be found in Chapter XII of *The Road to Wigan Pier*. The argument of this chapter was that although 'machine civilisation' can never be turned back (and although socialism can indeed be expected to benefit scientific research), it nevertheless contains grave dangers which need to be guarded against if the quality of human life is not to be permanently lowered. Orwell's biggest anxiety was that technological progress would end up reducing human beings to a state of 'soft' and 'flabby' torpor. Against the argument that socialism inevitably restores what John Ruskin had famously called 'joy in labour', Orwell insisted that the 'tendency' of modern technology is to rationalise production to the point where all traces of intellectual and aesthetic significance have been stripped from the experience of work. In a society which compels the worker to become the glorified superintendent of an automated labour process (and which also condemns him to live in a 'glittering Wells-world' from which nature has been largely expelled) it is more or less impossible to cultivate the 'hard' and 'brave' qualities which Orwell regarded as the foundation stones of a genuine civilisation: 'strength, courage, generosity, etc'.[69] Nor did Orwell believe that advanced technology would liberate people into a new world of creative and fulfilling leisure. While accepting that socialism would greatly reduce the length of the working week, he also insisted (*pace* William Morris) that it would ultimately prove very difficult to prevent the machine invading people's leisure time and doing as much damage to their recreations as it had once done to their work.

> The citizen of Utopia, we are told, coming home from his daily two hours of turning a handle in the tomato-canning factory, will deliberately revert to a more primitive way of life and solace his creative instincts with a bit of fretwork, pottery-glazing or handloom-weaving. And why is this picture an absurdity – as it is, of course? Because of a principle that is not always recognised, though always acted upon: that so long as the machine *is there*, one is under an obligation to use it. No one draws water from the well when he can turn on the tap.[70]

As is clear from this passage, Orwell's main fear was that technology had somehow acquired a momentum of its own. Human beings now invented machines even when there was no clear need to do so. If this situation were to be reversed under socialism, it would be necessary for mavericks like Orwell to form themselves into a 'permanent opposition' and campaign for technology to be used sensitively and sparingly. All of which brings us back to the brief passages which celebrated the common people's lack of intellectual distinction. When Orwell portrayed the English workers as the polar opposites of the scientific elite, instinctively attached to the life of the senses and suspicious of all forms of abstraction, he was surely implying that they would form a powerful counterweight to all forms of Bernalist technophilia in the society of the future. This belief occasionally betrayed him into some highly idiosyncratic observations about the value of education. Whereas most left-wingers believed that socialism would enable all men to become intellectuals, Orwell seems to have been concerned that too much education would strip the workers of their healthiest instincts. In a curiously invigorating (though also highly disconcerting) passage in *The Road to Wigan Pier*, he famously praised the working class for 'see[ing] through' the idea of formal education and insisted that 'I know now that there is not one working-class boy in a thousand who does not pine for the day when he will leave school. He wants to be doing real work, not wasting his time on ridiculous rubbish like history and geography.'[71] And yet, as George Woodcock has pointed out, there were other occasions on which Orwell's educational pronouncements were so mild as to be scarcely noticeable.[72] There was an especially interesting example towards the end of *The English People*. While insisting that a 'uniform educational system' (i.e. one in which children of all backgrounds and aptitudes are taught together) should be instituted for all pupils up until the age of about ten or twelve, Orwell also argued that educational streaming should be rigorously applied to the older age-groups.[73] It was not one of his more inspiring proposals.

On the relatively few occasions when Orwell spoke positively about science, he usually employed arguments which the SRS movement had done much to popularise. In spite of his hostility to the machine, he took it for granted that one of the main reasons for wanting socialism was that the free market had become a brake on technological development. While scarcely as utopian as a Bernal or a Hogben, he also recognised that the machines of the future would go a long way towards liberating human beings from unpleasant work – though he glumly acknowledged that they might never free us from the gruesome business of doing the dishes. Moreover, as Peter Huber has pointed out, there was a corner of his mind which regarded technology as one of the most potent enemies of totalitarianism. Since all dictatorships are founded on systematic lying, Orwell appeared to believe, it is clearly of the highest significance that science has invented a range of devices which can store truthful information in a comparatively indestructible form. For instance, while working at the BBC, he pointed out in a letter to Ritchie Calder that microfilms (the subject of a forthcoming broadcast) had the ability to 'prevent…libraries from being destroyed by bombs or by the police of totalitarian regimes'.[74] Yet even when he seemed closest to the spirit of the SRS movement, he could rarely resist taking its ideas and imbuing them with an anti-scientific twist. There was a particularly outrageous example in an article called 'What is Science?' which appeared in *Tribune* in 1945. Responding to a piece of correspondence from J. Stewart Cook, Orwell endorsed the idea that the general public should receive a much wider scientific education – one of the SRS movement's main demands.[75] Yet he followed this concession to orthodoxy with a swingeing attack on the political outlook of scientists, insisting that a knowledge of the natural world could often do as much to blunt political understanding as to promote it. Drawing his evidence from Robert Brady's *The Spirit and Structure of German Fascism* (a publication of the Left Book Club) he noted that German scientists had proved especially susceptible to the appeal of Hitler, and that 'the ability to withstand nationalism' was likely to be stronger in ordinary people than in the scientific elite.[76] Whereas Bernal had blamed the insularity of modern science on competition between capitalist states, Orwell seemed to regard it as a sort of professional deformation arising from scientific activity itself.

The Role of the Middle Classes

Having surveyed the most important characteristics of the common people, Orwell's other main goal in the writings on Englishness was to provide a brief snapshot of the wider class structure in England. What was the current state of the middle- and upper classes? To what extent could people from outside the working class be expected to participate in the socialist movement? Were the working-, middle- and upper classes really that different from each other? These were the questions which preoccupied Orwell in sections III to VI of 'England Your England' and in certain passages of *The English People*. Developing a theme which had first been broached in *The Road to Wigan Pier*, Orwell argued that the socialist movement would only be successful in England if it won the support of 'most of the middle class', especially the 'new indeterminate class of skilled workers, technical experts, airmen, scientists, architects and journalists' who were right at home in the 'radio and ferro-concrete age.'[77] It is often assumed that this interest in the middle-class distinguished Orwell from the rest of the British left, which (so the argument goes) remained obsessed with the industrial workers and wholly uninterested in the 'progressive' potential of other social strata. Yet this is to overlook the fact that a concern with winning middle-class support had been a central feature of Marxist politics at the time of the People's Front. Indeed, there were some striking parallels between *The Lion and the Unicorn* and Alec Brown's *The Fate of the Middle Classes* (1936), a rather breathless communist text which Orwell reviewed on two separate occasions in the months following its publication.[78] The purpose of the rest of this chapter is to examine Orwell's writings on the English class system in the light of Brown's earlier efforts.

Brown was already well known as an experimental novelist by the time he wrote *The Fate of the Middle Classes.* (Orwell ungenerously described his novel *Daughters of Albion* as a 'huge wad of mediocre stuff' in the *New English Weekly* in 1936.)[79] In 1934 he famously announced in *Left Review* that the socialist novel should be written exclusively in the language of the proletariat, on the grounds that 'LITERARY LANGUAGE FROM CAXTON TO US IS AN ARTIFICIAL JARGON OF THE RULING CLASS'.[80] This earned him a considerable amount of derision from his fellow communists, though (as we shall see in Chapter Four) it also sparked a lengthy debate which anticipated many of the arguments in Orwell's later writings on the political function of language. *The Fate of the Middle Classes* was less provocatively written, though its two main objectives were controversial enough: (1) to assess the likelihood of certain sections of the middle class going over to the side of communism, and (2) to identify the political, ideological and structural factors which had so far prevented them from doing so. Brown's argument was that modern capitalism had created a middle class consisting of three distinct groups, each of which had been fundamentally affected by the onset of the world slump. At the bottom of the heap was the so-called 'traditional' middle class, made up of shopkeepers, handicraftsmen and other 'small traders'. Wholly ineffective in their efforts to beat off the competition from big business, the majority of this group were now in danger of being sucked down into the working class.[81] More fortunate was the relatively small group of administrators who held elite positions in government and industry. Since most of these 'black-coated workers' were essentially surrogates for the bourgeoisie, 'piloting the ship' while the real bosses lived off a hoard of unearned income, their wealth and prestige had actually *grown* in the years since the Great War. As such, they were most unlikely to throw in their lot with the left. Brown's real interest was in the section of the middle class which came between the other two groups – the extensive network of 'brain workers' (teachers, scientists, writers etc.) who catered to all the educational, technical and cultural requirements of advanced capitalism. In a passage which echoed many of the assumptions of the SRS movement, Brown insisted that the onset of the slump had put Britain's intellectual workers in an intolerably frustrating position. Endowed by their professional training with a deep need to be creative, many of them had failed to find the sort of jobs that were capable of holding their interest. Highly trained scientists had settled for menial supervisory positions, writers of all kinds were hampered by a contracting market for their work, teachers languished on the dole. If the majority of disaffected intellectuals had yet to go over to communism, it was only because the ideology of the middle-class had imbued them with some disabling illusions about the extent of their influence. Because the bourgeoisie had devolved so much power to managers, scientists, technicians and so on, it had become natural for the middle class to believe that modern society was essentially run by themselves. These illusions of power were reinforced by the modern education system, which imbued its more successful products with an entirely misleading sense of their own intellectual eminence. According to Brown, the modern middle-class were instinctive voluntarists – they failed to understand that the ineluctable laws of capitalism would invariably prevent them from reshaping society according to their own desires. Yet this situation could not possibly last. A deepening of the capitalist crisis, combined with a vigorous intervention from the left, would surely convince even the most purblind member of the technical intelligentsia that communism was not merely necessary but also essential.

There were several ways in which Orwell's account of the class system coincided with (and was presumably influenced by) the one to be found in *The Fate of the Middle Classes.* The first part of Section IV of 'England Your England', in which Orwell provided a mordant commentary on the state of the ruling class, can almost be read as a four-page expansion of a throwaway remark in Brown's book. When Brown drew attention to the tendency of the modern bourgeoisie to delegate power to managers, technicians and scientists, he argued that one of the side effects had been a catastrophic decline of the bourgeoisie themselves: 'This inactivity of the bulk of the owning class – partly made possible by the fact that the new middle class was more and more running the complex apparatus of fully developed monopolistic capitalism – naturally resulted in a deterioration of the individuals composing the class, a deterioration of the class as a whole.'[82] Orwell took exactly the same position in his comments on bourgeois culture, ascribing the 'decay of ability in the ruling class'[83] to the fact that the dynamic entrepreneurs of the past had now been transformed into 'mere *owners*, their work being done for them by salaried managers and technicians.'[84] Orwell only differed from Brown in suggesting that the process of decline had been accelerated by a conscious choice. Faced with the realisation that they no longer had a role to play in the running of the modern economy, the ruling class had actually *decided* to become stupid, since this was the only way they could convince themselves of their continuing relevance: 'They could keep society in its existing shape only by being *unable* to grasp that any improvement was possible.'[85] When he shifted his attention to the middle classes, Orwell also found much to agree with in Brown's book. Like Brown, though with much less recourse to Marxist terminology, he accepted that (1) the middle classes could now be divided into two or three distinct groups, (2) that at least one of these groups (the so-called 'small traders') were in danger of disappearing altogether, and that (3) it was the broadly 'technical' and 'intellectual' groups that could be expected to go over to the left. However, despite accepting Brown's analysis in its broad outlines, Orwell also contributed some arguments of his own which went a long way towards distancing him from the communist position. The most important was about the precise circumstances in which the intellectual middle-class would be radicalised. While Brown had argued that Britain's scientists, technicians and teachers would end up converting to socialism because middle-class employment was under threat, Orwell insisted that the middle class was actually *expanding*. Writing in Section VI of 'England Your England', he famously observed that one of the 'most important developments' during the inter-war years had been the unprecedented spread of middle-class habits.[86] At a time when English culture had been permanently transformed by the 'mass-production of cheap clothes and improvements in housing',[87] it was becoming increasingly difficult to distinguish the middle classes from large sections of the proletariat and even from sections of the bourgeoisie. Class distinctions which had previously seemed inviolable were now being blurred by a 'general softening of manners'.[88] It was this which opened up the possibility of an alliance between the middle- and working-classes, since (or so Orwell implied) the cultural differences which had previously held them apart were no longer quite so evident. Whereas the communists spoke the language of class polarisation, insisting that the rich were getting richer and the 'middling types' sinking back towards the proletariat, Orwell put his hope for the future in the fact that large sections of British society were now converging on the centre ground.

There is one further parallel between Brown and Orwell which needs to be examined before we move on. This is the rather unusual fact that both men chose to illustrate their arguments about the middle class by invoking the work of H.G. Wells. References to Wells occur time and again in *The Fate of the Middle Classes*, beginning in the first few pages of the Introduction and extending right through to the Appendix. Brown's argument was that Wells embodied in an extreme form all the most troubling characteristics of the intellectual worker under advanced capitalism. His most obvious handicap was the sort of delusions of intellectual grandeur that were typical of the scientific elite. Convinced that 'We originative intellectual workers are reconditioning human life',[89] he had somehow persuaded himself that people of his own kind could reshape the world without meeting undue resistance either from existing rulers or from the impersonal laws of capitalism. The result was an astonishing ignorance of the way that modern societies actually work. Nowhere in Wells's writings was there any recognition that the free play of the scientific imagination could ever be stymied by the inherent limitations of a market society. According to Brown, Wells's excessive faith in the power of the literary and scientific intelligentsia resulted from the widespread habit of associating membership of the middle-class with the possession of high intelligence. Because admission to middle-class employment was now largely dependent on educational success (and because schools and universities breed intellectual snobbery in a peculiarly virulent form), it is inevitable that people like Wells will come to regard themselves as prodigies of intellectual flair – and also that they will venerate the intellect as a force which nothing on earth is ultimately capable of withstanding. In a mischievous attempt to deflate Wells's reputation for scientific prescience, Brown suggested that this species of intellectual fanaticism expressed itself in his novels in the form of a solipsistic indifference to the laws of nature: '…in the *Food of the Gods* there is no hint of the impossibility of a wasp just swelling to a yard long and still functioning; no hint of that most important truth that the organs of any species are all developed especially for that species, and as size increases or decreases from normal, the creature functions badly…the principal thing for Mr. Wells is not to start from reality and work with real elements, but to *invent something which is outside the normal world*'.[90] Brown also detected a curiously *unhistorical* element in many of Wells's novels. Whenever Wells evoked one of the central characteristics of life under capitalism (such as the division of society into classes) he invariably did so in a basically *static* form – there was no attempt to analyse things in their historical development. In so doing, Brown implied, he was able to dismiss capitalism from his thoughts by portraying it as a system fundamentally lacking in dynamism.

Although his two reviews of *The Fate of the Middle Classes* were not entirely complimentary, Orwell recognised in one of them that Brown's remarks about Wells were 'brilliantly done'.[91] It is therefore unsurprising that Orwell's subsequent writings on Wells should have echoed Brown's arguments. This was especially true of 'Wells, Hitler and the World State', the vigorously polemical essay which appeared in *Horizon* in August 1941. The core of the essay was Orwell's response to *Guide to the New World* (1941), a short book in which Wells had assessed the state of the war against Hitler and made some suggestions for 'constructive world revolution'. At a time when the German army had just scored some notable successes in Eastern Europe and Cyrenaica, Orwell found it astonishing that Wells should have (1) underestimated the strength of Hitler's military machine, and (2) suggested in all seriousness that the only solution to the problem of fascism was the immediate establishment of a World State. This breathtaking lack of realism was not so much the product of a defective imagination as of Wells's distinctive social position: 'Mr. Wells, like Dickens, belongs to the non-military middle class.'[92] Because Wells had been immersed for so long in the scientific ideology of his particular social group, he had lost all understanding of the dark forces which drove contemporary world affairs. He had every faith in the ability of the 'scientific man' to usher in a world of 'order, progress, internationalism, aeroplanes, steel, concrete [and] hygiene'; yet he failed to recognise that the so-called 'romantic man' (exemplified in the modern world by Hitler) had a much greater hold on the public imagination with his frankly atavistic vision of blood and honour.[93] The similarities between Orwell's arguments and those of Alec Brown are surely clear enough. There is the same emphasis on Wells as a representative figure of the scientific middle class; the same sense of amazement that he should have misunderstood the modern world so completely (though Orwell was more concerned with his softness on fascism than with his ignorance of the capitalist system); and the same limitless scorn for the sheer impracticality of his political vision. Where Orwell differed from Brown was in his assessment of Wells's historical achievement. While Brown had dismissed Wells as a scientific and historical ignoramus, Orwell looked back with admiration to the zenith of his career (roughly between 1890 and 1920) when he had helped to transform the modern world with the prescience of his political and scientific judgements. In spite of the unparalleled conservatism of Victorian and Edwardian society, Wells exploded the complacency of the age not simply by anticipating the radical changes that would shortly occur but also by imbuing them with an air of febrile excitement: '…[he] *knew* that the future was not going to be what respectable people imagined. A decade or so before aeroplanes were technically feasible Wells knew that within a little while men would be able to fly. He knew that because he himself *wanted* to be able to fly, and therefore felt sure that research in that direction would continue.'[94] Even when Orwell's arguments came closest to those of the communists, he was clearly incapable of sharing their disdain for the ornaments of 'bourgeois culture'. Wells was a 'wonderful man'[95] and any younger writer who tried to question his achievement had ultimately committed a 'sort of parricide'.[96]

2

THE POLITICS OF MASS COMMUNICATION

It is hardly surprising that George Orwell should have written so widely about the media and other forms of mass communication. As someone who felt a deep romantic attraction to working-class culture (and whose commitment to socialism was largely the result of this attraction), he was naturally interested in the way that things such as films, books, newspapers and comics helped to shape the working-class mind. Yet his attitude to the prevailing forms of mass communication was a curiously contradictory one. One the one hand he clearly believed that certain media texts reflected all the qualities which had attracted him to working-class culture in the first place – the warmth, the moral decency, the instinctive radicalism. He also argued that new forms of media technology could make an important contribution to some much-needed cultural reforms, such as the reshaping of the English language and the popularisation of serious literature. On the other hand, deeply influenced by Marxist approaches to culture, he consistently portrayed the media as one of the main means by which the ruling class disseminated its ideology. Nor did he believe that the media were necessarily getting any better. While most of his writings about contemporary popular culture were affectionate in tone, he feared that the media of the future (described in detail in *Nineteen Eighty-Four*) would primarily be used to reinforce the power of totalitarian governments. Orwell scholars have so far shown a curious reluctance to relate the writings on mass culture to their intellectual context.[1] By portraying Orwell as a sort of lone pioneer of Cultural Studies, they have perpetuated the idea that he was the only socialist of his day who saw the need to take popular culture seriously. Yet there were actually a number of left-wing intellectuals in the 1930s who wrote about the media, many of them associated in one way or another with the Communist Party. Communist writers contributed short pieces on the commercial arts to various editions of *Left Review*, to the publications of the documentary film movement and to C. Day Lewis's influential symposium *The Mind in Chains* (1937). The fascinating thing about much of this work was that it paralleled Orwell's combination of populist enjoyment and *Marxisant* despair. Although the English communists took it for granted that the products of the media were saturated in bourgeois ideology, they remained alert to those rare moments when they gave expression to a more questioning or oppositional perspective. There are three chapters in this book which examine Orwell's writings on popular culture, either in whole or in part. The purpose of this chapter is to explore Orwell's essays on the popular culture of his own day. By contrast, Chapter Four tries to show that Orwell ascribed a central role to the media in his various schemes for cultural reform, while Chapter Five looks at his gloomy predictions about the likely nature of mass communication in the totalitarian societies of the future. Each of these chapters argues that Orwell's understanding of popular culture was deeply influenced by communist writings.

Orwell's writings on the commercial culture of his own day can be divided into three categories. The first consisted of three essays on what might initially seem like unrelated subjects: 'Boys' Weeklies' (1940), 'Rudyard Kipling' (1942) and 'In Defence of P.G. Wodehouse' (1945). What bound these essays together was Orwell's concern to defend his subjects against the accusation that they displayed fascist (or *fascisant*) sympathies, and his attempt to show that each of them had gone a long way towards infecting the popular mind with a distinctive form of old-fashioned conservatism. The contrasting purpose of the essays in the second category was to trace the emergence in popular culture of a decidedly fascist or quasi-totalitarian outlook, especially in the area of detective fiction. The main documents here are 'The Detective Story' (1943) and 'Raffles and Miss Blandish' (1944), though it is also worth glancing at several shorter pieces, notably 'Pleasure Spots' (1946) and 'The Decline of the English Murder' (1946), in which Orwell inveighed memorably against the totalitarian potential of 'Americanisation'. The third category of writings showed off Orwell's populist side. In 'The Art of Donald McGill' (1941) and a handful of briefer pieces, Orwell's main objective was to show how certain popular forms displayed the same combination of innate decency and ethical irreverence which had attracted him to working-class culture. His main examples were the seaside postcard and the music-hall sketch. Before we can look at this body of work in detail, it is necessary to say something about the intellectual context in which Orwell was working. In particular, we will need to examine the obsessive emphasis on fascism in the Marxist criticism of the 1930s.

Conservatism or Fascism?

There would seem at first sight to be a purely political explanation for the fact that Orwell's writings on mass culture were preoccupied with the issue of fascism. At a time when Hitler's Germany, Franco's Spain and Mussolini's Italy posed a grave threat to European democracy, it was probably inevitable that left-leaning intellectuals would spend much of their time scanning the media for signs of fascist influence. Yet the mere existence of fascism is not enough to explain the particular themes which Orwell chose to explore. In particular, it fails to explain why so many of the essays on popular culture examine the nature of the relationship between fascism and old-fashioned conservatism. The most likely explanation for Orwell's obsession with this theme is that it had already been analysed at length by other radical critics. Especially relevant to a consideration of Orwell's work is the attempt of several British communists, notably John Strachey, Douglas Garman and Christopher Caudwell, to expose the *fascisant* elements in the work of modernist writers who might otherwise have been regarded as hard-line conservatives.[2] As is well known, a number of the leading British modernists (Eliot, Yeats, Lawrence etc.) had responded to the post-war crisis by espousing a militantly *traditionalist* form of conservatism. Horrified by the spectacle of mass democracy, unrestrained industrialism and cultural decadence (the latter symbolised by the rise of the cinema and the popular press), they had each concluded that European culture was far healthier in the hierarchical, agricultural and religious societies of the pre-industrial past.[3] The communists argued that cultural nostalgia of this sort was (1) suspiciously similar to the cultural politics of fascism, and (2) likely to lead its adherents into an explicit commitment to fascism before too much longer. An interesting example of the argument was developed by Douglas Garman in a famous essay on Eliot's *After Strange Gods*. In his early critical writings, notably 'Tradition and the Individual Talent' (1919), Eliot had encouraged writers to hold their own personalities in abeyance and recreate the 'classical' sensibility which dominated literary culture in pre-modern Europe.[4] While conceding that this defence of 'tradition' against 'modernity' was in some respects valuable, Garman was alarmed by the way that it had recently been supplemented by an emphasis on 'orthodoxy'. Worried that his vision of the classical past had been widely misinterpreted, or so Garman appeared to argue, Eliot had begun to look around for a strong institution that might be capable of enforcing it. Initially hopeful that the Anglo-Catholic church might fit the bill, he was now preparing to turn towards fascism – another ideology which sought to defend a traditional way of life by augmenting the power of authority: 'The graph of his personal development is closely parallel with that of fascism: just as the latter, having rejected democracy, strives to perpetuate the capitalist system in a disguised but more stringent form, so Eliot…turns to a creed which, while proclaiming its authority, gives full play to his individualist bent.'[5] Garman's argument was typical of a style of thought which saw little to distinguish nostalgia for the Middle Ages from the more dionysian cultural visions of a Hitler or a Mosley.

The Lure of Paternalism: Orwell on Boys' Weeklies

Orwell was evidently worried by the tendency of Marxist writers to blur the distinction between conservatism and fascism, even though he was occasionally guilty of it himself. The main purpose of 'Boys' Weeklies', 'Rudyard Kipling' and 'In Defence of P.G. Wodehouse' was to show that conservatism remained a powerful influence in British popular culture and that it needed to be understood on its own terms. Most of 'Boys' Weeklies' was taken up with an analysis of *Gem* and *Magnet*, two rival comics which had been established in the Edwardian period and still sold thousands of copies in 1939. Both comics were famous for weekly stories set in the imaginary public schools of Greyfriars and St Jim's. Nearly all these stories were intended to be humorous, emphasised the "supposed glamour" of public-school life for…all it is worth' (Orwell wrote as an ex-Etonian)[6] and focused on the more light-hearted or dramatic aspects of the school routine: '…horseplay, practical jokes, ragging masters, fights, canings, football, cricket and food'.[7] Even today, many years after it ceased publication, *Magnet* is still widely remembered in Britain for its central character Billy Bunter, the fat, unlucky and food-obsessed 'Owl' of Greyfriars whom Orwell regarded as a 'first-rate' comic creation. In his efforts to prove that '…the politics of the *Gem* and *Magnet* are Conservative, but in a completely pre-1914 style, with no Fascist tinge',[8] Orwell made it clear that Greyfriars and St Jim's were dignified paternalist institutions of a sort which any Tory traditionalist might find attractive. Each school was organised around a rigid hierarchy which placed boys from an aristocratic background firmly at the top. While most of the characters in the stories were wealthy (and no one from the working class ever put in an appearance, except as a criminal), it was usually boys with names like 'the Honourable Arthur A. D'Arcy' who cut the biggest dash. By always featuring the same characters in exactly the same settings, or so Orwell appeared to argue, *Gem* and *Magnet* both portrayed England as an unchanging paradise in which wealth and power passed seamlessly from one generation of the aristocracy to the next. They also expressed a view of the world that can best be described as morally authoritarian. The stories might always have been lighthearted but they invariably showed good behaviour being rewarded and bad behaviour being punished – even if the bad behaviour rarely amounted to much more than smoking, gambling or sneaking off to the pub. Along with the emphasis on moral authority went a deep strain of English patriotism, expressed in the axiom that 'foreigners are funny'.[9] Although the racism in the *Gem* and *Magnet* was never especially virulent (one of the central characters in the *Magnet* was actually an Indian, albeit of the 'comic babu' variety), it was taken for granted in the closed worlds of Greyfriars and St Jim's that all Frenchmen are 'excitable', all Chinese are 'sinister' and so on.[10] Moreover, as Orwell implied in a brilliantly evocative piece of writing, one of the comics' most noteworthy characteristics was their ability to associate the paternalist vision with an overwhelming feeling of *safety*, with the sense that life could be blissfully secure so long as one put one's faith in the benevolent bluebloods at the top of the system:

> The year is 1910 – or 1940, but it is all the same. You are at Greyfriars, a rosy-cheeked boy of fourteen in posh tailor-made clothes, sitting down to tea in your study on the Remove passage after an exciting game of football which was won by an odd goal in the last half-minute. There is a cosy fire in the study, and outside the wind is whistling. The ivy clusters thickly round the old grey stones. The King is on his throne and the pound is worth a pound. Over in Europe the comic foreigners are jabbering and gesticulating, but the grim grey battleships of the British Fleet are steaming up the Channel and at the outposts of Empire the monocled Englishmen are holding the niggers at bay. Lord Mauleverer has just got another fiver and we are all settling down to a tremendous tea of sausages, sardines, crumpets, potted meat, jam and

> doughnuts. After tea we shall sit round the study fire having a good laugh at Billy Bunter and discussing the team for next week's match against Rookwood. Everything is safe, solid and unquestionable. Everything will be the same for ever and ever. That approximately is the atmosphere.[11]

Orwell's account of the political content of *Gem* and *Magnet* was supplemented by some intriguing remarks about the way the comics affected their readers. Quoting from a number of letters in the correspondence pages which requested more information about life at Greyfriars and St Jim's ('What age is Dick Roylance?', 'How much did D'Arcy's monocle cost?', What are the Form captain's three chief duties?'),[12] Orwell concluded that many of the people who enjoyed the comics were 'living a complete fantasy-life.'[13] They had lost sight of the distinction between truth and fiction and seemed to assume that Greyfriars and St Jim's were more real than reality itself. Nor was this an accident. By using a range of more or less ingenious techniques, including those of tautology and stereotyping, the writers of *Gem* and *Magnet* had *deliberately* imbued their fictional creations with a sort of realistic solidity. Nearly every scene, character or episode in the two comics was painstakingly evoked in the most verbose and repetitive manner imaginable. The result was a sort of thickness of verbal texture which immediately created vivid images in the reader's mind. Moreover, the effect of realism was powerfully reinforced by the extravagant use of stereotypes, which reduced each character to a handful of easily envisaged characteristics – Bunter's corpulence, D'Arcy's monocle, Inky's Anglo-Indian solecisms and so on. Nearly twenty years before the emergence of Cultural Studies in Britain, Orwell had thus anticipated two major theoretical insights (one about the textual function of stereotypes and the other about the 'hyperreal' status of media representations) which his successors would explore with rather less essayistic flair.

Orwell clearly believed that the ability of *Gem* and *Magnet* to create 'extraordinary little world[s] of their own'[14] was an index of their political effectiveness. By enticing their young readers into a parallel universe of aristocratic whimsy, writers such as Frank Richards (the creator of Billy Bunter) ensured that they would absorb a conservative ideology without really thinking about it. This was a more alarming prospect than it might otherwise have seemed, since the fictional works which people encounter early in their lives often have a massive impact on their later outlook: 'It is probable that many people who would consider themselves extremely sophisticated and "advanced" are actually carrying through life an imaginative background which they acquired in childhood from (for instance) Sapper and Ian Hay.'[15] Yet there were other passages in 'Boys' Weeklies' which implied that *Gem* and *Magnet* often had a tendency to *undermine* their own message. Orwell made it clear that this was sometimes due to weaknesses in content and sometimes due to problems of form. As far as content was concerned, he attached great significance to the fact that neither *Gem* nor *Magnet* ever depicted behaviour of a genuinely disreputable kind, since this tended to sabotage their ability to preach an effective moral message. If the 'bad' pupils at Greyfriars and St Jim's were only ever punished for trivial offences, the argument seemed to go, it followed that a certain proportion of readers would view their behaviour as 'irresistibly fascinating' and even as a 'substitute for sex'. There were also ambiguities associated with the narrative structures which the two comics employed. One of the ways in which *Gem* and *Magnet* held the attention of their readers was by ensuring that it was possible to identify with nearly all the characters. Instead of creating stories around a single 'hero', they continually invited the reader to shift his attention from one mischievous schoolboy to another. When Orwell compared this technique to the stories in newer comics such as *Skipper* and *Hotspur*, each of which enacted its 'bully worship[ping]' outlook by forcing the reader to identify with a single character, he was effectively arguing that the significance of *Gem* and *Magnet* was that their mode of presentation conflicted with their authoritarian values. Even the use of racial stereotypes was hardly a foolproof method for inculcating English nationalism, Orwell implied, since the habit of persistently depicting foreigners in terms of a small number of disreputable characteristics would inevitably cause certain readers to ask: 'Can life really be that simple?'[16] By emphasising the difficulties which the comics had experienced in getting their message across, Orwell was again anticipating one of the most important themes of Cultural Studies – in this case the idea that all popular texts are 'polysemic'.[17]

The issue of polysemy draws our attention to another interesting parallel between Orwell and the communists. As I have tried to show elsewhere, one of the most important aspects of Marxist criticism in Orwell's day was its pioneering interest in the *ambiguity* of ideology. Implicitly rejecting Lenin's rigid distinction between 'bourgeois' and 'proletarian' forms of consciousness, some of the more adventurous British communists insisted (or at least implied) that no set of beliefs is ever entirely free of political contradictions. However much a particular ideology might reflect the interests of the ruling class, or so it was argued, it invariably contains elements which can be appropriated by oppressed groups and used to express a sceptical or subversive attitude towards the status quo. This principle was heavily to the fore in the outpouring of writings on the 'English radical tradition' which occurred after 1935. Anxious to show that the English people had often been motivated by a primitive form of communist consciousness (a belief summed up in the slogan 'communism is English'),[18] writers such as Jack Lindsay, Edgell Rickword and Christopher Hill paid close attention to the role of ideas in the popular rebellions of the past. While not denying that the Peasants' Revolt of 1381, the Wilkesite uprisings of the 1760s or the Chartist agitations of the 1840s had their roots in material conditions, they also insisted that each instance of plebeian revolt had been underscored by a conscious subversion of the dominant ideology. Just as the disaffected peasants of the Middle Ages appropriated the egalitarian element in Christianity and bent it to their own ends, so the rebellious workers of the capitalist age took liberalism's emphasis on liberty, equality and fraternity and inflected it to the left. When Orwell emphasised the element of ambiguity in popular texts, it was this nascent tradition of polysemic criticism with which he was aligning himself. Like the communists (and also like the 'Gramscian' exponents of Cultural Studies who came after him), he was implicitly celebrating the capacity of ordinary people to read popular texts against the grain of their declared ideological position. At the same time one gets the impression that polysemy had a psychological significance for Orwell which it might not have had for other writers. Whereas the communists prided themselves on their ideological consistency, Orwell was famously contradictory in his beliefs. Nowhere is this clearer than in his affectionate sketch of the world of Billy Bunter, where he simultaneously denounces conservatism while implying that aspects of it (especially its emphasis on paternalism) are actually rather attractive. The unstated argument is that socialism can only assume a truly humane form if it enriches itself with ideas from other traditions. In so far as polysemic texts united contradictory meanings in a single semantic space, it seems likely that Orwell regarded them as a powerful support for his pluralistic instincts. By unpicking the disparate meanings in a boys' comic or a seaside postcard, he perhaps reassured himself that his political inconsistencies reflected a basic English distaste for ideological fanaticism. At any rate his willingness to learn from the conservative tradition was fully on display in many of his other writings on popular culture, not least the great essays on Kipling and Wodehouse.

'Good Bad Books': The Politics of Rudyard Kipling and P.G. Wodehouse

If *Gem* and *Magnet* obviously qualified as examples of mass communication, Rudyard Kipling and P.G. Wodehouse were both writers who hovered on the verge of mass appeal. Orwell regarded them as 'good bad' writers who had secured a sizeable popular audience for literary art of a fairly high order.[19] The striking thing about his essay on Kipling was its argument about the cultural circumstances in which totalitarianism had arisen. Defending him against the charge that his support for British imperialism was effectively proto-fascist, Orwell argued that Kipling had always displayed the sort of instinctive hatred of tyranny that was typical of nineteenth-century conservativm. As a deeply religious man who abhorred the idea that human beings should play at being God, he regarded any attempt to exercise untrammelled power as a blasphemous assault on a divine prerogative – and one which would inevitably end in disaster. His related belief, summed up for Orwell in the following stanza from 'Recessional', was that human beings should always temper their earthly ambitions with a substantial measure of religious humility:

> If, drunk with sight of power, we loose
> Wild tongues that have not Thee in awe,
> Such boastings as the Gentiles use,
> Or lesser breeds without the Law –
> Lord God of hosts, be with us yet,
> Lest we forget – lest we forget![20]

Orwell's implied point was that stanzas such as this indirectly tell us a great deal about the historical developments which gave rise to totalitarianism. At the time when Kipling was acting as a cheerleader for the British Empire, or so the argument seemed to go, totalitarianism was not really possible because human beings were still restrained by their belief in God. It was only the collapse of religious faith (an otherwise necessary and beneficial occurrence) which enabled certain individuals to develop that unquenchable lust for power which Orwell regarded as the motive force behind both Stalinism and fascism. Orwell also took great pleasure in portraying Kipling as a model of literary activism from whom the contemporary 'pansy left' could learn some valuable lessons. In an age of mass indifference to literature, Kipling had managed to appeal to the public by writing numerous poems (not all of them very good) in which poetic diction had been grafted onto everyday feelings.

He had *ennobled* the outlook of the common man by transfiguring it in verse. His desire to reach out to the public was not so much the product of a temperamental quirk as of his status as a man of action. As an ardent apologist for British imperialism, one who had himself contributed to the subjugation of India, Kipling had an urgent desire to justify the existing order to as many people as possible. If the socialist writers of the 1930s had failed to make an impression on mass consciousness, it was precisely because their attitude was one of permanent opposition – they simply had no record of practical achievement to defend. Kipling's generation of imperialists might have been odious but at least they were 'people who did things…they changed the face of the earth'.[21]

'In Defence of P.G.Wodehouse' was slightly less controversial than 'Rudyard Kipling', though its theme was broadly the same – the need to ensure that conservative ideas in popular art were scrupulously distinguished from those of a more fascist nature. The essay was occasioned by the political controversy in which Wodehouse had been caught up since the beginning of the war. When Belgium fell to the Nazis in 1940, Wodehouse was immediately arrested at his holiday home in Le Touquet and sent to an internment camp. He subsequently agreed to give five humorous talks on German radio, allegedly (though this is still a matter of debate) in return for being released from the camp and allowed to live in a plush hotel in Berlin. Although the broadcasts were largely non-political, they nevertheless caused outrage in Britain and Wodehouse was widely accused of having fascist sympathies. At the time when Orwell came to his defence, just three or four months before the Nazis were defeated, a number of politicians and journalists had begun to repeat the demand that Wodehouse should be soundly punished once the war was over. Aside from suggesting that he was guilty of little more than 'stupidity', Orwell defended Wodehouse by portraying him as a signal instance of the *non-political* conservative who is bound to his country by deep ties of patriotism. He was essentially a stalled adolescent who had never moved beyond the simple ideology which he had imbibed at public school. Whichever of his books one reads (and Orwell surveyed his entire output) one inevitably finds a lighthearted emphasis on the decency of the aristocracy, the need to avoid work at all costs and the joys of cricket. Since the importance of loving one's country is a central tenet of the public-school code, it is simply inconceivable that he could ever have sided with the Nazis:

> He *may* have been induced to broadcast by the promise of an earlier release (he was due for release a few months later, on reaching his sixtieth birthday), but he cannot have realised that what he did would be damaging to British interests. As I have tried to show, his moral outlook has remained that of a public-school boy, and according to the public-school code, treachery in time of war is the most unforgivable of all the sins.[22]

Although 'In Defence of P.G. Wodehouse' is not generally regarded as one of Orwell's more important essays, there are several reasons why it retains its relevance for a contemporary audience. The first is that it does a virtuoso job of extracting a political message from an ostensibly 'non-political' body of work. By demonstrating that such unlikely characters as Jeeves, Wooster and PSmith were all the bearers of a conservative ideology, Orwell showed that there is no such thing as 'simple entertainment' and that all popular texts convey a political message of one sort or another. As such, 'In Defence of P.G. Wodehouse' is a perfect essay to give to the large number of people (many of them students) who criticise Media and Cultural Studies for 'reading too much' into popular entertainment. There is also the issue of the historical status of conservatism. In showing that Wodehouse had not progressed ideologically since his schooldays, Orwell drew attention to the fact that he had managed to overlook nearly all the most important political developments of the modern age – the rise of fascism among them. The burden of his argument was not that conservatism is brutal or indecent, simply that it is *out of date*. Finally, it is worth taking note of the political circumstances in which the essay was written. Orwell's decision to write his essay was prompted by the belief that Wodehouse had fallen victim to a dangerous mood of vengeance which began to grip the country in the closing stages of the war. As early as 1944, chiefly in his 'As I Please' column in *Tribune*, Orwell had warned against the demand that the Axis powers (and all those who supported them) should be treated as brutally as possible once the war was won. His point was not simply that humiliating one's defeated enemies is the best way of laying the foundations for future wars (unlike other people in Britain he had not forgotten the lessons of the Treaty of Versailles), but also that the desire for vengeance was all of a piece with the totalitarian outlook which posed the biggest threat to humanity's future.[23] It goes without saying that his opposition to the more extreme forms of war psychosis is as relevant today as it was in 1945.

Fascism and the Detective Story: Orwell's Debt to Alick West

If Orwell often took issue with the communist habit of detecting fascist and *fascisant* sympathies in modern cultural forms, he also took his lead from it in a number of his most important writings on popular culture. This was especially true in 'The Detective Story' (1943) and 'Raffles and Miss Blandish' (1944), two brilliant essays which traced the evolution of the detective novel over a period of about seventy years. There were some marked similarities between Orwell's arguments and those of the communist writer Alick West, who contributed a two-part essay on 'The Detective Story' to *Left Review* in 1938.[24] Although it is most unlikely that Orwell deliberately plagiarised West, it seems almost certain that West's ideas were turning themselves over in his mind when he began to formulate his arguments. This can best be illustrated by a detailed summary of the two bodies of work.

West's essays on detective fiction appeared about a year after his book *Crisis and Criticism* (1937), one of the founding works of Marxist literary theory in Britain. In some respects they provide a textbook illustration of the emergent Marxist emphasis on the polysemy, instability and ideological ambiguity of cultural production. Whereas a number of his Marxist contemporaries had described the detective novel as a degraded expression of capitalism in crisis,[25] West set out to rescue it from critical disdain by showing that (1) it was effectively a by-product of important developments in 'serious' literature, and (2) it was by no means a purely reactionary form and had often displayed an intriguing blend of what Raymond Williams might have called 'hegemonic' and 'emergent' elements since its beginnings in the eighteenth century. His essay began with a subtle exploration of the first of these points. According to West, the thriller could only emerge once the serious novel had broken with traditional forms of first-person narrative, since it is impossible to generate the requisite level of 'suspense' if a story is narrated through the eyes of one of its characters: 'If the hero himself relates his adventures in the first person, the reader already knows he has come safely through them…'[26] The decisive event in the birth of the thriller can thus be regarded as Samuel Richardson's invention of the 'epistolary' novel (that is, a novel in which the story is told through a series of letters), because this made it possible to write about characters whose ultimate fate had not been advertised at the beginning of the book. Also of importance was the poetry of leading Augustans such as Pope and Young, who created an inherently suspenseful form of literature by oscillating wildly between rapture and ennui. Moreover, in using his novels to illustrate the idea of 'serendipity' (that is, the ability to make far-reaching deductions on the basis of scanty physical evidence), Walpole had created the circumstances in which the detective could be portrayed as a prodigy of intellectual flair.

Having thus linked the birth of the thriller to important shifts in the literary culture of the eighteenth century, West went on to propose that the detective novel had gone through three main stages of development. Each of these stages had brought about subtle changes in the *politics* of the form. The first, which began in 1764 with the publication of the 'first thriller' (Horace Walpole's *The Castle of Otranto*) and lasted until about 1840, reflected the intelligentsia's highly ambivalent attitude towards the romantic movement and its attack on the status quo. A novel like William Godwin's *Caleb Williams* (1794) idealised the criminal and portrayed him as a 'far greater man' than the detective, yet its seditiousness was not altogether total – the detective came out on top at the end. By contrast, the dominant mood of the second phase (c.1840–c.1900) was the desire to see the existing order protected at all costs. Terrified by the growth of the labour movement and the prospect of revolution, middle-class readers exulted in the spectacle of a brilliant detective solving crimes with breathtaking intellectual flair. This was the period in which Sherlock Holmes could identify a criminal simply by inspecting the knees of his trousers. By the start of the twentieth century, on the other hand, the detective novel was beginning to revert to the ambivalence of its first period. The work of Wallace or Chesterton might not have been as seditious as *Caleb Williams* but it often created the impression that the criminal was far more interesting than the forces of law and order. This was partly because it took great pains to conceal his identity until the closing stages of the narrative, swathing him in a certain irresistible glamour as a consequence; but it also resulted from new ways of representing the detective. The modern crime novel was not so much a tribute to individual genius as a study of bureaucracy: its attention had shifted from the inspired amateur to 'mass investigation by the police.'[27] Moreover, it is difficult to admire the police when chance has replaced the intellect as the main means by which crimes are solved: '...a man repairing telephones wires happens to look into the window of a room where the criminals think themselves unobserved, and his evidence gives a vital clue.'[28] Although West was not entirely comfortable with modern detective novels, seeing them as 'finally dull, even though one cannot lay them down',[29] he insisted that their sympathy towards the criminal represented a 'sign of revolt against decaying capitalism'.[30]

He also seemed to believe that they went a long way towards illustrating fundamental Marxist assumptions about the relationship between human beings and their environment. Whenever a criminal is brought to justice in a modern crime novel, West argued, it is usually because he has failed to erase all traces of his criminality from the areas in which he moves: 'The interrelation between a crime and its environment are [*sic*] so intricate that no one can commit a crime and isolate it from its environment; at some point or other he makes a contact with social reality, which he forgets or cannot obliterate: he has to travel, buy things, telephone.'[31] By thus drawing attention to the sheer difficulty of manipulating the social world, the crime novel provides a powerful illustration of the role of material circumstances in shaping human fortunes. Its ultimate message is that 'social being determines consciousness'.

In 'The Detective Story' and 'Raffles and Miss Blandish', Orwell retained the broad argument of West's essays but came to an entirely different set of political conclusions. Like West, he set out to compare the detective novels of his own day with those of the past, though he ignored the age of Godwin and settled for a straight comparison between the 'vintage' works of the nineteenth century and the 'mass produced' novels of the period between 1920 and 1940. He also followed West in arguing that the main difference between the two periods was that reverence towards the detective had now given way to fascination with the criminal. If the 'earlier writers…made their detectives into exceptionally gifted individuals, demi-gods for whom they felt a boundless admiration',[32] their modern counterparts had adopted an 'equivocal attitude towards crime'.[33] Although this argument was obviously not distinctive enough for us to say with any confidence that Orwell had derived it from West, the truly remarkable thing was the way that he (Orwell) echoed West's essay when seeking to substantiate it. Where West had insisted that the modern crime writer boosts the criminal and diminishes the detective by (1) swathing the criminal in mystery by concealing his identity until the end of the book, (2) replacing the individual detective with the bureaucratic police organisation, and (3) emphasising the role of chance in the solution of crimes, Orwell wrote as follows:

> The most annoying thing about the writers of modern detective stories is their constant, almost painful effort to hide the culprit's identity…[34]

> [Edgar] Wallace was one of the first crime-story writers to break away from the old tradition of the private detective and make his central figure a Scotland Yard official...His own ideal was the detective-inspector who catches criminals not because he is intellectually brilliant but because he is part of an all-powerful organisation.[35]

> ...in Wallace's most characteristic stories the 'clue' and the 'deduction' play no part. The criminal is always defeated either by an incredible coincidence, or because in some unexplained manner the police know all about the crime beforehand.[36]

The issue which divided Orwell from West was that of how the transition from one stage to another should be evaluated. Whereas West saw the nineteenth-century thriller as little more than a vessel of bourgeois ideology, Orwell believed that writers such as Arthur Conan Doyle, Ernest Bramah and R. Austin Freeman had contributed something unique and valuable to the development of English literature. What he particularly seemed to admire was the mood of unflustered intellectualism which ran through their writings. The important thing about the detective stories of the 'Golden Age' was not so much the crime under investigation, nor even the issue of whether a criminal would ultimately be caught. It was rather the sheer pleasure which the detective invariably took in solving an intellectual puzzle. For instance, in a book such as *The Adventures of Sherlock Holmes* (1892), Conan Doyle made it perfectly clear that Holmes regarded detection as an end in itself. Not only was Holmes wholly uninterested in women (an important sign of his 'monkish' commitment to the life of the mind), he was also an *amateur* – someone who tried to solve crimes purely for the love of it, with no regard for material rewards or wider institutional loyalties. He was the symbol of a 'more leisurely age' in which people could devote themselves to their chosen tasks without feeling unduly rushed or pressurised. At the level of style, Orwell went on to argue, this sense of leisureliness tended to express itself through a deliberate cultivation of verbosity. Many of the best passages in Conan Doyle, Bramah and Freeman had practically nothing to do with the plot, but simply existed so that the author could build up an impression of the detective's intellectual brilliance. Orwell's example was the famous passage in 'The Blue Carbuncle' in which Holmes examined a hat and then spoke at length about the identity of its likely owner, regardless of the fact that 'the hat...has only the vaguest connection with the main events'. There seems little doubt that Orwell admired this sort of writing because it corresponded to his deep nostalgia for the England of his boyhood.[37] As a socialist who always harboured the darkest suspicions about science and technology (see Chapter One), he seems to have regarded the period between 1880 and 1914 as the only one in which technology had been used on a truly humane scale. Although 'machine civilisation' had progressed to the point where a great deal of avoidable misery had been taken out of life, it had not yet threatened people's need for continuity, tranquillity and a sense of closeness to nature. When Sherlock Holmes sank into his armchair and meditated for hours about his latest case, he was simply expressing the spirit of an age that knew how to benefit from technology but not be enslaved by it – the same spirit which Orwell captured so memorably in the middle section of *Coming Up For Air*. Here again one detects a definite strain of traditional conservatism in Orwell's argument.

The differences between Orwell and West became especially pronounced when Orwell turned his attention to the detective fiction of his own day. Whereas West regarded cynicism towards the police as a sign that capitalist rule was under threat (even though the purpose of modern crime fiction was 'to divert a confused desire for social change into safe channels'),[38] Orwell saw it as a harbinger of moral and political catastrophe. He focused his remarks on James Hadley Chase's *No Orchids for Miss Blandish* (1939), a novel set in the USA in which a wealthy young woman is abducted and brutally raped by gangsters. By the time the gangsters are tracked down and murdered by the police, the woman in question (the 'Miss Blandish' of the title) has become so attached to one of her captors that she commits suicide rather than face life without him. Orwell had a number of objections to the entire sub-genre of thrillers to which this 'cesspool' of a book belonged. The first was that it posed an enormous threat to the distinctive moral outlook of the common people. If ordinary people were still inclined to behave better than their social superiors, or so the argument went, it was primarily because they had not fallen prey to moral relativism. By clinging to the belief that the distinction between right and wrong should be rigorously applied at all times and in all places, they had remained immune to the specious arguments which allowed intellectuals to justify the barbarism of the age. The problem with books like *No Orchids for Miss Blandish* was that they presented the relativist case in a peculiarly seductive form, implying that the only morality which truly mattered was that which served as a cover for one's personal interests. Orwell's broader point, reminiscent of the communist orthodoxy he had elsewhere sought to oppose, was that the work of writers like Chase expressed the same psychological outlook that had engendered the rise of fascism. The truly sinister thing about the modern crime novel was the *gratuitousness* with which it depicted brutal acts of violence. Once the reader has immersed himself in the orgy of rapes, murders and shootings which disfigure a book like *Orchids for Miss Blandish*, he can have little doubt that Chase's characters (and probably Chase himself) are motivated by a 'love of cruelty and wickedness *for their own sakes*.'[39] It was precisely this exultation in untrammelled power that Orwell would later describe in *Nineteen Eighty-Four* as the 'why' rather than the 'how' of totalitarian politics. As a sort of capstone to his argument, Orwell also pointed out that *No Orchids for Miss Blandish* was an 'impudent plagiarism of William Faulkner's novel, *Sanctuary*.'[40] This might well have been a deliberate response to West's attempt to confer legitimacy on the crime story by relating it to developments in high culture.

While Orwell recognised that the totalitarian outlook had taken root throughout the world, his specific point in 'Raffles and Miss Blandish' was that it had spread rapidly in the West through the medium of American popular culture. James Hadley Chase was not an American himself but he had made 'a complete mental transference to the American underworld.'[41] His book was typical of a new type of popular art, exemplified by gangster movies and the so-called 'Yank mags', which belied the USA's reputation for liberalism by emphasising the naked worship of power. Orwell's implied point was that America had proved susceptible to a semi-fascist outlook because its liberal principles could easily be subverted by people of an illiberal frame of mind.[42] In a society which ascribed immense importance to the idea of social mobility, there was always a danger that the desire for personal success would curdle into the assumption that 'anything is "done" so long as it leads on to power.'[43] In this sense, 'Raffles and Miss Blandish' anticipated the critique of meritocracy which writers such as Michael Young began to develop in the 1950s. Nor was it the only piece of writing in which Orwell expressed his concern about the 'Americanisation' of British popular culture. His article 'Decline of the English Murder' repeated the argument of 'Raffles and Miss Blandish' in a slightly more whimsical form.[44] The reviews he wrote for *Time and Tide* in 1940 and 1941 were full of scorn for the sheer implausibility of Hollywood movies, though it is clear that he enjoyed many of these films on their own terms.[45] And in his little-known essay 'Pleasure Spots' (1946), he traced the links between the artifice of American life and the threat to individual liberty. 'Pleasure Spots' was Orwell's only analysis of what can perhaps be called the topography of incipient totalitarianism. Surveying the restaurants, holiday camps and other commercial spaces in which the citizens of post-war America spent much of their leisure time, he implied that most of them had been designed with the purpose of destroying the culture of individualism. By herding their 'inmates' into large groups, they obscured the characteristics which distinguished one person from another. Their insistence on playing music at all times made it impossible for people to think clearly or even to hold a proper conversation. And by making use of the most hideously synthetic materials on the market (coloured glass, electric light and plastic), they helped to inculcate a mood of supreme indifference towards the natural world. The latter characteristic was especially important, or so Orwell implied, because the sense of 'awe', 'mystery' and 'littleness' which people experience in the presence of nature is one of the most effective antidotes to totalitarian conformity. Faced with the thought that 'hundreds of pleasure resorts...are now being planned', Orwell could only console himself by pointing out that the advent of the nuclear age made it 'unlikely that they will be finished.'[46] It was a disconcerting reminder of the sheer misanthropy to which he sometimes fell prey in the last few years of his life.

Seaside Postcards and the Virtues of the Common People

Most of Orwell's writings on the media and mass communication were pessimistic. While he clearly felt a certain affection for boys' comics, popular newspapers, detective novels and the like, the main message of his essays on these topics was that the media are 'censored in the interests of the ruling class.'[47] Like most other socialist writers of the 1930s, he was inclined to explain this state of affairs by pointing to the economic structure of the culture industry.[48] Since the majority of media companies are owned and controlled by the wealthy, or so the argument went, it is more or less impossible that mainstream journalists, fiction writers or broadcasters will ever be free to express a radical or anticapitalist perspective. And yet, at the same time, there was another strand in Orwell's writings on popular culture which interpreted certain media texts as a straightforward expression of the virtues of the common people. The essential document in this context was 'The Art of Donald McGill' (1941), an essay of fewer than 4000 words in which Orwell analysed the lurid 'seaside postcards' to which he had been devoted since his teens. The main theme of the essay was essentially an ethical one. As we shall see in a moment, Orwell's conclusion after surveying the postcards of McGill and others was not only that the English working class still subscribed to a fairly strict moral code (a point which partly contradicted his own argument in 'England Your England') but also that they possessed a shrewd realism about moral issues that was not evident in their social superiors. Because 'The Art of Donald McGill' was so idiosyncratic, it has usually been regarded as a unique event in the history of the English essay – a sort of virtuoso *jeu d'esprit* on a subject which no one but Orwell would ever have dreamed of addressing. While this is true up to a point, it overlooks the fact that Orwell was actually contributing to a debate which other writers on the left had already launched. The debate in question concerned the role of vulgarity and sensationalism in the popular media. There were some especially striking parallels between 'The Art of Donald McGill' and the work of the communist intellectual Charles Madge, whose essay 'Press, Radio and Social Consciousness' (1937) raised similar themes but came to very different conclusions.

There are at least two reasons why it is safe to assume that 'Press, Radio and Social Consciousness' had come to Orwell's attention. The first is that he either referred or alluded to the symposium in which it appeared on a number of occasions, notably in his essay 'Inside The Whale' (1940).[49] The second is that Madge's work as a co-founder of the Mass Observation movement (a pioneering collective of amateur anthropologists who collected sociological data throughout Britain) was of considerable interest to him.[50] Although Madge's essay touched on a number of aspects of media culture, its main purpose was to draw attention to an element of political ambiguity in popular newspapers. On the one hand, Madge insisted, it is clearly the case that the economic structure of the press has deeply reactionary consequences. Since the newspapers are owned by large commercial organisations which can only turn a profit by selling advertising space, it is more or less inevitable that the ideas they express will be those of the ruling class. However, the need to secure a mass readership has also obliged the newspapers to cultivate a mental atmosphere (to use one of Orwell's favourite phrases) which goes some way towards subverting those ideas. The leitmotif of the popular newspaper in Britain is a 'vulgar and sensational' ethos which reflects the unconscious preoccupation with sex and violence that characterises the working-class mind in modern conditions. When bourgeois ideology is juxtaposed against this ethos, when the prejudices of the ruling class are absorbed into the 'strange poetry' of the proletarian unconscious, there is every chance that the reader will adopt a critical distance from what he reads and begin to question the shibboleths of capitalist society: 'The newspaper-reader is temporarily in the state described by Coleridge as a "willing suspension of disbelief"...it means we regard it [i.e. the news] not as objective fact, but as poetic fact. It also means that when we stop reading, the news ceases to have the same hard, inescapable force that the objective fact has; it becomes a poetic memory, affecting our feelings but not our actions.'[51] In a sort of sub-Reichian twist to his argument, Madge also seemed to believe that cheap newspapers would ultimately have a dramatic effect on working-class morality. By appealing to desires that would otherwise have remained suppressed, they create 'formidable psychological reserves of dissatisfaction' which must one day subvert the ethic of self-denial on which capitalism depends. Moreover, in their endless search for new sources of sensationalism, they frequently dredge up material which portrays the existing system in a more morbid light than ever:

> Even when ostensibly benevolent, capitalism cannot help being the bearer of evils; and even when, vice versa, it is simply out to win a big circulation, the newspaper cannot help being a good influence, and eventually an influence subversive of itself. Though it may carry political propaganda and exploiter-class advertisement on one page, on another it will print the story of a starving unemployed family, simply because it is a good human story. The class-basis of the proprietors determines the politics; the class-basis of the readers at least helps to determine the rest of the news.[52]

Whereas Madge saw the 'sensational and vulgar' material at the heart of the popular media as a sort of cultural acid, profoundly subversive in its capacity to corrode bourgeois ideology and tempt ordinary people away from their puritanism, Orwell interpreted it in a much more conservative fashion. The first few pages of 'The Art of Donald McGill' lovingly described the most common scenarios in McGill's postcards, making it clear that McGill took a 'humorous' but not 'witty' delight in satirising society's most morally esteemed activities – getting married, having children, behaving respectfully towards the old. Yet the clear message of the essay was that the orgy of garish colours, porcine women and obscene jokes in seaside postcards was not so much a challenge to established morality as a way of reaffirming it. McGill's satires only strike us as funny because they take the continued existence of a 'fairly strict moral code' for granted: 'This [a postcard satirising a newly married couple] is obscene…but it is not immoral. Its implication – and this is just the implication *Esquire* or the *New Yorker* would avoid at all costs – is that marriage is something profoundly exciting and important, the biggest event in the average human being's life.'[53] Moreover, the element of vulgarity in his work reflected a deep moral wisdom which is common among working people but rare in the middle and upper classes. By sending up established values in a way which did very little to subvert them, McGill evoked the deep shades of grey which invariably characterise our moral outlook – the fact that each of us is simultaneously Don Quixote (a principled defender of moral order) as well as Sancho Panza ('a little fat man' who values self-indulgence and personal survival more than moral honour). Orwell seemed to believe that this sense of moral complexity is especially pronounced among ordinary people, who translate it into a determination both to observe existing standards but not to be irrationally beholden to them. As such, the moral vision of the working class is similar to the one enunciated in Chapter Seven of Ecclesiastes: 'Be not righteous over much…why shouldst thou destroy thyself? Be not overmuch wicked, neither be thou foolish.'[54] Orwell also endorsed the expression in McGill's postcards of a fairly bleak vision of human limitations, one which again reflected the innate good sense of working people. When McGill peopled his drawings with images of physical grotesquerie, including women with enormous bottoms and pathetic husbands with emaciated torsos and false teeth, he was effectively expressing the proletarian conviction that 'youth and adventure – almost, indeed, individual life – end with marriage.'[55] The scion of a middle- or upper-class home might still regard life after the age of twenty-five as an opportunity for personal fulfilment; but his working-class counterpart will probably abandon all his personal ambitions once the first flush of youth has passed. To be working class and married is to live almost solely for one's children.

Although 'The Art of Donald McGill' is not an especially political essay, it is easy to see why a socialist of Orwell's stamp might have been attracted to the 'world view' expressed in McGill's postcards. As a writer who was always suspicious of the doctrine of human perfectibility, not least because it had infected the socialist movement with the sort of intolerance that ultimately gave rise to Stalinism, Orwell perhaps saw the element of working-class fatalism in seaside postcards as a useful antidote to utopian illusions. Moreover, since he seems to have suffered from what his friend Richard Rees called a 'hypersensitive conscience',[56] there was also perhaps a sense in which he regarded the socialist movement as a potent source of guilt. With its manichaean habit of portraying the workers as wholly good and the bosses as irredeemably evil (along with its its insistence that socialism would expunge all forms of selfishness from human nature), the socialist movement must sometimes have struck Orwell as an intolerably demanding moral taskmaster, continually reminding him of his own failure to behave with absolute integrity. In this context, McGill's Ecclesiastean moral code must have provided reassuring evidence that the working class would never be tempted by the inhumane strictures of a black-and-white morality. Indeed, 'The Art of Donald McGill' goes a long way towards challenging some of the more simplistic assumptions about Orwell's attitude to morality. Ever since V.S. Pritchett described him as a 'secular saint' in an obituary notice in the *New Statesman* in 1950,[57] there has been a tendency to regard Orwell as a *soi-disant* moral guardian of the most uncompromising kind. Inclined on the one hand to assess his own behaviour by impossibly high standards, he was also (or so the argument goes) brutally hard on anyone who called the basic standards of Judaeo-Christian civilisation into question. No one who has read Orwell's attacks on the 'shrieking little poseurs' and 'pious sodomites' of the British left can doubt that there is an element of truth in all this; but there is another side to the story which is much more important. While Orwell was indeed an opponent of moral relativism (a point which came out clearly in 'Raffles and Miss Blandish'), he was also obsessively scrupulous in distinguishing genuine infractions of morality from less serious misdemeanours. His writings were littered with passages in which he defended the unlikeliest people against charges of degeneracy, even when he risked considerable moral or political censure by doing so. For instance, in a remarkable review of Charles du Bos's *Byron and the Need of Fatality* in *The Adelphi* (September 1932), he argued that Byron's infamous leaning towards incest was a 'fairly trivial matter', apparently on the grounds that he (Byron) 'had no feeling of perversion in what he did'.[58] And eight years later, even while arguing that Britain would not survive the war unless it turned towards socialism, he insisted on pointing out that the English ruling class were '*morally* fairly sound'.[59] Although Orwell was inclined to use words such as 'evil', 'frightful' and 'abominable' a bit too readily, he was no apostle of saloon-bar prejudice. As 'The Art of Donald McGill' proves, his writings are a powerful riposte to moral fanaticism of all kinds.

3

LITERATURE AND COMMITMENT

Nothing illustrates Orwell's ambivalence towards cultural Marxism more powerfully than his writings on literature. In the period when Orwell wrote his most important pieces of literary criticism, his contemporaries in the Communist Party spent much of their time trying to achieve two things. The first was to show that many of England's greatest writers had displayed a definite tendency towards political radicalism, sometimes to the point where their work could even be described as communist. The second was to identify the reactionary elements in the outlook of the leading modernists, most of whose work was dismissed as a symptom of capitalist society in decline. It is no exaggeration to say that much of Orwell's criticism took its lead from these two bodies of work. The great essays on Dickens and Swift can be read as direct responses to communist writings on English literary radicalism (the former came perilously close to plagiarising a book by T.A. Jackson), while essays such as 'Inside the Whale', 'W.B. Yeats' and 'Gandhi and Mayfair' reworked a number of Marxist arguments about the politics of modernism. At the same time, however, Orwell's criticism was also marked by a distinctly unfashionable emphasis on the dangers of mixing politics with art. Although most of the English communists paid lip-service to the idea that Marxist content was no guarantee of literary greatness, their day-to-day critical judgements were often fiercely partisan. Even writers as sophisticated as Alick West, Ralph Fox and Christopher Caudwell occasionally gave the impression that their main criterion for judging a book was whether or not it reflected the current line of the Communist Party. In a notorious essay in C. Day Lewis's symposium *The Mind in Chains* (1937), Edward Upward even went so far as to suggest that 'no book written *at the present time* can be "good" unless it is written from a Marxist or near-Marxist viewpoint.'[1] By contrast, while accepting that the creative writer and the literary critic had no choice but to be political in the modern age, Orwell wrote a whole series of pieces in which he warned against the dangers of excessive partisanship. This chapter tries to clarify Orwell's approach to literature by (1) exploring his hostility to the cult of political commitment, (2) assessing his contributions to work on English literary radicalism, and (3) surveying his interpretation of modernism.

The Perils of Commitment

Although Orwell was primarily a literary critic rather than a theorist of literature, he outlined the general ideas which informed his criticism in a series of essays and broadcasts. The most important of these were probably 'The Frontiers of Art and Propaganda' (1941), 'Literature and Totalitarianism' (1941), 'Literature and the Left' (1943), 'Why I Write' (1946), 'The Prevention of Literature' (1946) and 'Writers and Leviathan' (1948). Orwell's argument in these pieces was an interestingly ambiguous one. On the one hand he insisted that all works of literature are intrinsically political and have definite political effects. On the other hand, suspicious of the excessively partisan approach of some of his Marxist contemporaries, he also warned that certain types of political commitment can end up having a disastrous effect both on literary criticism and on literature itself. As we shall see, Orwell's anxiety about the 'invasion of literature by politics'[2] was largely a consequence of his early exposure to the art-for-art's-sake movement, whose ideology he had only partly outgrown.

When Orwell argued that all literature should ultimately be regarded as political, he was advancing a similar case to that of the English Marxists. His basic assumption was that the majority of literary works tend to 'reflect' the existing social (and especially economic) circumstances, primarily in the sense that they contain 'propaganda in some form or other' whose purpose is to legitimise the status quo.[3] He further argued that a writer's political message goes a long way towards determining the style of his work, even though he opened his essay on Yeats with the complaint that 'Marxist criticism has not succeeded...in...trac[ing] the connection between "tendency" and literary style.'[4] Largely unimpressed by the communist experiments in 'Socialist Realism', Orwell nevertheless accepted that certain works can offer a critical perspective on the status quo and make a powerful case for social reform. What distinguished Orwell from the communists was the belief that the political interpretation of literature, though undoubtedly an advance on purely intrinsic forms of criticism (e.g. that of George Saintsbury), might ultimately wreak havoc on literary culture if applied too narrowly. His main argument was that the outlook of the successful writer is invariably at odds with the outlook of the effective politician. Since the dawn of the modern age, or so Orwell insisted, it has been customary to regard literature as a means of individual self-expression. The writer under capitalism has been expected to provide an accurate record of what he thinks and feels, and this has meant that 'sincerity' has become a necessary (though not sufficient) condition of literary excellence: 'The worst thing we can say about a work of art is that it is insincere...Modern literature...is either the truthful expression of what one man thinks and feels, or it is nothing.'[5] The problem with political movements is that they can only achieve success by peddling half-truths and lies to a credulous public. If a writer commits himself wholeheartedly to a political movement, in the sense of seeking to express its distinctive outlook and principles in his creative writings, he invariably poisons the wellsprings of his inspiration by subordinating his own beliefs to the strategic distortions of his colleagues. Because political commitment is the enemy of self-expression, it is also the enemy of great art.

Orwell took it for granted that no responsible writer in the middle of the twentieth century would ever wish to withdraw from politics. At a time when totalitarianism is flourishing and even the most purblind intellectual has become aware of the 'enormous injustice and misery of the world',[6] serious writers have a moral obligation to participate in political movements and to address political themes in their work. If they wish to protect themselves against the worst effects of political commitment, their only option is to draw a rigid distinction between their activism and their writing. When a writer engages in ordinary political activity, he must simply reconcile himself to all the dishonesty and low cunning that go with it – no man can have clean hands in the fight for a better society. But the one thing he must never do is become a hired propagandist at the service of his particular cause. When a writer explores political themes in his work, his first commitment must always be to the truth and not to the half-truths and lies of the practical politician. He must always evoke political realities in all their ambiguity and complexity, even if this involves being ruthlessly candid about his own side's deficiencies. The only person who can write decently about politics is not the 'good Party man' of Marxist lore but the curmudgeonly outsider who cocks a snook at all existing orthodoxies. More generally, Orwell also addressed the issue of how the economic rewards of authorship could be increased. Noting that few authors made a decent living from the royalties on their books, he attacked the assumption that people like himself should have to resort to journalism in order to subsidise their more serious work: 'Journalism…makes concentration on one subject and prolonged spells of work very difficult.'[7] Rejecting the idea that authors should seek patronage from the wealthy or grants from the state (and ignoring the issue of how writers would make their living under socialism), Orwell insisted that the only practical solution to the writer's dilemma was reform of library financing. If the cost of subscribing to a library were slightly increased and the public obliged to pay a 'small fee' whenever they borrowed a book, it would then be possible to pay a royalty to the author whenever his work was checked out. Orwell made an amusing attempt to browbeat his readers into supporting this scheme by appealing to their puritanism. Pointing out that most people were happier to spend money on drinking, smoking and visiting the cinema than on reading a book, he sardonically implied that regular drinkers were infinitely nobler than their more respectable counterparts in the 'reading public'. The former were at least willing 'to pay for [their] beer' (Orwell was himself a fan of English bitters),[8] whereas the latter expected to get their literary pleasures for free. It says something for the solidly practical cast of Orwell's mind that similar proposals for the reform of libraries were later passed into law.[9]

If Orwell believed that political commitment posed a major threat to the integrity of literature, he also feared its consequences for the quality of literary criticism. According to Orwell, the besetting sin of the *engagé* critic is to evaluate literature by political rather than aesthetic criteria. His tendency is always to praise a book if it accords with his own beliefs and dismiss it if it expresses an uncongenial point of view, regardless of its merits as a piece of writing. Orwell often condemned such communist writers as Christopher Caudwell, Philip Henderson and Edward Upward on precisely these grounds. Indeed, the persistence with which he accused them of political bias is one of the main reasons why their influence on him has gone undetected. However, his most important remarks on bias in criticism occurred in a celebrated essay on an altogether weightier critic. In 'Lear, Tolstoy and the Fool' (1947), the main themes of which had first been rehearsed in a BBC talk entitled 'Tolstoy and Shakespeare' (1941),[10] Orwell set out to discover why Leo Tolstoy had treated Shakespeare's plays with such contempt in his little-known pamphlet *Shakespeare and the Drama* (1903). How was it, Orwell inquired, that Tolstoy had been able to defy the received aesthetic wisdom and dismiss Shakespeare as a 'vulgar hack'? His conclusion was that Shakespeare had enraged Tolstoy (and thereby clouded his aesthetic judgement) by exposing the limits of his political beliefs. As is well known, Tolstoy embraced an ideology of extreme asceticism in his final years. Convinced that it was only possible to do the will of God by eschewing all material comforts and attending selflessly to the needs of others, he divested himself of his considerable wealth and adopted the lifestyle of an ordinary Russian peasant. The results were famously disastrous. Orwell's argument was that Tolstoy found it impossible to read Shakespeare dispassionately because he realised that in *King Lear* (a play singled out for especially virulent criticism in *Shakespeare and the Drama*) the whole idea of world-renunciation had been exposed as a sham. When Lear sloughed off his regal status and sank into a life of poverty, Shakespeare had roundly attacked him for turning his back on the wellsprings of human happiness: 'Don't relinquish power, don't give away your lands.'[11] If even a genius like Tolstoy could corrupt his aesthetic judgement by adhering too rigidly to a particular set of political beliefs, or so Orwell seemed to imply, it behoves all the rest of us to take special care not to fall into the same trap. Since Orwell had himself made a deliberate effort to renounce his class background (though never as fanatically as Tolstoy), he no doubt regarded his enthusiasm for *King Lear* as a reassuring sign that his own judgement retained its integrity.

As has often been pointed out, Orwell's ambivalence towards the political interpretation of literature had a great deal to do with the residual influence of the art-for-art's-sake movement.[12] As a schoolboy at Eton and later as an aspiring young author, Orwell had absorbed many of the assumptions which began to creep into literary culture at the time of Walter Pater, Oscar Wilde and the other so-called 'aesthetes'.[13] The most important of these was that 'art' and 'society' are irreconcilably opposed to each other. Since modern societies have treated art with a total lack of respect, or so the aesthetes argued, it is necessary for the artist to protest against his marginal status by taking it to provocative new extremes. Not only must he demonstrate his contempt for all forms of social activity (economics, politics and so on), he must also turn his private quest for 'beauty' into the sole subject matter of his art. The artist is an apostle of privacy or he is nothing. At the level of theory, the aesthetes launched a frontal assault on the idea that the purpose of art is somehow to 'reflect' the external world. Anxious to drive a wedge between art and society, they argued that the best works of literature create a sort of parallel universe in which the reader can take sanctuary from the unpleasant realities of his everyday life: 'Art is our spirited protest, our gallant attempt to teach Nature her proper place' (Oscar Wilde).[14] Although Orwell came to reject ideas such as these, not least because the notion of the autonomous artist could simply not be sustained in an age as hair-raisingly political as his own, there is no doubt that his grounding in aestheticism was the main factor which prevented him embracing the political theory of literature too uncritically. By imbuing him with the unshakeable conviction that art and politics must always be uncomfortable bedfellows, the ideology of the art-for-art's sake movement served to remind him that (1) a political writer is likely to be worthless unless he commands a high level of literary skill, (2) it is possible to derive aesthetic pleasure even from those works whose political message one disagrees with, and (3) the best political writers are those who view their particular movement from the perspective of a querulous outsider.

There were also passages in Orwell's work which strongly implied that the assumptions of the art-for-art's sake movement could still have progressive consequences, regardless of their theoretical weakness. For instance, in a fascinating review of Julian Green's *Personal Record 1928–1939* (1941), Orwell seemed to argue that aesthetes like Green provide a model of civility against which the utilitarian spirit of the age can be judged. By virtue of being wholly and unashamedly useless, they provide a salutary contrast to the horrible obsession with efficiency which dominates the industrial world: '...the ghostly sincerity of this book is deeply appealing. It has the charm of the ineffectual, which is so out of date as to wear an air of novelty.'[15] Moreover, there are obvious Wildean overtones to the passages in *Nineteen Eighty-Four* in which Winston gazes at the old paperweight which he buys from Mr Charrington's junk-shop. At least a century old (and therefore a piquant reminder of a time before the Party), the paperweight was made from 'soft, rain-watery glass' and contained a sprig of pink coral.[16] What Winston seemed to value most was the way it set itself apart from contemporary London, enticing the viewer into an alternative (and infinitely beautiful) world from which all political impurities had been expunged:

> Winston did not get up for a few minutes more. The room was darkening. He turned over towards the light and lay gazing into the glass paperweight. The inexhaustibly interesting thing was not the fragment of coral but the interior of the glass itself. There was such a depth of it, and yet it was almost as transparent as air. It was as though the surface of the glass had been the arch of the

> sky, enclosing a tiny world with its atmosphere complete. He had the feeling that he could get inside it, and that in fact he was inside it, along with the mahogany bed and the gate-leg table, and the clock and the steel engraving and the paperweight itself. The paperweight was the room he was in, and the coral was Julia's life and his own, fixed in a sort of eternity at the heart of the crystal.[17]

Simply by illustrating the aesthete's maxim that a work of art should always create a world of its own, the paperweight defied the crushing sameness of a totalitarian culture. At a time when the Party insisted that there were no alternatives to the status quo, it reminded Winston that there are *always* different ways of organising our lives. The aesthete might be foolishly irresponsible in his contempt for politics, Orwell implied, but his yearning for alternative realities makes him a natural enemy of tyranny.

The Radical Tradition in English Literature

The attempt to identify a radical tradition in English literature has preoccupied Marxist critics in Britain since the end of the nineteenth century. Eleanor Marx and Edward Aveling published a book-length study of *Shelley's Socialism* as early as 1888,[18] while many of the CPGB's early newspapers and journals (notably the *Sunday Worker* and *Communist Review*) made a point of carrying introductory articles on writers such as Burns, Blake and Shakespeare. Yet it was not until the 1930s that Marxist intellectuals recounted the history of literary radicalism with any degree of thoroughness. As we have seen in Chapter One, the outpouring of work on the 'English radical tradition' began in earnest in 1935 and took its lead from Georgi Dimitrov's seminal speech to the Seventh Congress of the Communist International. Proclaiming the need for communist parties throughout the world to adopt a 'People's Front' strategy against fascism, Dimitrov pointed out that fascist organisations had gained an advantage over the left by portraying themselves as the true inheritors of their respective national traditions. It was therefore necessary for Marxists to restore the historical balance by drawing attention to the rich traditions of popular and artistic radicalism in their countries of origin. In the four years between the CPGB's adoption of the People's Front strategy and its temporary abandonment of it in 1939, British communists produced influential monographs on three radical writers (Morris, Dickens and Bunyan) as well as a flurry of articles on other literary radicals in journals such as *Left Review* and the *Daily Worker*.[19] The investigation of literary radicalism was continued after the war in the journal *Our Time* (founded in 1941) and reached new heights of sophistication in the writings of Marxist historians such as Christopher Hill, Arnold Kettle and E.P. Thompson. Most of these writers acknowledged a debt to the pioneering work of the 1930s.

There are several ways in which Orwell's writings on the radical tradition in English Literature can be linked to those of the communists. His two most important essays on individual British authors were probably 'Charles Dickens' (1940) and 'Politics vs Literature: An Examination of *Gulliver's Travels*' (1946). The first of these was a direct response to T.A. Jackson's *Charles Dickens: The Progress of a Radical* (1937), an influential communist text which Orwell famously accused of 'stealing' Dickens for political purposes. As we shall see, Orwell's strategy was shamelessly to distort Jackson's book while using one of its main arguments as the basis for a new hypothesis about the nature of Dickens's radicalism. By contrast, 'Politics vs Literature' was a mischievous riposte to one of the main assumptions on which the communist investigation of English radicalism had been based. Whereas the communists had set out to prove that none of the great writers of the past displayed fascist or proto-fascist sympathies, Orwell argued that the great interest of *Gulliver's Travels* was that it explored the outlook of right-wing authoritarianism *from the inside*. Far from being a precursor of the modern socialist or anti-imperialist, Swift was a bad-tempered misanthrope whose books provided the left with a rare insight into the mental habits of its deadliest political enemies. The purpose of the rest of this section is to bring these issues into focus by (1) providing a brief account of the influence of *Charles Dickens: The Progress of a Radical* on 'Charles Dickens', and (2) comparing Orwell's writings on Swift to those of communist writers such as Edgell Rickword and Rex Warner. I will also try to flesh out Orwell's understanding of the radical tradition by glancing at some of his shorter writings on English authors, notably the important essays on Charles Reade, Tobias Smollett and Samuel Butler.

Dickens as Moralist

The first point which Orwell made in 'Charles Dickens' was that over the years a large number of critics had misleadingly projected their own beliefs onto Dickens's work, on the grounds that 'Dickens is one of those writers who are well worth stealing.'[20] One of his two examples was T.A. Jackson, perhaps the greatest self-taught British Marxist of his generation,[21] whose recent book *Charles Dickens: The Progress of A Radical* was said to portray its subject as a man of communist sympathies. The virulence of Orwell's attack has tended to obscure the fact that the argument of 'Charles Dickens' was actually very similar to that of Jackson, even though he (Orwell) was ultimately advancing a quite different case about Dickens's radicalism. Although Jackson's book is too disorganised and digressive to be straightforwardly summarised, its main concern was to portray Dickens as a cultural radical with a powerful faith in the possibilities of working-class power. Dickens, or so the argument went, instinctively understood that the cultural poverty of the Victorian age was rooted in its capitalist base. Since entrepreneurs have no choice but to be parsimonious with their investments (a situation summed up by Mr Gradgrind's injunction to 'buy in the cheapest market and sell in the dearest'),[22] and since a society's values are invariably based on those of the dominant economic system, it follows that the main characteristic of everyday life under capitalism will be a brutal suppression of emotion. The consequences of a compassionless culture are particularly severe for children, whom the system (in the form of such schoolmaster-ogres as Dr Blimber, Mrs Pipchin and Wackford Squeers) treats as undisciplined beasts whose spirit has to be broken at an early age.[23] According to Jackson, who was unfairly described by Orwell as making 'spirited efforts to turn Dickens into a bloodthirsty revolutionary',[24] Dickens responded to the crisis of Victorian culture by calling for power to be taken out of bourgeois hands and devolved to working people. As soon as the workers are assigned a more central role in society, or so Dickens allegedly believed, their natural generosity of mind would pose a major threat to the more self-denying traditions of the ruling class. Working on this assumption, Jackson put forward the startling argument that the various stages in the evolution of Dickens's writings can be precisely correlated with the various stages in the development of Victorian radicalism. The first, roughly between 1836 and 1842, was one of unbounded optimism. At a time when Chartism enjoyed mass support and male wage-earners seemed on the verge of winning the vote, Dickens wrote a series of novels (*Pickwick Papers*, *Oliver Twist*, *Nicholas Nickleby*) in which class hierarchies were treated as a purely accidental feature of modern society, soon to be replaced by a more fluid set of economic and political relationships. Among the most important characters in these books were benevolent employers such as Pickwick and Brownlow who were held up as models of democratic virtue. The argument of the books was essentially a moral one. If only the people at the top of society behaved more responsibly, Dickens appeared to suggest, then inequalities would rapidly be reduced and the capitalist system would work perfectly well.[25] However, the subsequent retrenchment of English radicalism was rapidly to engender a darkening of Dickens's mood. In the years between the collapse of industrial Chartism in 1842 and the failure of the Second Charter in 1848, most of his novels (especially *Dombey and Son*) began to explore the factors which prevent the wealthy from voluntarily surrendering their power. One of his main themes at this point was the nature of pride, seen as the natural ally of hierarchy.[26] Moreover, the final period of his career (stretching from 1848 through to his death in 1872) saw the growing pessimism of the second period harden into outright despair about the possibility of social change. Looking on as the challenge of Chartism collapsed, Dickens now came to believe that British institutions were specifically designed to prevent ordinary people from exercising power. He illustrated this view with great trenchancy in *Bleak House* (1853), which showed how the legal system seeks to exclude the uninitiated by adopting procedures of a wholly unnecessary complexity.[27]

Without ever acknowledging that he owed a debt to Jackson, Orwell relied heavily on his insights while developing his own account of Dickens's work. At the heart of 'Charles Dickens' was a blatant attempt to appropriate one of Jackson's most important arguments while considerably extending its scope. As we have seen, Jackson believed that (1) the early Dickens was a 'moralist' who thought that society would change for the better so long as the people at the top of the system behaved more responsibly, but also that (2) he had grown out of his moralism once the true nature of British institutions became clear to him. Orwell's argument was that Dickens had indeed been a moralist but that he retained his moralism throughout the whole of his career. Always sympathetic to the underdog (though never entirely comfortable with the organised working-class), he had nevertheless rejected the path of social reform and put all his faith in a change of heart on the part of the elite: 'His whole "message" is one that at first glance looks like an enormous platitude: If men would behave decently the world would be decent.'[28] In support of this reading, Orwell put forward his own version of Jackson's argument about the three stages into which Dickens's work can be divided. Whereas Jackson had argued that Dickens began as a moralist (stage one), then came to doubt the willingness of the elite to change its ways (stage two) and finally became an uncompromising critic of British institutions (stage three), Orwell argued that the three stages in his career were actually defined by subtle changes to his original moral outlook. In his 'early optimistic period', Dickens clearly believed that British society would soon be redeemed by the philanthropy of the high and mighty.[29] The main characteristic of the 'rather despondent' novels of the 1850s was not an abandonment of moralism so much as a new emphasis on 'the helplessness of well-meaning individuals in a corrupt society.'[30] Casting a gloomy eye over the worst cases of Victorian injustice in novels such as *Great Expectations* and *Hard Times,* Dickens was obviously coming to doubt whether a few enlightened members of the establishment could indeed effect a sea-change in human affairs. However, by the time he entered his third period (exemplified by *Our Mutual Friend*), he had returned once more to his early faith in the moral capacities of the elite: 'Dickens's thoughts seem to have come full circle...individual kindliness is the remedy for everything.'[31]

Orwell buttressed his account of Dickensian moralism in a couple of passages which were surely written in direct response to the corresponding passages in Jackson's book. The first concerned that 'recurrent Dickens figure, the Good Rich Man.'[32] As we have seen, Jackson believed that wealthy philanthropists were integral to Dickens's early period because they symbolised the ability of the elite to eschew self-interest. Characters such as Pickwick, Brownlow and the Cheerybles went out of their way to shower wealth and opportunity on their less fortunate brethren, in the process acquiring the status of 'good fairies'. Orwell broadly endorsed this argument but was rather more critical of what he took to be Dickens's lack of realism, noting that 'Even Dickens must have reflected occasionally that anyone who was so anxious to give his money away would never have acquired it in the first place.'[33] Where Orwell and Jackson really parted company was in their estimation of the role of the Good Rich Man in Dickens's subsequent writings. In line with his assumption that all traces of moralism had disappeared from Dickens's outlook after the first period was complete, Jackson insisted that there were no benevolent employers at all in the novels written after 1842. By contrast, Orwell argued that the Good Rich Man had simply taken a slightly less extravagant form in the novels of the second period ('...[he] has dwindled from a "merchant" to a rentier'), only to be triumphantly revived at the eleventh hour in *Our Mutual Friend*:

> Nevertheless in the last completed novel, *Our Mutual Friend* (published 1864–5), the good rich man comes back in full glory in the

> person of Boffin. Boffin is a proletarian by origin and only wealthy by inheritance, but he is the usual *deus ex machina*, solving everybody's problems by showering money in all directions. He even 'trots' like the Cheerybles. In several ways *Our Mutual Friend* is a return to the earlier manner, and not an unsuccessful return either.[34]

The other passage of Jackson's to which Orwell seemed to reply directly concerned the representation of political violence in *Barnaby Rudge* and *A Tale of Two Cities*. Writing at a time when the CPGB still subscribed to an insurrectionary strategy for achieving socialism, Jackson insisted that Dickens became more attracted to the idea of violent revolution as his disillusionment with British institutions deepened. Whereas *Barnaby Rudge*, published in 1841 but written in 1839, seemed to dismiss the Gordon Rioters of 1780 as a bunch of drunkards and madmen, *A Tale of Two Cities* (1859) portrayed the *canaille* of 1789 in a much more favourable light.[35] By contrast, Orwell argued that Dickens felt a hatred for those who would seek change by force which remained constant throughout his career. The Gordon Riots are indeed presented in *Barnaby Rudge* as the work of an evil mob; but even in *A Tale of Two Cities*, which acknowledged that the French masses had legitimate grievances, it was strongly implied that the French Revolution might have been avoided if the aristocracy had only taken its responsibilities more seriously. The 'profound horror' which Dickens displayed in the face of 'mob violence' tells us all we need to know about his suspicion of political action.[36] This argument tied in with the more fundamental disagreements between Orwell and Jackson. The most important of these related to Dickens's attitude towards the working class. While accepting that his work could in some ways be interpreted as an attack on industrial capitalism, Orwell completely rejected the idea that Dickens was a sort of instinctive populist who wished to see power devolved to the workers. He was actually a rather typical member of the 'shabby genteel' classes who suffered from many of the ordinary snobberies of the age. Intensely concerned about the plight of the dispossessed, he could never quite free himself from the belief that people of his own kind were superior to those who laboured with their hands. His attitude in this regard became especially clear when he wrote about sexual relationships between working-class men and bourgeois women, since (in Orwell's memorable formulation) this 'is a thing too painful to be lied about, and consequently it is one of the points at which the "I'm-not-a-snob" pose tends to break down.'[37] The relationship between Uriah Heep and Agnes Wickfield was portrayed with a good deal of knee-jerk middle-class squeamishness, while other socially unequal trysts were usually treated simply as an occasion for humour. The limited nature of Dickens's sympathy towards the workers was further illustrated by (1) his semi-feudal attitude towards servants, (2) his almost complete failure to write about work (either of the agricultural or industrial variety), and (3) his seeming equation of the good life with ceaseless leisure and shameless luxury. On the other hand, Orwell seemed to agree with Jackson that Dickens had written brilliantly about the oppression of children, echoing his point that he (Dickens) had succeeded in satirising nearly all the 'systems' of education which prevailed during the Victorian period. However, whereas Jackson clearly regarded Dickens's writings on education as an extraordinary act of moral prophecy, Orwell felt that they had been partly vitiated by their 'woolly vagueness' and their failure to advance an educational perspective of their own.[38]

Since Orwell agreed with Jackson that the need to change society is ultimately more important than the need to change people's attitudes, why should he have gone out of his way to emphasise Dickens's moralism? Why did he write so warmly about a man who allegedly made no contribution whatsoever to the debate about social reform? The rather ironic answer is that he regarded Dickensian moralism as an important antidote to totalitarian habits of thought. In a slightly obscure passage towards the end of the essay, Orwell argued that the 'moralist' is likely to find it easier than the 'politician' to keep his humane instincts alive. If a man believes that human beings have been treated badly as a matter of choice, the argument seemed to go, his sympathy for them is likely to remain strong. Nothing illustrates this more powerfully than Dickens's writings, which are basically unpolitical but 'always and everywhere' on the side of the oppressed. By contrast the habit of explaining oppression solely in terms of social structure is always inherently dangerous, since it often leads to an obsession with impersonal historical forces at the expense of real people:

> Most revolutionaries are potential Tories, because they imagine that everything can be put right by altering the *shape* of society; once that change is effected, as it sometimes is, they see no need for any other...The common man is still living in the mental world of Dickens, but nearly every modern intellectual has gone over to some or other form of totalitarianism. From the Marxist

> or Fascist point of view, nearly all that Dickens stands for can be written off as 'bourgeois morality'.[39]

Orwell's implied point was that socialist societies can only flourish if they combine political reform with a Dickensian emphasis on moral responsibility. The grim alternative is Stalinist barbarism. Since Jackson was one of Britain's most egregious apologists for Stalinism, shamelessly defending the Moscow Trials in the pages of *Left Review*,[40] he might well have been one of the 'modern intellectuals' whom Orwell had in mind when he formulated this argument. At any rate, the amusing thing about 'Charles Dickens' is that it ripped Jackson's argument about moralism out of context and used it to launch a stinging attack on the movement to which Jackson belonged. It was a characteristic piece of Orwellian mischief.

Swift as 'Tory Anarchist'

Orwell's implicit point in 'Charles Dickens' was not that the communists were wrong to see Dickens as a radical, simply that their understanding of his radicalism was badly flawed. Elsewhere in his writings on English literature, taking his desire to outrage the communists to more extreme lengths, he came perilously close to a mischievous endorsement of precisely those fascist and *fascisant* arguments about culture to which the Party intellectuals were responding. As we have seen, Dimitrov had urged communists to write about the radical tradition in order to disprove the assumption that the values of the past were essentially fascist values in embryo. By contrast, Orwell seemed happy to admit that many of Britain's greatest writers had anticipated the fascist outlook. He insisted that the value of writers such as Swift and Gissing was not that they were 'progressive' but that they depicted the mentality of right-wing authoritarianism *from the inside.* The contrast between Orwell's writings on Swift and those of communists such as Rex Warner and Edgell Rickword is especially instructive. In the brief essays which they contributed to *Left Review* in the 1930s, Rickword and Warner both tried to rescue Swift from his reputation for hardline conservatism.[41] Despite being a Protestant cleric of solidly aristocratic background who served the government of Lord Oxford as a propagandist, Swift was portrayed by the communists as one of emergent capitalism's most uncompromising critics. In particular, he was credited with deep insight into capitalism's parlous effects on international affairs and individual liberty. Appalled by the sheer viciousness of market competition, or so the argument went, he soon came to realise that war, imperialism and abuses of state power were an inevitable consequence of the new bourgeois order. He also had a deep respect for the common people which reflected itself in the plain style of his political pamphlets. Swift's hostility to capitalism was partly ascribed to a sort of high-minded aristocratic resentment. As the representative of a pre-modern ruling class which the emerging bourgeoisie had done much to undermine, it was more or less inevitable that he would come to deplore 'the irresponsibility of man towards man which results when every item of personal worth has been translated into "exchange value".'[42] Moreover, in a surprising argument which reflected his own expertise in Classics, Warner went so far as to suggest that Swift's radicalism had been profoundly influenced by his classical education. Especially important was his interest in the philosophy of the Greek Stoics, who believed that human beings are inherently level-headed, group-minded and capable of sorting out their differences in a peaceable manner. Since the Augustan ruling class had proved spectacularly incapable of living up to these principles, Warner implied, Swift's hatred towards them had been all the more intense. At the same time, while praising his capacity for invective, the communists were anxious to dispel the idea that Swift had been a hater of humanity in general. In contrast to Dr Johnson's famous portrait of Swift as a man grown deranged by personal bitterness (see *The Lives of the Poets*), they effectively argued that his loathing of the elite was inversely proportional to his admiration for the powerless. 'This is not the record of a misanthrope', wrote Warner in an account of Swift's involvement in the campaign for Irish independence, 'but of a "defender of liberty".'[43]

Orwell's writings on Swift could hardly have been more different. 'Politics vs Literature' explicitly repudiated the idea that Swift should be regarded as a representative of the radical tradition: 'We are right to think of Swift as a rebel and iconoclast, but except in certain secondary matters, such as his insistence that women should receive the same education as men, he cannot be labelled "Left". He is a Tory anarchist, despising authority while disbelieving in liberty, and preserving the aristocratic outlook while seeing clearly that the existing aristocracy is degenerate and contemptible.'[44] By defining Swift as a 'Tory anarchist' (a label he had once applied to himself), Orwell was effectively turning the communist argument on its head. Whereas Warner and Rickword believed that Swift's aristocratic background made him deeply suspicious of capitalism, Orwell insisted that it had actually infected him with a virulent dose of traditionalist conservatism. For one thing it made him utterly contemptuous of the emerging scientific culture. At various places in *Gulliver's Travels* (1726), especially in the celebrated passages on the Academy of Lagado and the island of Laputa, he somewhat inconsistently portrayed scientists as (1) self-obsessed charlatans preoccupied with useless knowledge, (2) vulgar utilitarians engaged in a pointless race to invent new gadgets, and (3) presumptuous know-it-alls who wrongly believed that their expertise in science qualified them to pronounce on quite different areas of activity, such as religion and politics. Orwell explained Swift's hatred of science in terms of his aristocratic reverence for the past. Because he regarded science as the enemy of historical consciousness, not least because of its awesome capacity to transform the human environment, he greatly feared that it would end up destroying people's knowledge of the achievements of the pre-modern age. The twist in Orwell's argument was that Swift felt a special reverence for the Classical period and wrote about figures such as Brutus, Socrates and Junius with an 'almost unreasoning admiration'.[45] There was perhaps a conscious dig here at people like Rex Warner, who (as we have seen) interpreted Swift's knowledge of the classics in a rather more positive light. Far from providing him with a humane ethical perspective from which to criticise the excesses of modern capitalism, Orwell seemed to imply, Swift's classicism had actually turned him into a sentimental antiquarian.

Orwell's biggest disagreement with the communists centred on Swift's attitude towards authority. While accepting that Swift had been a formidable critic of the governing class of his day, he rejected the idea that this somehow signalled a liberal (or proto-socialist) concern for human rights. The only reasonable explanation for Swift's attacks on Walpole or the Duke of Monmouth was that his own faction had been excluded from power by the hated Whigs. Moreover, in his aristocratic anxiety to guard against change, he had come perilously close not simply to anticipating the politics of totalitarianism but also to endorsing them. Writing at a time when no state could impose total control on its subjects, he had conjured a vision of political dictatorship in Book III of *Gulliver* which uncannily foreshadowed the worst excesses of modern fascism:

> He [Swift] has an extraordinarily clear prevision of the spy-haunted 'police State,' with its endless heresy-hunts and treason trials, all really designed to neutralise popular discontent by changing it into war hysteria. And one must remember that Swift

> is here inferring the whole from a quite small part, for the feeble governments of his own day did not give him illustrations ready-made...There is something queerly familiar in the atmosphere of these chapters, because, mixed up with much fooling, there is a perception that one of the aims of totalitarianism is not merely to make sure that people will think the right thoughts, but actually to make them *less conscious.*[46]

Orwell did not make it entirely clear whether Swift approved of this sort of totalitarianism, though he described sections of Book III as an 'attack' on it. Nevertheless, the core of his argument was that Swift undoubtedly approved of the rather different type of totalitarianism which he portrayed in his sketch of the Houyhnhnms in Book IV. The Houyhnhnms have generally been seen as organising themselves along anarchist lines, since theirs was a society without laws or formal mechanisms of punishment. Orwell's point was that Swift's race of 'noble horses' had in fact arrived at the 'highest stage of totalitarian organisation' by making public opinion the primary means of social control.[47] Rehearsing the critique of anarchism which libertarian admirers such as George Woodcock, Vernon Richards and Nicholas Walter found so distressing,[48] he argued that a society which accepts the need for laws is likely to be more liberal than one which does not, since it allows (or potentially allows) the individual to behave as he sees fit so long as what he does is legal. By contrast an anarchist society has to rely on 'exhortation' as a means of binding people together, with the almost inevitable result that pluralism is squeezed out by the desire to conform: 'When human beings are governed by "thou shalt not", the individual can practise a certain amount of eccentricity: when they are supposedly governed by "love" or "reason", he is under continuous pressure to make him behave and think in exactly the same way as everyone else.'[49] What Swift really admired about the Houyhnhnms was that they agreed about practically everything and discussed very little. Their language contained no word for 'opinion', nor did they suppose that the pursuit of the truth required a judicious sifting of all the available evidence. Each of them believed that 'reason' provides a series of self-evident truths which every member of the community has a duty to obey. By portraying Swift as someone for whom disagreement was little more than 'sheer perversity', Orwell was mischievously transforming Warner's 'defender of liberty' into an apostle of what de Tocqueville or Mill might have called the tyranny of the majority.

There is no doubt that Orwell admired Swift enormously. On one occasion he even said that '*Gulliver's Travels* has meant more to me than any other book ever written.'[50] But how can this be explained? How could a libertarian socialist have been so attracted to an Augustan cleric whose suspicion of freedom was only matched by his hatred of science? Judging by the evidence of 'Politics vs Literature' (as well as a number of passages in other writings), the answer is that Orwell regarded Swift's pessimism as a salutary corrective to the panglossian dogmas of the left. Rejecting the efforts of Rickword and Warner to rescue their man from the accusation of misanthropy, Orwell was happy to go along with the Johnsonian line that Swift's ideas can ultimately be traced to a deep hatred of humanity. Indeed, he recognised that Swift's misanthropy was of a peculiarly uncompromising kind, arising out of visceral disgust at the grim realities of human biology: 'Swift was presumably impotent, and had an exaggerated horror of human dung: he also thought about it incessantly, as is evident throughout his works.'[51] Although Orwell did not endorse this vision of humanity (and even acknowledged that its author 'only just passes the test of sanity'),[52] his point was that Swift's extremism casts light on a corner of the mind which every human being needs to face up to. While the majority of people believe that human nature is basically good, nearly all of us occasionally feel that the body is disgusting and that human beings are incapable of behaving well. Since 'both horror and pain are necessary to the continuance of life on this planet',[53] Swift's work should therefore be regarded as a powerful warning against the suppression of our more uncomfortable assumptions. It is easy to see how remarks like this can be linked to Orwell's dislike of left-wing utopianism, even though he made no reference to his socialism in 'Politics vs Literature'. By forcibly reminding us of humanity's darker instincts, or so Orwell implied, Swift helps to insulate us against the naïve belief in human perfectibility which ultimately results in Stalinist barbarism. It was hardly an argument with which the communists would have agreed.

Literature and Antinomianism

Orwell's writings on Dickens and Swift were supplemented by a series of much shorter essays on English authors, most of them written either as broadcasts for the BBC or as free-standing contributions to *Tribune*. Many of these pieces identified an element of radicalism in the outlook of their chosen subjects, though not necessarily of a sort that was distinctively socialist. In a radio talk on *Macbeth* (October 1943), Orwell praised Shakespeare for anticipating the terrible paranoia and dread to which the tyrants of the twentieth century have invariably fallen victim: 'He [Macbeth] is in fact a sort of primitive medieval version of the modern Fascist dictator.'[54] Charles Reade was commended for his store of 'penny-encyclopaedic learning',[55] which Orwell perhaps associated with the no-nonsense empiricism and love of privacy that figured as hallmarks of the English character in *The Lion and the Unicorn.* Bernard Shaw was mentioned in dispatches for his savage indictment of war, his attack on Victorian moralism and his gift for combining 'political purpose' with genuine artistry.[56] More interesting still were the handful of literary essays in which Orwell gave indirect expression to his well-disguised streak of antinomianism. As we have already noted, Orwell had a typical outsider's regard for people who openly defy the most cherished values of their age, seeing them (arguably at any rate) as hard-line defenders of personal liberty from whom less adventurous souls can learn valuable lessons in independent thinking. His love of well-meaning licentiousness was expressed to high comic effect in a superb essay on Tobias Smollett (September 1944), in which 'Scotland's best novelist' was said to find 'duelling, gambling and fornication...almost morally neutral.'[57] The arch-aesthete Oscar Wilde was praised for exposing the hollow foundations of Victorian respectability (though Orwell also noted that his studious defiance of sexual convention had eventually been the death of him),[58] while Samuel Butler's famous assault on the Victorian family was implicitly endorsed in a BBC broadcast for sixth-form students in 1945.[59] Orwell even proposed that a strain of moral ambiguity could occasionally be found in entire literary genres. Surveying the history of English comic writing in 'Funny, But Not Vulgar' (1944), he disarmingly observed that the purpose of humour is to rid humanity of its delusions of grandeur by attacking its most important values: 'A joke['s]...aim is not to degrade the human being but to remind him that he is already degraded.'[60] Something similar was implied in the brief essay on 'Nonsense Poetry' (1945), where the work of Edward Lear was said to express the 'amiable lunacy' of an 'unhappy' and 'solitary' man.[61] At the same time, anxious to absolve himself of a charge of nihilism, Orwell also emphasised that the strain of absurdity in humorous writings has a definite progressive edge. One of the great pleasures of the comic tradition is that it allows us to see the 'mighty' brought down with 'a bump' ('Every joke is a tiny revolution...'),[62] while the 'they' so often invoked in nonsense verse are usually dry authority figures whom we enjoy seeing humiliated. In a striking illustration of his wish to keep moral chaos within limits, Orwell noted that his favourite verses by Lear were those which substituted a 'touch of burlesque or perverted logic' for out-and-out anarchy.[63]

Orwell's sneaking regard for antinomianism also explains some of his wider literary tastes, including his admiration for several of the more disreputable figures in the history of American literature. He seems to have been especially drawn to Mark Twain and Walt Whitman, whose work he valued for reflecting the extraordinary spirit of freedom which accompanied the expansion into the American West in the mid- to late-nineteenth century. In his fine essay 'Mark Twain – The Licensed Jester', published in *Tribune* in November 1943, Orwell argued that the frontier culture of Twain's time was one of the least restrictive in human history. As thousands of people migrated Westwards and established makeshift communities along the route, it was more or less impossible for traditional forms of authority to make themselves felt. The state was extraordinarily weak; employers had no real means of disciplining their workers; the churches were widely ignored and weighed down by doctrinal disagreements. The result was that 'human beings felt free, indeed *were* free, as they had never been before and may not be again for centuries.'[64] Knowing full well that their misdemeanours were likely to go unpunished, people developed a 'strange and sometimes sinister individuality' which owed little to the established morality.[65] This was the quality which Twain managed to capture in the variety of criminals, labourers and adventurers who populated novels such as *The Innocents at Home*, *Roughing It* and *Life on the Mississippi*. Orwell hinted at the political significance of these novels when he said that they show 'how human beings behave when they are not frightened of the sack.'[66] By describing the men of the American West in all their devil-may-care irreverence, or so it was implied, Twain had provided the modern workers with a sort of Platonic image of political independence which could inspire their struggles for a better society. After several decades in which anti-Americanism has become entrenched on the left, we often forget that many British radicals in the period between the American Revolution and the New Deal regarded the USA as a potent source of libertarian inspiration. Orwell's remarks about Twain (as well as his eulogy on Whitman in 'Inside the Whale') reminds us that the power of America's faith in individual liberty should not be underestimated.

The Politics of Modernism

The communist writers of the 1930s generally took a dim view of developments in modern literature. The idea that 'bourgeois literature' had recently undergone a terrible decline first took root in Britain during the Class-against-Class period (1928–1933), receiving powerful expression in the work of John Strachey, Montagu Slater and John Cornford.[67] After 1934 it played a central role in the various attempts to win support for the aesthetic of Socialist Realism. Following the lead of the various speeches at the Soviet Writers' Congress, especially those of Zhdanov and Bukharin, British communists began to portray modernism as a sort of diseased sham-literature to which Socialist Realism provided the only alternative. These were the years in which writers such as Joyce, Eliot and Lawrence were routinely dismissed as semi-fascist exemplars of a 'dying culture'. At first sight, Orwell's attitude towards modern literature seemed to have nothing in common with that of the Marxists. An unabashed admirer of the leading British modernists, he openly attacked the likes of Philip Henderson and D.S. Mirsky for failing to recognise their greatness.[68] Yet his own writings on modernism were themselves sometimes marred by a note of political intolerance. This was especially true of 'Inside the Whale' (1940) and several other essays written at about the same time, many of which echoed the communist tracts that Orwell had been reading over the previous couple of years. The purpose of this section is to bring these echoes into clearer focus. It will look in turn at (1) Orwell's analysis of the fashionable modernist writers of the 1920s, (2) his controversial account of the work of Henry Miller, and (3) his scathing critique of the so-called 'Auden school' of literary radicals.

Aestheticism and Reaction

Orwell's work is littered with appreciative references to the modernist writers who came to prominence in Britain in the 1920s. In an autobiographical note which he contributed to an American dictionary of contemporary authors in 1940, he even went so far as to describe Joyce, Eliot and Lawrence as being among the handful of writers whom 'I care most about and never grow tired of'. This makes it all the more surprising that his most important writings on modernism should have adopted such a jaundiced tone. In 'Inside the Whale' and a handful of other essays and broadcasts, notably 'The Rediscovery of Europe' (1942), 'W.B. Yeats' (1943) and 'Benefit of Clergy: Some Notes on Salvador Dali' (1944), Orwell went out of his way to accuse the modernists of political irresponsibility. His argument was based on the implicit recognition that many of the modernists were unhealthily obsessed with the issue of literary form. Like their predecessors in the art-for-art's sake movement, Orwell seemed to suggest, they rejected the idea that literature 'reflects' reality and instead regarded the poem, story or novel as a sort of self-enclosed world of its own. They therefore assumed that the main purpose of the literary work was to draw attention to what we might now call its 'autonomy', showing how language invariably distorts the 'real world' even as it seeks to record it:

> When one looks back at the 'twenties, nothing is queerer than the way in which every important event in Europe escaped the notice of the English intelligentsia...In 'cultured' circles art-for-art's-saking extended practically to a worship of the meaningless. Literature was supposed to consist solely in the manipulation of words. To judge a book by its subject-matter was the unforgivable sin, and even to be aware of its subject-matter was looked on as a lapse of a taste. About 1928, in one of the three genuinely funny jokes that *Punch* has produced since the Great War, an intolerable youth is pictured informing his aunt that he intends to 'write'. 'And what are you going to write about, dear?' asks the aunt. 'My dear aunt,' says the youth crushingly, 'one doesn't write *about* anything, one just *writes*.'[69]

Why should this obsession with the autonomy of literature have taken such deep root in the years between the wars? Orwell's implied answer was that most of the modernists had been infected by a 'tragic sense of life'.[70] Unlike Wells, Shaw and the other cheerful proseltyisers who dominated English literature in the Edwardian period, men like Eliot, Lawrence and Yeats were crippled by pessimism. None of them had any faith in science, technology or the idea of progress. Having convinced themselves that real life was not to be trusted, it was more or less inevitable (or so Orwell implied) that they would take refuge in the idea that literature was somehow hermetically sealed from the world around them. The twist in Orwell's argument was that the belief in aesthetic autonomy had condemned the modernists to a species of political obscurantism. Because they refused to accept that literature could represent the world accurately, none of them had come close to addressing the important issues of the day. In an age of economic slump, imperialist war and fascism, they had wilfully resorted to subject matters and beliefs that were mind-numbingly recondite. Eliot became an Anglo-Catholic and harped on about the importance of 'tradition'; Lawrence conceived a bizarre belief in the redemptive power of sexuality; while even Joyce (Orwell's personal favourite) devoted most of his work to 'the vision of a Catholic who has lost his faith.'[71] Disillusioned by human nature and the naive optimism of their literary forebears, the modernists had arrived at a state of complete political irrelevance by way of a pointless belief in the opacity of language.

While many of these ideas about modernism today seem self-evident, they were not widely shared on the left in the 1930s. The majority of Marxist critics tended to ignore the modernist interpretation of literary form, instead confining themselves to gloomy comments about the political content of individual works. Yet Orwell's account of modernism was anticipated in all its essentials by Philip Henderson's *The Novel Today* (1936), a Marxist text which he (Orwell) reviewed with scant sympathy in the *New English Weekly*.[72] Although Henderson's work was often treated with hostility even by fellow members of the Communist Party,[73] it clearly owed a great deal to the ideas which had first been outlined at the Soviet Writers' Congress in 1934. *The Novel Today* was structured around a contrast between the bourgeois or 'romantic' novel and the socialist or 'revolutionary' novel – the former seen as irredeemably decadent and the latter as infinitely promising. In order to draw out the differences between the two trends, which broadly corresponded to the Soviet distinction between modernism and Socialist Realism, Henderson essayed his own contribution to the venerable debate about the relative characteristics of classicism and romanticism. Falling some way short of the critical sophistication which had animated the debate in the post-war years (especially in the work of T.E. Hulme and Eliot), he simply proposed that the goal of the classical writer is to understand the world around him while the goal of the romantic writer is to evoke his inner states. If the bourgeois novel had undergone a precipitous decline since the beginning of the century, Henderson argued, it was precisely because most of its practitioners had fallen victim to the romantic temptation to turn their backs on the real world and seek sanctuary in inner space. Everyone from D.H. Lawrence to Marcel Proust had shown a baleful incapacity to look reality in the eye. By contrast, the revolutionary novel was at least inspired by a solidly classical desire to comprehend contemporary politics.[74] What linked Henderson to Orwell was the recognition that the 'romanticism' of the modernist novel had usually been a consequence of the belief in literature's autonomy. In a series of ingenious readings, not all of them very convincing, Henderson insisted that the work of most of the leading modernists gave either direct or indirect expression to the assumption that language can never mirror reality. Marcel Proust had woven his novels out of 'an interior world of imagination and private sensibility',[75] concerned only to idealise his memories of a pointless and slothful life. Virginia Woolf aimed at the 'musicalization of reality', superimposing the 'rhythm and texture of music' on the chaos of real time.[76] Even James Joyce had evoked a sense of 'aesthetic stasis' in his writings, though only with dubious success.[77] Like Orwell, Henderson took it for granted that aestheticism of this sort was wholly incompatible with the representation of political realities. Indeed, there were interesting rhetorical similarities between the sentence in *The Novel Today* in which he summarised his case and one of Orwell's most important pronouncements in 'Inside the Whale'. While scarcely evidence of plagiarism on Orwell's part, they go a long way towards corroborating the view that Henderson's book played a major role in shaping his understanding of modernism:

> Today the tendency is to take the attitude of Proust still further, for literature to become still more abstracted and introspective, to fly to the past, the future, to fantasy – anywhere, in fact, rather than honestly face 'the story of social relations…what is going on everywhere'.[78]

> Our eyes are directed to Rome, to Byzantium, to Montarpanasse, to Mexico, to the Etruscans, to the Subconscious, to the solar plexus – to everywhere except the places where things are actually happening.[79]

Although Orwell accused the modernists of turning their backs on the real world, he was also aware that the beliefs which they expressed in their work had important and occasionally 'sinister' political implications. Following the lead of communist writers such as John Strachey, Douglas Garman and Edgell Rickword, he often argued that the ideas of Hulme, Eliot and other leading modernists bore important family resemblances to the dogmas of fascism. His subtlest exploration of this theme occurred in the brief essay on Yeats which appeared in *Horizon* in January 1943. Written in response to V.K. Narayana Menon's *The Development of William Butler Yeats* (1942), Orwell's essay was primarily concerned with teasing out the political implications of Yeats's interest in the occult. Noting that Yeats had combined his taste for astrology, mediumship and reincarnation with support for the Irish Blueshirts, Orwell suggested that there are several reasons why someone who subscribes to an occult philosophy might also be predisposed to supporting fascism. The most important is that fascism and occultism both tend to promulgate a cyclical view of history. In many of his writings, or so Orwell argued, Yeats expressed the belief that each stage in human history is destined to repeat itself: 'the central idea of his philosophical system seems to be our old friend, the cyclical universe, in which everything happens over and over again.'[80] Orwell's point was that the doctrine of the cyclical universe provides fascism with an important metaphysical prop, since it calls into question the liberal (or Marxist) belief that history is heading inexorably towards ever greater amounts of freedom. If a return to the hierarchical and authoritarian societies of the past is more or less inevitable, it is easy enough for a fascist thinker to steel himself against mass democracy by clinging to the belief that an 'age of tyranny' will soon be upon us once more. Orwell also noted an important parallel between the occult and fascist attitudes towards knowledge. Just as the occultist believes that esoteric doctrines should be confined to a gifted elite, so the fascist insists that only a small group of natural leaders have enough knowledge to govern society: 'Those who dread the prospect of universal suffrage, popular education, freedom of thought, emancipation of women, will start off with a predilection towards secret cults.'[81] Finally, in a remark which betrayed an uncharacteristic ignorance of esoteric doctrines, Orwell argued that occultists and fascists are bound together by a 'deep hostility' towards the Christian ethic. It has not often been recognised that a sort of furtive and embarrassed interest in the paranormal was a recurring feature of Orwell's life and work. At Eton he occasionally participated in magical rituals and allegedly feared that he had caused the death of a fellow pupil.[82] Later on he corresponded with Sir Sacheverell Sitwell on the subject of poltergeists, asked Rayner Heppenstall to draw up an astrological chart for his son Richard and wrote admiringly about the Victorian medium Daniel Dunglas Home.[83] He also endowed Winston in *Nineteen Eighty-Four* with the capacity to see the future in his dreams. No doubt he would have written more about the paranormal if people like Yeats had not convinced him that fascism and occultism were ultimately two sides of the same coin.

Modernism in the Age of Dictatorship

As well as assessing the political impact of the modernist writers of the 1920s, Orwell also tried to predict how modernism might develop in the coming age. His most important attempt to gaze into the future occurred in 'Inside the Whale', specifically in his extended comments on the work of the American novelist Henry Miller. Although Miller is not now regarded as a major writer, he enjoyed considerable notoriety in some circles after the publication of his novel *Tropic of Cancer* in 1935. Banned in Britain until the 1960s on grounds of obscenity, the book is a violently picaresque account of the debauched and bohemian lifestyle which Miller adopted in the Paris of the 1920s. Orwell summed up its contents well when he wrote that '…it is a story of bug-ridden rooms in workingmen's hotels, of fights, drinking bouts, cheap brothels, Russian refugees, cadging, swindling and temporary jobs.'[84] The argument of 'Inside the Whale' was that Miller had captured something essential about the spirit of the age and in so doing had set the standard for the literature of the immediate future. Orwell's starting point was precisely the taste for moral anarchy which has been noted elsewhere in this chapter. What he admired about Miller was his habit of portraying human beings in all their irredeemable *lowness*. Whereas other novelists employed a 'Geneva language' and aimed to reinforce humanity's most flattering illusions about itself, Miller could be relied upon to 'drag the *real-politik* of the inner mind into the open' – the fact that a clear majority of human beings are habitually cruel, coarse and grossly self-indulgent.[85] Without in any way being the most gifted writer of the age, he had nevertheless made an exhilarating attempt to reject the novel's commitment to elevated subject matter and open it up to all sorts of scrofulous and lavatorial material. Yet the true significance of his work lay not so much in its subject matter as in his attitude towards it. According to Orwell, Miller was essentially an apostle of *passivity*. Far from revolting against the parade of squalor to which he exposed his readers, he seemed happy to accept everything with an attitude that ranged from near-mysticism to amused resignation. The message of *Tropic of Cancer* was that nothing can be changed and that the individual would be well-advised to 'sit on [his] bum.'[86] This was the source of Miller's significance as a contemporary novelist. At a time when totalitarian conformity is everywhere gaining ground against liberty, Orwell argued, the only successful writers will be those who follow Miller's example and plaintively say 'I accept' to everything which exists:

> The literature of liberalism is coming to an end and the literature of totalitarianism has not yet appeared and is barely imaginable. As for the writer, he is sitting on a melting iceberg; he is merely an anachronism, a hangover from the bourgeois age, as surely doomed as the hippopotamus...It seems likely, therefore, that in the remaining years of free speech any novel worth reading will follow more or less along the lines that Miller has followed – I do not mean in technique or subject-matter, but in implied outlook. The passive attitude will come back, and it will be more consciously passive than before. Progress and reaction have both turned out to be swindles. Seemingly there is nothing left but quietism – robbing reality of its terrors by simply submitting to it. Get inside the whale – or rather, admit you are inside the whale (for you *are*, of course). Give yourself over to the world-process, stop fighting against it or pretending that you control it; simply accept it, endure it, record it. That seems to be the formula that any sensitive novelist is now likely to adopt.[87]

Although Orwell regarded Miller as a genuinely new type of novelist, he also recognised that his work was in some ways similar to that of a handful of earlier writers. He detected a particular resemblance between *Tropic of Cancer* and Joyce's *Ulysses*, not least because both novels had gone out of their way to 'expose the imbecilities of the inner mind'.[88] The comparison between Miller and Joyce hints at one of the more important sources which Orwell might have drawn on when writing 'Inside the Whale'. There is a very close resemblance between Orwell's account of *Tropic of Cancer* and the famously abusive reading of *Ulysses* which Karl Radek adumbrated at the Soviet Writers' Congress in 1934. (Radek's attack on Joyce was frequently quoted by British communists, several of whom adapted aspects of its argument in their own work).[89] Taking Joyce as his example of all that was objectionable about bourgeois modernism, Radek argued that the goal of *Ulysses* was to provide a wholly unselective portrait of the nature of everyday life. By trying to record everything which his protagonist Leopold Bloom had thought, said or done in the course of 24 hours, Joyce had written a book that could reasonably be compared to a 'heap of dung, crawling with worms, photographed by a cinema apparatus through a microscope.'[90] In spite of its pretentious allegorical content and its numerous references to ancient myths, it focused almost exclusively on meaningless conversations, petty rituals and lowering physical detail. The inevitable result was that human beings were portrayed as inherently trivial creatures who knew in their bones that 'there is nothing big in life.'[91] Nor was this attack on human nature without its political significance. By insisting that human beings are incapable of moral grandeur, Radek argued, Joyce was encouraging them to adopt an attitude of 'neutrality' towards the political events of the day. Since the entire world was currently under threat from fascism, it followed that *Ulysses* was unwittingly doing a great deal to disable its readers in the face of tyranny. If we substitute 'passivity' for 'neutrality' (which effectively means the same thing), it is clear that Orwell's argument about Miller simply weaves Radek's observations about Joyce into a more sophisticated pattern. The only thing which really distinguishes the two men is the issue of how the new tendency in modernist literature should be assessed. Whereas Orwell endorsed the passive attitude (though not the political circumstances which gave rise to it) on the grounds that it was the only one likely to produce significant literature in the modern age, Radek saw it as a cultural sickness which would destroy the novel and bring political catastrophe in its wake.

The Auden Group as Fifth Columnists

While Orwell clearly regarded the modernists as the most important writers of the inter-war period, he was also aware of the younger *Marxisant* authors who had come to prominence in the 1930s. An important section of 'Inside the Whale' contained an assessment of what we would now call the 'Auden Circle', several of whose members had conducted an uneasy flirtation with the Communist Party. These pages were among the most scathing that Orwell ever wrote. His broad argument was that Auden and his associates were not really sincere in their political commitments, since they used their support for communism to express a range of impulses which were largely reactionary and which would not have been tolerated without a radical coloration. For instance, Orwell famously insisted that their support for the USSR was basically a consequence of displaced patriotism. Raised in their bourgeois homes and their public schools to put love of country before everything else, people like Auden, Stephen Spender and C. Day Lewis longed to be the loyal servants of a nation state. Their only problem was that they could no longer give their loyalty to England, since the inglorious history of the post-war period had gone a long way to shattering their illusions about it. Their solution was to transfer their allegiance to Stalin's Russia, which they worshipped every bit as cravenly as earlier generations had worshipped England: '…the "Communism" of the English intellectual is something explicable enough. It is the patriotism of the deracinated.'[92] Orwell also implied that membership of the communist movement had allowed Auden and his peers to satisfy a sort of vicarious craving for violence. Having been raised in very comfortable circumstances, or so the argument seemed to go, they had developed a need to experience the thrill of violence without behaving violently themselves. With its history of purges, barricades and civil wars, Soviet Russia provided them with a spectacle of political brutality which could at once be secretly enjoyed and kept firmly at arm's length. Orwell illustrated this outlook with a blistering attack on Auden's poem 'Spain' (1937), one of the few genuinely great poems to have been written in response to the Spanish Civil War. 'Spain' was structured around a contrast between the anticipated glories of the socialist future ('To-morrow…all the fun under Liberty's masterful shadow…')[93] and the miserable tasks which the current generation had to perform in order to bring that future about. When he wrote about 'the conscious acceptance of guilt in the necessary murder',[94] Auden strongly implied that one of the tasks he had in mind was that of committing political assassinations. Orwell responded as follows:

> …notice the phrase 'necessary murder'. It could only be written by a person to whom murder is at most a *word*. Personally I would not speak so lightly of murder. It so happens that I have seen the bodies of numbers of murdered men – I don't mean killed in battle, I mean murdered. Therefore I have some conception of what murder means – the terror, the hatred, the howling relatives, the post-mortems, the blood, the smells. To me, murder is something to be avoided. So it is to any ordinary person. The Hitlers and Stalins find murder necessary, but they don't advertise their callousness, and they don't speak of it as murder; it is 'liquidation', 'elimination' or some other soothing phrase. Mr Auden's brand of amoralism is only possible, if you are the kind of person who is always somewhere else when the trigger is pulled. So much of left-wing thought is a kind of playing with fire by people who don't even know that fire is hot.[95]

Why should the work of the Auden Circle have been so badly compromised by these undercurrents of patriotism and bloodlust? Orwell's answer was that people like Auden had yet to transcend the ideology of their schooldays. Echoing the work of his friend Cyril Connolly, who famously argued in *Enemies of Promise* (1937) that English writers had been condemned to mediocrity by their state of 'permanent adolescence',[96] he implicitly portrayed Auden, Spender and Day Lewis as overgrown public schoolboys who were still in thrall to the hearty banalities of the Officer Training Corps. Indeed, in a mischievous attempt to characterise the *ethos* of their writings, he even argued that Auden's early poems conjured an 'atmosphere of uplift' that owed a great deal to Kipling: 'It is pure scoutmaster, the exact note of the ten-minutes' straight talk on the dangers of self-abuse.'[97] Although Orwell stopped short of dismissing Auden as a sort of Stalinist Baden-Powell with a hammer and sickle emblazoned on his khaki shorts, his verdict on Auden's poetry was probably the most unfair of his career – not least because one of the poems he cited in support of it was actually written by C. Day Lewis![98] It says a great deal for Auden's sense of Christian charity that he later claimed to miss Orwell intensely.

Orwell's argument about the Auden Circle was not quite as original as it seemed. Marxist critics had already said something very similar about Britain's younger writers, though their case differed in one important respect. Whereas Orwell claimed that Auden and his peers had tried to vent their immature impulses by latching onto communism, the communists insisted that their real commitment was actually to *fascism*. The most interesting version of this argument can be found in Edgell Rickword's article 'Straws for the Wary: Antecedents to Fascism', which appeared in the first issue of *Left Review* in October 1934. Rickword began by claiming that the young writers of the age had fallen victim to a mood of irrationalism which gripped British culture in the wake of World War One. (His argument applied not simply to the Auden Circle but to other fashionable writers such as Herbert Read and Aldous Huxley.) Shocked that an allegedly rational civilisation could have plunged the world into carnage, they had grown suspicious of the intellect and 'set to work to re-assert the primacy of belief'.[99] Among other things this had trapped them at a 'predominantly adolescent' stage of their development and reinforced their fascination with 'dressing-up, the gang-spirit...[and]...devotion to the Leader'.[100] The great appeal of fascism, or so Rickword implied, was that it enabled the young intellectuals to vent their adolescent desires behind a cloak of political respectability. The existence of fascist regimes in Germany and Italy provided a focus for their patriotism; while their boyish hunger for violence was more than satisfied (albeit vicariously) by the fascist drive-to-war: 'This [i.e. the work of Aldous Huxley] is an example of the helpless type of intellect which, though it may detest war, yet thinks of it as "inherent in human nature," and in many cases gets an emotional kick out of this looking down on the mass of slaughtering humans from its own icy heights of dispassionate understanding.'[101] By taking arguments such as these and claiming that it was actually communism which catered to the warped psychological needs of Britain's young writers, Orwell was performing precisely the sort of audacious polemical manoeuvre which made him so unpopular among members of the CPGB. It is difficult to believe that he was not completely aware of what he was doing.

Implicit in 'Inside the Whale' was the belief that many of Britain's younger writers were effectively fifth columnists in the camp of left-wing radicalism. Ostensibly committed to making the case for change, or so Orwell seemed to imply, people like Auden, Spender and Day Lewis actually intended to *undermine* the left by portraying it in unpalatable terms. This sort of argument was stated more explicitly in a review of Lionel Fielden's *Beggar My Neighbour* which appeared in *Horizon* in September 1943, though on that occasion Orwell aimed his fire at a prominent anti-imperialist rather than a Marxist. While Fielden's book *appeared* to make the case for Indian independence, Orwell nevertheless dismissed its author as a modish impostor who was 'actually desirous of the exact opposite of the thing he advocates.'[102] If Fielden had been serious about persuading his Western audience that imperialism was a bad thing, he would not have resorted to the manichaean fiction that Indians are wholly good while Europeans are entirely corrupt. Nor would he have portrayed Indian civilisation as predominantly 'spiritual', since it was clear that the Indian people could only free themselves from British rule by throwing off their Gandhian illusions about passive resistance and resorting to force. Here too there were some interesting parallels between Orwell's arguments and those of the communists. The idea that a number of radical writers were effectively working for the other side had first appeared in *The Intelligentsia of Great Britain* (1935), a violently opinionated book by the Anglo-Russian critic D.S. Mirsky which Orwell recommended in *The Road to Wigan Pier.*[103] Written at the time of the 'Class Against Class' policy (though only published three years after its abandonment), Mirsky's book was intended to show that the only genuine socialists in Britain were those who belonged to the CPGB. It therefore contained a chapter in which a variety of non-Party Marxist intellectuals were accused of conscious treachery. G.D.H. Cole and A.L. Rowse were criticised for encouraging the workers to support the Labour Party, knowing perfectly well that it would never introduce socialism. A group of unnamed literary classicists were condemned for treating Marxism simply as a theory of society and not as a programme for political change. (It is possible that Mirsky was thinking about Edgell Rickword, Douglas Garman and other former contributors to *The Calendar of Modern Letters*.) And, most interestingly of all, John Middleton Murry was attacked for trying to recast Marxism in the language of religion, specifically in his book *The Necessity of Communism* (1932). When Murry claimed that middle-class intellectuals like himself could bring an element of 'disinterestedness' to the revolutionary movement, Mirsky argued, he was actually trying to dilute the militant instincts of the workers by exposing them to the cold shower of bourgeois caution.[104] If arguments like this seemed to stick in Orwell's mind, it was perhaps because (1) Murry had been his first editor at the *Adelphi,* and (2) he had himself made great play of the need to attract the middle-class to the socialist movement. It is also possible that Mirsky's book forced him to confront a certain ambivalence in his own attitude to socialism. At any rate, it is not necessary to resort to psychoanalytic explanations to believe that the sheer violence of his attacks on Auden and Fielden was in part the consequence of projection.

4

REFORMING ENGLISH CULTURE

As we have seen, Marxist literary criticism in the 1930s was often heavily prescriptive. Taking their lead from the various speeches at the Soviet Writers' Congress in 1934, British communists such as Alick West, Ralph Fox and Christopher Caudwell were intent on making the case for a new form of socialist art. Even when they appeared to be writing about purely theoretical or critical issues, they were usually developing arguments which bolstered the case for Socialist Realism. There was no such attempt to promote a new form of literature in the work of George Orwell. Not only did Orwell believe that the very term 'Proletarian Literature' was something of an oxymoron (a view he expressed in a radio dialogue with Desmond Hawkins in 1940),[1] he also had no clear idea of how writers could incorporate socialist themes into their work without threatening their literary integrity. But this is not to say that his writings were entirely lacking in a prescriptive element. In a handful of important essays, notably 'New Words' (1940), 'Poetry and the Microphone' (1943), 'Propaganda and Demotic Speech' (1944) and 'Politics and the English Language' (1946), Orwell made a powerful case in favour of two related objectives: (1) the need to expand the scope of the English language, and (2) the need to popularise serious literature by exploiting the potential of modern broadcasting technology. Although Orwell is not generally seen as possessing much philosophical intelligence, one of the interesting things about these writings was their clear debt to some of the most philosophical passages in the work of the English communists. In particular, Orwell seems to have been strongly influenced by the famous attempts of West and Caudwell to provide a Marxist account of the fundamental characteristics of language and poetry. The purpose of this chapter is to place the prescriptive element in Orwell's writings in this wider philosophical context, as well as to examine his debt to communist writings on the relationship between language and class.

Reforming the English Language

Orwell's writings on the need to reform the English language can broadly be divided into two categories.[2] The first explored the idea that English is extremely bad at expressing the 'subjective' side of human experience and needs to be restructured accordingly. The second proposed that English is now being used with a horrific lack of clarity and that political life is being corrupted as a result. Orwell's concern with the subjective side of English was clearly influenced by communist writings on the history and philosophy of language, especially those which traced the origins of language to the economic practices of primitive societies. Since literature was still widely regarded in the 1930s as a record of private experience, it was common for the Marxist writers of the day to be told that their political perspective on the arts was little more than vulgar philistinism. When writers such as West and Caudwell made the case for Socialist Realism, they tried to repudiate this charge by pursuing a range of philosophical, historical and critical arguments which proved (or purported to prove) that literature was political at its very core. One of their favourite strategies was to resort to arguments of a broadly anthropological kind. Drawing on the work of anthropologists and linguists such as E.B. Tylor, G.A. de Laguna and Ludwig Noiré, they surveyed the history of primitive societies and insisted that poetry and language *both had their origins in economic activity*. The most influential version of this argument was formulated by Caudwell in *Illusion and Reality* (1937), a book which Orwell had in his library at the time of his death.[3] The opening chapter of *Illusion and Reality* proposed that poetry had originally been invented to adapt human instincts to the needs of production. Since human beings are not instinctively predisposed to work, it followed that primitive societies could only survive by modifying people's instincts and persuading them to take active steps to secure the necessities of life. Caudwell's argument was that poetry made an important contribution to this process by projecting a vision of economic paradise. In portraying a world of verdant fields, fruit-laden trees and abundant harvests, it helped to transform the outlook of primitive man by persuading him that his environment could indeed be made compatible with his deepest desires – but only if he worked for it.[4] Going further back in history, Caudwell then took the even more radical step of insisting that language itself had been rooted in economic necessity. Far from being the by-product of instinctual, religious or mimetic drives, the power of articulate speech had only emerged when primitive communities needed to find a reliable means of co-ordinating their economic practices. Caudwell tried to substantiate his case by drawing attention to what he took to be the combination of subjective and objective elements in all forms of language. Whenever language is utilised, even in a purely scientific context, it always tells us something about the 'common perceptual world' (that is, the complex of events and objects which exist independently of the speaker or writer) as well as registering a response in the sphere of the 'common affective world' (that is, it evokes the attitude of the speaker or writer towards the events and objects to which he refers). This combination of subjective and objective factors can be regarded as the ultimate proof that language originally grew out of economics, or so Caudwell argued, since all acts of production seek to remake the external world in the image of human desires.[5]

Language and the Inner Life

Orwell's essay on 'New Words' also examined the relationship between the subjective and objective elements in language, though its starting point was a sharp sense of language's limitations. Orwell implicitly agreed with Caudwell that English is very good at evoking the external world. There is no shortage of serviceable words for the 'material objects' which exist outside us, man-made or otherwise. The big problem is that there are no words at all for evoking what Caudwell had called our 'common affective world'. Dreams, non-verbal thought processes, the deep emotional convictions which often form the basis of our actions – all these things have usually proved 'practically unamenable to language.'[6] Not even the greatest writers have succeeded in describing what 'goes on inside the brain', since in practice they have all tried to mimic their inner states by 'using words in a tricky roundabout way, relying on their cadences and so forth'.[7] Orwell's startling proposal was that intellectuals should therefore make a systematic attempt to devise an entirely fresh vocabulary for mankind's subjective experiences: 'The solution I suggest is to invent new words as deliberately as we would invent new parts for a motor-car engine.'[8] In a rare statement of faith in the possibilities of modern communications technology, he argued that this could only be done properly by making extensive use of the cinematograph. If words are indeed to be found for our innermost feelings, the argument seemed to go, we have to be sure that everyone is aware of precisely what they refer to. It is not enough to attach a word to a feeling on the assumption that everyone knows what the feeling is, since common meanings can only be generated when the referents of individual words are somehow made tangible: 'What is needed is to *show* a meaning in some unmistakeable form, and then, when various people have identified it in their own minds and recognized it as worth naming, to give it a name.'[9] This is the context in which the cinematograph becomes relevant, Orwell argued, because the great unacknowledged potential of film is its peerless capacity to make consciousness visible:

> Everyone must have noticed the extraordinary powers that are latent in the film – the powers of distortion, of fantasy, in general of escaping the restrictions of the physical world. I suppose it is only from commercial necessity that the film has been used chiefly for silly imitations of stage-plays, instead of concentrating as it ought on things that are beyond the stage. Properly used, the film is the one possible medium for conveying mental processes. A dream, for instance…is totally indescribable in words, but it can quite well be represented on the screen…What is wanted is to discover the now nameless feelings that men have *in common*. All the powerful motives which will not go into words and which are a cause of constant lying and misunderstanding, could be tracked down, given visible form, agreed upon, and named.[10]

There are interesting echoes in this passage of an argument which had first been formulated by Siegfried Kracauer, the German Marxist whose writings on film gave an extremely sophisticated gloss to the Soviet preference for realism over modernism. One of the two most important defenders of cinematic realism in the early days of film theory (the other was André Bazin), Kracauer argued that the great virtue of film is that it allows us to record aspects of reality that our minds are not otherwise capable of registering. These include what he called 'special modes of reality' – that is, states of consciousness which are so intense or unusual that they ordinarily 'overwhelm' the individual.[11] By emphasising the ability of the cinematograph to convey an accurate impression of our inner lives, Orwell was therefore adopting a position which Kracauer would broadly have agreed with. Although Kracauer's main theoretical writings were all published after 'New Words', he had already produced a large number of essays while working as a cultural critic in the Weimar

Republic. We cannot know for sure whether Orwell was familiar with any of these essays; but it is surely significant that the one film he mentioned by name was Robert Wiene's *The Cabinet of Dr Caligari* – the expressionist masterpiece which Kracauer famously condemned for corrupting the principle of realism and paving the way for Hitler. At any rate, Kracauer's writings were probably familiar to many of the critics whom Orwell would have met while working as a film reviewer for *Time and Tide.* They would also have been known to communist intellectuals such as Ralph Bond, Ivor Montagu and James Klugmann, several of whom admired the cinema of the Weimar Republic and tried to spread awareness of it among British radicals. It is perfectly possible that Orwell had heard of Kracauer as a result of their efforts.

Having argued the case for the systematic invention of new words, Orwell went on to make an even more startling proposal about the form the words should take. The starting point of his argument could hardly have been more different from what Roger Fowler has called 'mainstream linguistics since Saussure',[12] which famously assumes that the relationship between signifier and signified is inherently arbitrary. Dismissing the idea that words are made up of a 'mere arbitrary collection of letters',[13] Orwell insisted that the majority of words (or at least the most expressive ones) actually bear a definite physical resemblance to the things they refer to. His example was the word 'plummet', which somehow seems to embody the act of plummeting in its very shape.[14] According to Orwell, the invention of new words should therefore be characterised by a careful effort to exploit the physical correspondences between language and reality. It is not enough either to conjure new words out of old ones or thoughtlessly to pluck an inappropriate combination of sounds out of the air. Orwell tried to substantiate his case by employing an argument which clearly owed a great deal to the anthropological element in Marxist criticism. When the communists set out to prove that language had its origins in economic activity, they often paid considerable attention to the role of gestures in the primitive system of production. For instance, in the anthropological chapters of *Crisis and Criticism* (1937), Alick West insisted that gestures had been the main means of co-ordinating economic activity in the period before the emergence of language.[15] It was only after the invention of tools that they ceased to play a major role, since it was obviously impossible for the hand to gesture freely while simultaneously using an axe or a scraper. Faced with the need to find a new means of co-ordinating their activities, primitive communities had therefore elaborated what West called their 'pantomimic gestures of the tongue' (that is, the more or less inarticulate sounds which had always accompanied primitive labour) into something more genuinely referential.[16] The result was the birth of language. Orwell took these sort of arguments and bent them into bizarre new patterns. Recognising that gestures had indeed been primitive man's most important means of communicating 'before he had words', he insisted that '…like any other animal he [i.e. primitive man] would cry out at the moment of gesticulating, in order to attract attention.'[17] Since all gestures tend to mimic the actions to which they refer, or so Orwell insisted, it follows that the sounds which accompany them must also display some mimetic characteristics. When primitive communities sought to translate gestures into words (Orwell did not discuss the circumstances in which this had occurred), they were simply elaborating on sounds which already bore a marked physical resemblance to their referents. Language had been mimetic at the very moment of its inception because it was rooted in gesture and all gestures are inherently imitative. While the communists often admitted that there was no firm evidence for their anthropological arguments, none of them had ever suggested anything as bizarrely speculative as this.

Why should Orwell have ascribed such importance to this uncharacteristically quixotic proposal for reforming the English language? It is clear that his motives were primarily political, even though there are no explicit references to politics in 'New Words'. In the first place he obviously believed that the limitations of language necessarily give rise to linguistic dishonesty. Since we have no words to describe our subjective responses to things (responses which are largely responsible for our actions), it follows that we usually resort to a species of fiction when seeking to explain our behaviour: 'When you are asked "Why do you do, or not do, so and so" you are invariably aware that your *real* reason will not go into words, even when you have no wish to conceal it; consequently you rationalize your conduct, more or less dishonestly.'[18] Remarks like this can probably be linked to Orwell's wider concern about the parlous state of political language, which we will return to in the next section. What he seemed to be implying in 'New Words' is that our lack of a subjective vocabulary makes political dishonesty all the more likely, since the political writer who deliberately distorts his message is merely brushing with the grain of language. If the structure of our language makes it more or less inevitable that we will lie whenever we open our mouths, or so the argument seemed to go, we can hardly expect political discourse to evince much concern for the truth. Orwell also seemed to believe that the existing state of the language gives rise to dangerous misunderstandings about human nature. Deprived of a vocabulary with which they can evoke their inner lives, many people naturally come to underestimate the role of consciousness (as opposed to environmental influences) in shaping their behaviour: '…it is a fact that some people seem unaware of being influenced by their inner life, or even of having any inner life.'[19] Orwell was probably motivated at this point by a distaste for behaviourism, whose influence could be detected in the work of many Marxist writers in the 1930s – not least that of Christopher Caudwell. By insisting that most human behaviour consists of conditioned, ineluctable and automatic responses to external stimuli, behaviourism must have struck Orwell as a terrifying denial of human freedom and perhaps as the handmaiden of totalitarianism. Inventing a new vocabulary for subjective experiences was therefore a crucial element in rebutting a philosophy which reduced human beings to the status of salivating dogs. Moreover, Orwell seemed to regard his proposals for linguistic reform as an important antidote to religious superstition. Whenever human beings seek to take a 'direct rational approach to…[their] difficulties', they often convince themselves that their behaviour is dangerously hubristic and that divine displeasure will follow in due course:

> All the bosh that is talked about our national genius for 'muddling through', and all the squashy god-less mysticism that is urged against any hardness and soundness of intellect, mean au fond that it is *safer not to think*. This feeling starts, I am certain, in the common belief of children that the air is full of avenging demons waiting to punish presumption. In adults the belief survives as a fear of too-rational thinking. I the Lord thy God am a jealous God, pride comes before a fall etc. – and the most dangerous pride is the false pride of the intellect…any attack on such a fundamental thing as language, an attack as it were on the very structure of our own minds, is blasphemy and therefore dangerous.[20]

If the attempt to invent a new vocabulary is successful, Orwell implied, it will therefore have been shown that the systematic application of reason is not merely possible but also desirable. The political implications of this argument are clear. In the face of widespread scepticism about the ability of human beings to plan economic activity, Orwell perhaps saw the reform of language as a sort of dress rehearsal for the creation of socialism. This brings us to his more famous writings on the state of English, notably the great essay 'Politics and the English Language', each of which is more straightforwardly political than 'New Words'.

The War against Obscurity

Orwell's most important ideas about language were contained in 'Propaganda and Demotic Speech' (1944), 'Politics and the English Language' (1946) and the section entitled 'The English Language' in *The English People* (1947). By the time these pieces were written, Orwell had abandoned the vaulting ambition displayed in 'New Words'. Instead of advocating a concerted effort to provide English with a vocabulary for subjective experiences, he now wished simply to start a debate about rescuing the language from widespread misuse. His main argument about the current state of English is extremely well known, not least because 'Politics and the English Language' has been compulsory reading for generations of students and journalists. If the language is now being used with a hideous lack of clarity, or so Orwell claimed, it is largely because contemporary politics is divorced from common decency. Anxious to divert the public's attention from the immorality of their actions and their proposals, politicians and writers have resorted to 'sheer cloudy vagueness' in order to 'name things without calling up mental pictures of them.'[21] The bombing of villages is described as 'pacification'; the violent uprooting of entire communities is passed off as the 'rectification of frontiers'; the imprisonment or murder of political dissidents is glossed as the 'elimination of unreliable elements'.[22] The point about this sort of language is that it coarsens thought even as it conceals it. The more a person hides the true nature of his actions from himself, or so the argument went, the greater the likelihood that his behaviour will get even worse: 'It [i.e. our language] becomes ugly and inaccurate because our thoughts are foolish, but the slovenliness of our language makes it easier for us to have foolish thoughts.'[23] The decline of English can therefore be seen as both a symptom and a cause of the twentieth century's descent into barbarism.

Much of 'Politics and the English Language' was devoted to a scathing analysis of the bad linguistic habits which tend to make prose obscure. Among the 'swindles and perversions' to which Orwell paid most attention were (1) metaphors which have been used so often that they no longer suggest a clear visual image, (2) the use of 'operators or false verbal limbs' instead of simple words (e.g. 'make contact with' instead of 'contact'), (3) the preference for excessively formal or foreign-sounding words, and (4) the frequent resort to polysemic terms such as 'romantic', 'sentimental' and 'natural' which ultimately have no real meaning at all.[24] Orwell was especially critical of what he called the 'jargon peculiar to Marxist writing',[25] noting that much of it consisted of poor translations from German, French and Soviet sources. Yet the message of his essay was that the decline of English is by no means irreversible. Rejecting the idea that a decadent civilisation can only be rescued by thoroughgoing social change, Orwell insisted that individual writers can do a great deal to restore clarity to the language of public affairs. The best course of action is for the writer to decide what he wants to say before trying to put it into words (a piece of advice which reflects Orwell's commitment to what linguists call 'linguistic instrumentalism'),[26] simply by thinking in terms of 'pictures or sensations'.[27] He should then try to express himself as clearly and concretely as possible by adhering to six simple rules, all of which have now been quoted so often that most of us can recite them in our sleep:

> (i) Never use a metaphor, simile, or other figure of speech which you are used to seeing in print.
> (ii) Never use a long word where a short one will do.
> (iii) If it is possible to cut a word out, always cut it out.
> (iv) Never use the passive where you can use the active.
> (v) Never use a foreign phrase, a scientific word or a jargon word if you can think of an everyday English equivalent.
> (vi) Break any of these rules sooner than say anything outright barbarous.[28]

Orwell's arguments in 'Politics and the English Language' have received far more coverage than those in 'Propaganda and Demotic Speech' and *The English People*. This is probably because the latter writings seek to relate the decline of the language to the existence of the class system. More precisely, they both ascribe the ghastliness of modern English to the cultural prominence of the upper classes – something which Orwell stopped short of doing in 'Politics and the English Language'. Orwell's point was that words are most likely to be used clearly by people who have a practical relationship with the world around them. Since the upper classes are not required to work for a living, it follows that their use of language is correspondingly 'anaemic'.[29] By contrast, the language of the working class retains its simplicity and freshness. Obliged to communicate effectively in order to perform their everyday tasks, working people instinctively prefer concrete words to abstract ones and continually invent metaphors which create a vivid image in the mind's eye: 'A useful word like *bottleneck*, for instance, would be most likely to occur to someone used to dealing with conveyor belts: or again, the expressive military phrase *to winkle out* implies acquaintance both with winkles and with machine-gun nests.'[30] If the health of English is ever to be restored, it is necessary to end the cultural dominance of the ruling class and increase the cultural influence of the workers – a point I will return to shortly. Orwell also expressed his concern that the degraded state of English had led to a dangerous reliance on terms imported from America. Because of the 'vivid, almost poetic quality' of much American slang (and also because American English seems more classless than its Anglo-Saxon equivalent), many Englishmen are trying to lend a new dynamism to their speech by using terms such as 'stooge', 'stool pigeon' and 'cop'.[31] As necessary as this sometimes is, it also brings great problems in its wake. For one thing, American English is often stupidly euphemistic and needlessly verbose. It also lacks a wide and precise vocabulary, especially in relation to 'natural objects and localities.'[32] The more it is used as a substitute for the language of England, Orwell implied, the greater the likelihood that it will reinforce all the problems of vagueness and imprecision that it was intended to solve.

Once we realise that Orwell's anxieties about the state of English were closely related to his interest in class, it becomes clear that his writings on language are not quite as idiosyncratic as they sometimes appear. They actually form part of a lengthy debate about the linguistic virtues of the lower orders which effectively began in the early years of the nineteenth century, when William Wordworth famously announced in his Preface to *Lyrical Ballads* (1800) that English poetry could only be revived by resorting to the 'language of the middle and upper classes of society'.[33] The debate was given a distinctively Marxist tinge by the communist critics of the 1930s. An especially virulent exchange about the merits of working-class language occurred in the pages of *Left Review* in 1934, in a series of articles responding to the Founding Statement of the British Section of the Writers' International. Putting an English gloss on the ideas of the Soviet Proletkult movement (which had enjoyed a brief vogue among British communists in the early 1920s), the novelist Alec Brown insisted that serious literature in Britain had usually been written in a ruling-class 'jargon' that was wholly incomprehensible to ordinary people. Socialist writers should therefore make a deliberate effort to reject the language of the established literary tradition, instead submitting to the 'proletarianisation of our actual language.'[34] Brown summarised his argument in three upper-case slogans whose air of arid dogmatism was all too typical of his critical persona:

> LITERARY ENGLISH FROM CAXTON TO US IS AN ARTIFICIAL JARGON OF THE RULING CLASS; WRITTEN ENGLISH BEGINS WITH US...WE ARE REVOLUTIONARY WORKING-CLASS WRITERS; WE HAVE GOT TO MAKE USE OF THE LIVING LANGUAGE OF OUR CLASS...ALLUSIVE WRITING IS CLIQUE WRITING: WE ARE NOT A CLIQUE.[35]

Brown's ideas received a mixed response from some of the other contributors to *Left Review*. The poet Hugh MacDiarmid argued that the duty of communists was to raise working people to the highest cultural levels, in order that they could then go on to understand Marxism in its most sophisticated forms. When Brown implied that the impoverished language of the workers was actually extremely rich, he was guilty of reinforcing the terrible cultural deprivation which capitalism had imposed upon them. There was no such thing as 'Marxism without tears' (the phrase was Lenin's).[36] Montagu Slater admitted that Brown had raised 'an important point' in his original contribution, but rejected the idea that Marxists had nothing to learn from the history of English literature: 'Among our jobs is that of making the stored-up literary labour of the past usable by the present.'[37] Douglas Garman agreed with Slater about the value of Britain's literary heritage, waspishly observing that Brown's style of writing was 'itself an unfortunate example of jargon.'[38] Brown drew his main support from the critic J.M. Hay, who argued that the superiority of plebeian speech was a direct consequence of working people's economic experiences. Hay's implied point was virtually identical to the one which Orwell made almost ten years later in *The English People*. If working people usually reject abstract terms in favour of a vividly concrete style of expression, it is precisely because 'the concrete word is rooted deep in the practical acts of everyday life and has, because of its practical roots, developed a wide range of secondary associations which give it colour and psychological force.'[39] But this is not to say that the sole task of the Marxist writer is to translate working-class speech into an appropriate written form. Since spoken language is lacking in the complex structures which allow sophisticated thoughts to be clearly expressed, Marxist writers must aim to combine the invigorating clarity of working-class language with the formal resources of 'our great heritage of written English.'[40]

The debate in *Left Review* seems to have been widely discussed among British socialists, so there is every chance that Orwell would have encountered it. It is even more likely that he read Ralph Fox's *The Novel and the People* (1937), a book which launched an eloquent defence of the Brown/Hay thesis some three years after MacDiarmid, Slater, Garman and others appeared to have seen it off. Widely hailed as a turning point in the development of Marxist literary theory in Britain, *The Novel and the People* expressed Fox's view that the novel is the main imaginative form through which Marxists can convey their message. A chapter entitled 'The Lost Art of Prose' discussed the sort of language in which the socialist novel should be written. Like 'Politics and the English Language', it began from the assumption that the obscurity of official English is largely a consequence of the immorality of modern politics: 'This art of prose is a dying one in our own day, for in order to call things by their right names, you must not be afraid of things you have to describe… Cobbett used language to express life, the B.B.C. uses it to conceal life.'[41] The only option for the socialist writer is to irradiate his work with the 'folk language' of the masses, since the 'only people in our country [with] the necessary experience of life' to speak clearly are those who work for a living.[42] Rejecting the idea that the greatest works of literature had been written in the patois of the ruling class, Fox strengthened his defence of plebeian speech by insisting that the English tradition would never have displayed such linguistic vitality without the influence of ordinary people. Nearly all the great authors from Chaucer onwards have taken their lead from the 'popular, almost proverbial' habits of speech which exist among the lower orders, to the point where '…it is difficult to judge whether they have actually created proverbial language or whether they merely used proverbial language.'[43] Scholars and critics have obscured literature's debt to ordinary speech by emphasising the importance of the King James Bible; but the point which needs to be grasped is that the language of the King James Bible was itself a reflection of early-modern vernacular.[44] If the link between literature and ordinary speech had recently broken down, Fox argued, there were nevertheless a number of bourgeois writers who had tried to revive it. One of them was Rudyard Kipling, an unlikely hero for a British communist, whose work reflected many of the developments in working-class vocabulary which accompanied the rise of 'power machinery'. Orwell was to say something fairly similar in his essay on Kipling in *Horizon*.

How exactly were the 'official' languages of literature and public affairs to be opened up to the purifying influence of working-class speech? This was an issue on which Brown, Hay and Fox were largely silent. Although Fox threw out the tantalising suggestion that 'it may be that here the poets will take the lead',[45] he gave no indication of the circumstances in which they would do so. There were times when Orwell was similarly vague. Having insisted in *The English People* that 'language ought to be the joint creation of poets and manual workers',[46] he went on to argue that a close alliance between the two groups had existed in the 'feudal past' and needed to be revived. Although the echoes of the *Scrutiny* group were unmistakeable (Leavis and his co-thinkers are another overlooked influence on Orwell), the point was not dwelled upon. It was only in 'Propaganda and Demotic Speech' that Orwell suggested a definite strategy for restoring popular language to national influence. While accepting that the conventions of speech could never form the basis of written language or even of a successful broadcast talk (a point which linked him to Hay and Fox), he nevertheless argued that formal language would benefit enormously from an infusion of demotic vigour. The first step in the process is to ensure that the characteristics which distinguish speech from writing are fully understood. The best way of doing this is to exploit the potential of modern recording technology. What is needed is to persuade a dozen fluent speakers to sit in front of a microphone and talk at length without a script. Efforts should also be made to record a range of conversations between a number of different people. The resulting material should then be transcribed and subjected to a thorough linguistic analysis, with a view to uncovering 'the rules of spoken English'. Once these rules have been discovered, it will be relatively easy (or so Orwell implied) to achieve a new conversational ease in all forms of writing.[47] If these proposals gave off a definite whiff of crankishness, they were nevertheless important for confirming what 'New Words' had already made clear – that Orwell regarded media technology as a crucial component of any strategy for cultural reform. His other writings on the political value of electronic recording would be rather more persuasive.

Bringing Poetry to the People

It is something of a truism that George Orwell was one of the few serious writers of the twentieth century who appealed to a mass audience. *Animal Farm* and *Nineteen Eighty-Four* are among the best known novels of the age, even if their political significance has occasionally been lost on the thousands of schoolchildren who have had to read them. What has less often been recognised is that Orwell spent at least three years of his career as a committed populariser of other people's work. As a Talks Producer in the Indian Section of the BBC between 1941 and 1943, he wrote a series of highly informative broadcasts which tried to spread knowledge of English Literature to listeners in the subcontinent. After resigning from the BBC he spent two years as the Literary Editor of *Tribune*, where he continued his efforts at popularisation by aiming a classic series of essays on English authors at the intelligent but not necessarily 'educated' members of the British Labour Movement. His experiences at the BBC inspired a remarkable pamphlet entitled *Poetry and the Microphone* (1945), which argued that modern broadcasting technology provides enormous opportunities for introducing serious poetry to a mass audience. This section brings our consideration of the prescriptive elements in Orwell's thinking to an end by (1) identifying the assumptions about poetry on which *Poetry and the Microphone* was based, and (2) clarifying the pamphlet's main arguments.

Given that he wrote almost nothing about the popularisation of other literary forms, why should Orwell have devoted an entire pamphlet to the theme of popularising poetry? There are probably two good answers to this question. The first is that Orwell had made a genuine effort to devise new ways of broadcasting poetry while working for the BBC. His biggest innovations occurred in a programme called *Voice* which ran for six episodes on the Indian Service between August and December 1942. *Voice* was based on the idea that the listener was eavesdropping on an editorial meeting at a 'more or less highbrow' literary magazine. Each programme brought together a range of critics and authors for a seemingly casual but actually precisely scripted conversation about an aspect of literature. The extremely distinguished contributors included Herbert Read, T.S. Eliot, Dylan Thomas, Stephen Spender, William Empson, George Woodcock, Mulk Raj Anand and Orwell himself. The first programme encompassed a range of issues but each of the succeeding programmes addressed a single theme: war poetry, the literature of childhood ('not...literature written *for* children but *about* childhood...'),[48] American literature, the influence of the Orient on

English Literature and Christmas.[49] The majority of discussions centred on poetry (especially contemporary poetry), though occasionally a piece of prose was brought in for the sake of balance. While the standard of the discussions was not perhaps as high as Orwell seems to have believed, it was nevertheless the case that the contributors made a genuine effort to introduce their listeners to general ideas about the nature of poetry. The following extract is reasonably representative, not least because it illustrates Orwell's great gift for plain-speaking provocation:

> ORWELL: Has anybody any opinions on that? [The participants had just listened to a reading of 'In Memory of Ann Jones' by Dylan Thomas.] I suppose the obvious criticism is that it doesn't mean anything. But I also doubt whether it's meant to. After all, a bird's song doesn't mean anything except that the bird is happy.
> EMPSON: Lazy people, when they are confronted with good poetry like Dylan Thomas's, which they can see is good, or have been told is good, but which they won't work at, are always saying it is Just Noise, or Purely Musical. This is nonsense, and it's very unfair to Dylan Thomas. That poem is full of exact meanings, and the sound would have no effect if it wasn't…
> ANAND: But it's also true that his poetry has become a good deal less obscure in an ordinary prose sense lately. This poem, for instance, is much more intelligible than most of his later work. Listen:
>
> Her fist of a face died clenched on a round pain:
> And sculptured Ann is seventy years of stone.
>
> That has a meaning that you can grasp at first hearing, hasn't it?
> ORWELL: Yes, I admit you grasp at a glance that this is a poem about an old woman, but just listen again to the last five lines:
>
> These cloud-sopped, marble hands, this monumental
> Argument of the hewn voice, gesture and psalm
> Storm me forever over her grave until
> The stuffed lung of the fox twitch and cry Love
> And the strutting fern lay seed on the black sill.
>
> The last two lines in particular defy interpretation and even the syntax is a bit funny. But as sound, that seems to me very fine.[50]

If Orwell's pride in *Voice* was one of his reasons for wishing to write *Poetry and the Microphone*, the other was arguably a belief that there is something intrinsic to poetry which demands that it be popularised. Although he made very few general statements about poetry in the pamphlet itself, it is clear from scattered statements in the rest of his work that he regarded poetry as being rooted in the life of the people. This is especially evident in a review of Jack Lindsay's pamphlet *A Perspective for Poetry* which appeared in the *Manchester Evening News* in November 1944. The pamphlet was one of the first works in which Lindsay outlined his belief that culture is a form of 'productive activity' and Orwell described it as 'one of the ablest pieces of Marxist literary criticism that have been written for some years past.'[51] Although it is not entirely clear whether Orwell understood the full implications of Lindsay's case, he focused his attention on the anthropological arguments with which the pamphlet began. According to Orwell, Lindsay's main point was that the poet had originally reflected the 'collective consciousness' which allegedly existed in primitive societies. While certainly regarded as an 'exceptional being', he was not 'isolated' from his fellow men and served as an exemplar of the wider community. When the group loyalties of the primitive tribe were disrupted by the emergence of class differences, it followed that the poet lost his 'freedom' because his vocation was now 'at odds' with the established social structures. Lindsay's conclusion (at least in Orwell's opinion) was that the poet can only recapture his full creative powers by committing himself to socialism, since it is only under socialism that he can once again experience the egalitarian and classless conditions in which he initially thrived. The important point is that Orwell had no major disagreements with any of these arguments. On the one hand he claimed that 'In very broad terms there is little doubt that Mr. Lindsay's theory is correct', while on the other he affirmed that 'The poet is most free, least isolated from his fellows, when he is helping the historical process along'.[52] In an uncharacteristically Zhdanovist touch he even described Lindsay's pamphlet as an 'effective counterblast' against the 'frank declarations of irresponsibility' which had tarnished the work of Britain's younger poets.[53] (He was presumably thinking of Dylan Thomas and other members of the so-called 'Apocalyptic' school.) Where Orwell differed from Lindsay was in his response to the political implications of the argument. Lindsay was wrong to imply that the modern poet should join the Communist Party, or so Orwell argued, because in practice the world communist movement is (1) unlikely (and perhaps unwilling) to create a classless society of any kind, and (2) too insistent that the writer should tell lies in the service of his cause. The ultimate proof of the communist movement's artistic bankruptcy was the fact that since the Russian Revolution it had '...produced so little worthwhile literature.'[54]

If Orwell agreed with the communists that poetry should be popularised because it had once been the property of the entire community, he still managed to imbue the anthropological argument with an ingenious anti-communist twist. In 'The Prevention of Literature' (1946), the most virulently anti-communist of all his major essays, he seemed to argue that the communal roots of poetry give the poet a definite advantage over the prose writer in a totalitarian age. Since prose is a form which reflects the mind of an individual, or so Orwell argued, it necessarily falls into desuetude in any society which seeks to abolish individualism. By contrast, the fact that 'good verse...is not necessarily an individual product' (a legacy of the fact that 'primitive peoples compose verse communally') means that it tends to find the group-minded culture of Stalinist or fascist societies less injurious.[55] Even under the most intrusive and draconian of governments, there is a sense in which the poet is brushing with the grain of the prevailing culture, even though his work is unlikely to be of the highest quality. Moreover, he derives a further advantage from the relative intellectual simplicity of his chosen form, which makes it 'easy...to keep away from dangerous subjects and avoid uttering heresies.'[56] It also helps that state censors and the like tend to be indifferent to poetry and that totalitarian governments usually maintain a high demand for 'patriotic songs', 'heroic ballads celebrating victories' and 'elaborate exercises in flattery'.[57] What Orwell was perhaps implying was that poetry should be popularised because (1) it is the only literary form which is likely to survive the Stalinist horrors of the coming age, and (2) it will be less likely to surrender to Stalinist ideology if it is firmly rooted in the culture of the people. More broadly, he also attached great political significance to the specifically *national* dimension of poetry. In a talk entitled 'Modern English Verse' which he delivered on the Indian Service of the BBC in June 1943, he noted that 'Poetry is of all arts the most national, or I should rather say local...'[58] Unlike prose, music and painting, which aspire to a universality that allows them to transcend their culture of origin, poetry is always tied down to a 'particular time' and a 'particular place'. Indeed, its national particularities are so pronounced that often it can only be understood (or at least properly understood) if the reader is familiar with the historical circumstances which helped to shape it. In other words, the argument seemed to go, poetry exemplifies national character in a way which is untrue of any other art form. Given that Orwell believed very strongly in the progressive aspects of the English character (and given that he presumably believed that poetry reflects them in an emotionally heightened form), he perhaps came to regard the popularisation of poetry as a powerful means of reinforcing his own people's most cherished radical instincts. In this sense, *Poetry and the Microphone* is a sort of companion piece to *The Lion and the Unicorn.*

Orwell's argument in *Poetry and the Microphone* was that the broadcasting of poetry on the radio could go a long way towards winning a mass audience for the form by rescuing it from 'obscurity and cleverness'. For most of its history, or so it was claimed, poetry had been a central part of oral culture and had therefore had to be immediately understandable. Obscurity (and the loss of a popular audience) only set in when poetry became largely confined to the page. If modern poets wish to shed the 'unintelligibility' and 'intellectual pretentiousness' which have turned their work into the preserve of an elite, they have no choice but to revert to the habit of writing poems which can easily be read aloud. In practice this can be achieved far more effectively by broadcasting on the radio than by appearing in front of a live audience, since the 'special advantage of the radio' is 'its power to select the right audience, and to do away with stage-fright and embarrassment'.[59] Whereas a poet at a live reading is likely to feel intimidated by the proximity and size of his audience, he can sustain himself in a broadcasting studio with the pretence that he is speaking only to one person. He can also be confident that his listeners are interested in what he has to say, since people sitting at home are under no compulsion to pay him any attention – especially when their radios can easily be turned off. More importantly, the broadcaster enjoys an advantage over his audience in a way that the live performer does not. While the live performer invariably has to reflect the mood in the room, address what he regards as his least intelligent listeners and 'ingratiate [himself] by means of the balleyhoo known as "personality"' (a wonderful Orwellian phrase),[60] the broadcaster can read his poems without taking any of these things into consideration. Orwell accepted that the common people's hostility towards modern poetry was as about as 'complete as it could be', but he took succour from the fact that sub-poetic forms such as nursery rhymes and ballads still commanded a measure of popular affection. Given that people seemed happy to listen to doggerel of the most worthless kind (Orwell wrote with particular exasperation about a 'piece of patriotic balderdash' which had been recited on the BBC while he was writing his pamphlet),[61] it was surely possible that a measure of 'strategy…and subterfuge' could persuade them to listen to more elevated material.

Having made the case for devoting more airtime to poetry, Orwell bolstered his argument with an attack on what we might now call technological determinism. Of all the possible objections to the idea of reciting poetry on the radio, Orwell claimed, the most powerful is probably the belief that broadcasting technology is somehow intrinsically degrading. After listening to the endless 'tripe' which pours from the 'loudspeakers of the world', some of it disseminated by democracies and some by dictatorships, it is natural for people to assume that 'it is for that and nothing else that the wireless exists'.[62] The challenge for reformers is thus to make it clear that the 'capabilities of an instrument' are not reducible to 'the use it is actually put to.'[63] The poor quality of radio broadcasts has nothing to do with the limitations of technology and everything to do with existing patterns of media organisation. Since the world's broadcasting companies are owned either by governments or by private monopolies (both of which have a vested interest in sustaining a trivial popular culture), it follows that the programmes they produce will be 'vulgar, silly and dishonest'. It would be relatively easy to use the same technology to produce programmes of a more stimulating type, if only the political will existed. However, instead of calling for the broadcasting industries to be organised along different lines, Orwell insisted that there were increasing possibilities for creative work even in the context of the existing companies. According to Orwell, whose argument broke decisively with the more pessimistic forms of left-wing media criticism, media companies are increasingly resistant to censorship by virtue of their immense size. The more it becomes necessary to staff large bureaucratic organisations with vast numbers of workers (many of them intellectuals), the more difficult it becomes to monitor their output closely. Even in an organisation like the BBC, associated in the public mind with 'genteel throaty voices' and the prejudices of the establishment, there will inevitably be 'loose ends and forgotten corners' in which culturally ambitious or politically subversive work can be done.[64] (It seems likely that Orwell was thinking of his own experience in the India Service.) By rejecting technological determinism and claiming that media companies were becoming too big to censor effectively, Orwell was clearly anticipating two of the most important arguments which the New Left would employ in the post-war years to bolster their calls for cultural reform.[65] Moreover, when he wanted to illustrate his claim that more creative work was being done in the media industries than ever before, he referred to the '...Government pamphlets, A.B.C.A. [The Army Bureau of Current Affairs] lectures, documentary films and broadcasts to occupied countries which have been issued during the past two years [i.e. 1941–1943]'.[66] He was surely aware that much of this work had been done by communists.

There is one other way in which *Poetry and the Microphone* links up with the work of the British communists. At one point, acknowledging that public distaste for poetry was part of a wider cultural malaise, Orwell tried to distinguish his argument from what he called the 'Marxist', 'Anarchist' and 'religious' belief in the existence of cultural crisis. While accepting that the communist thesis was 'undoubtedly true' in 'broad detail', he rejected the idea that Britain could only be restored to a semblance of cultural health once socialism had been achieved. Given that 'aesthetic improvement is...a necessary part of the general redemption of society' (a tantalising thought which Orwell refused to expand),[67] it is necessary to make at least an effort to swim against the tide of cultural decay. The obvious point about Orwell's argument was that it misunderstood the communist line. The communist onslaught on the 'decadence' of capitalist civilisation had indeed been ferocious (and nowhere more so than in books by John Strachey, Philip Henderson and D.S. Mirsky which Orwell had written about); but the whole burden of communist cultural policy was that artists could still do good work if they adopted the conventions of Socialist Realism. Living in a capitalist society was no barrier to artistic greatness, the communists had argued, so long as the artist followed the lead of the 1934 conference. What all this highlights is the sheer complexity of Orwell's response to the work of the communist critics. Quite apart from modifying or rejecting arguments which he had interpreted correctly, Orwell was also inclined to respond to arguments which the communists had never actually made. It is a fascinating example not merely of the depth of the Marxist influence on Orwell, but also of the way that many of his most compelling critical positions were rooted in what Harold Bloom might have called 'creative misreading'.

5

THE TOTALITARIAN FUTURE

The issue which most sharply divided the socialist left in Orwell's day was the nature of the Soviet Union. Whereas the various organisations of the hard left were united by their hatred of capitalism, their commitment to the class struggle and their faith in Marxism as a tool of historical, political and cultural analysis, they disagreed bitterly over whether the USSR could even be described as socialist. The majority of British Marxists accepted the Communist Party's line that the USSR was the 'hope of the world', though there is evidence that they did not always do so without misgivings. A much smaller group, most of whom belonged either to the Independent Labour Party or one of the tiny Trotskyist parties, took the view that the Stalinist system was little better than a monstrous perversion of the socialist ideal. Orwell agreed with the anti-Stalinists from the beginning and wrote bitter attacks on the USSR from 1936 onwards. At the same time (and unlike some of his more propaganda-minded contemporaries) he was interested not simply in denouncing Stalinism but in understanding it. What is it about socialism that makes it susceptible to totalitarian distortions? Are dictators like Stalin primarily motivated by political or psychological considerations? By what means do totalitarian governments enforce their rule? Although Orwell gave different answers to these questions at different times, his mature theory of totalitarianism was largely contained in *Nineteen Eighty-Four* – the novel which Bernard Crick once described as a 'masterpiece of political speculation' which is worthy of comparison to Hobbes's *Leviathan*.[1] Orwell chose to skewer the authoritarian strain in modern socialism not by writing directly about the USSR (something he had already done at length) but by conjuring a dystopian fantasy in which Britain is governed by a socialist dictatorship that takes Stalin's methods to new extremes.[2] In doing so he created a book which did more than any other to shape the West's understanding of the USSR during the Cold War.

Nineteen Eighty-Four has probably received more critical attention than any other modern novel.[3] Scores of academics and critics have discussed its main themes and tried to identify the sources which influenced it. As a result of their work we know that Orwell's understanding of totalitarianism was shaped by an enormous variety of texts, including several dystopian novels (e.g. *The Iron Heel* by Jack London and *We* by Yevgeny Zamiatin), James Burnham's controversial treatises on the so-called 'managerial society' and a range of obscure pamphlets by American Trotskyists. We also know that Orwell derived a lot of inspiration simply from observing the behaviour of his peers on the left. Appalled by what he regarded as their contempt for democracy, or so the argument goes, Orwell coolly surveyed the communists, pacifists and fellow-travellers of his own day and projected their characteristics onto the Oceanian ruling class. Indeed, it is only in their writings on *Nineteen Eighty-Four* that scholars have acknowledged the possibility that Orwell was influenced by the British communists. However, since practically none of them has known very much about the intellectual culture of the CPGB, their understanding of this influence has generally been vague. Most of them have assumed that Orwell was primarily motivated by a sort of furious but impressionistic hatred of communists, not by a detailed knowledge of their ideas and activities. They have also taken it for granted that the communist influence on Orwell was a largely negative one, in the sense that he (Orwell) only ever responded with scorn to what the communists said, wrote or did. The purpose of this chapter is to give a more nuanced account of the communist influence on Orwell's understanding of totalitarianism. It will focus primarily on *Nineteen Eighty-Four* but also on several of the essays which anticipated its main themes. I will try to show that a number of Orwell's ideas had clearly been anticipated in the writings of the CPGB's cultural thinkers, and that sometimes (though by no means always) Orwell was seeking to extend communist ideas and not simply to treat them as degraded symptoms of the totalitarian mind. Sections One and Two examine Orwell's explanation for the rise of totalitarianism and his account of how totalitarian governments work. (It will be seen that he ascribed particular importance to the specifically *cultural* methods by which Stalinist conformity is enforced.) Section Three turns to issues of a more literary nature, arguing that the form of *Nineteen Eighty-Four* was deeply influenced by (1) contemporary Marxist writings on the nature of dystopian literature, and

(2) the conventions of the socialist novel. Section Four brings the chapter to an end by challenging the idea that *Nineteen Eighty-Four* was a work of unalloyed pessimism. Its main argument is that Orwell's undoubted gloom about the prospects of Stalinist advance was balanced by a cautious optimism about the capacity of dissenting individuals (and ultimately of working people as a whole) to keep the spirit of liberty alive.

The 'Why' of Totalitarianism

As we have seen, Orwell aspired not only to describe the workings of dictatorship but also to explain why totalitarian systems should have existed in the first place. To use Winston's language in *Nineteen Eighty-Four*, he sought to address the 'why' as well as the 'how' of Stalin's Russia, Hitler's Germany or Big Brother's Oceania. His explanation for totalitarianism contrasted sharply with the left-wing orthodoxy of the day. Most radical intellectuals in the 1930s and 1940s insisted that the purpose of dictatorship was to advance a definite social objective, such as the defence of capitalism (in the case of fascism) or the consolidation of socialism (in the case of Stalinism). Orwell's argument was much gloomier. If governments throughout the world were now surrendering to the totalitarian virus, it was precisely because modern elites felt an overwhelming need to possess untrammelled power *for its own sake.* When Stalin purged the USSR of 'rotten elements' or Hitler dispatched his opponents to concentration camps, they were not so much pursuing a rational political strategy as luxuriating in the sheer pleasure of dominating other people: 'It is not easy to find a direct economic explanation of the behaviour of the people who now rule the world. The desire for pure power seems to be much more dominant than the desire for wealth.'[4] Orwell further argued that powerlust of this sort was a distinctively modern phenomenon, entering human affairs for the first time towards the end of the nineteenth century. His basic assumption was that totalitarianism had been an unintended consequence of the decline of religious faith. When the majority of people believed in God, or so it was implied, they tended to experience a sort of awed humility in the face of divine power which made it most unlikely that they would seek absolute power for themselves. By contrast, once the belief in God had disappeared, it was more or less inevitable that the unscrupulous and ambitious would begin to regard themselves as secular divinities. Modern culture had 'rendered unto Caesar the things that are God's' and the unforeseen result was the nightmare of the concentration camp.[5] Although

Orwell believed that a religious revival was neither likely nor desirable (not least because the collapse of religious illusions made it impossible for the ruling class to hoodwink the poor with the prospect of heavenly bliss), there were times in his writings on totalitarianism when the note of religious despair seemed wholly comparable to that of the 'silly clever' Catholic intellectuals whom he attacked elsewhere: 'There is no wisdom except in the fear of God; but nobody fears God; therefore there is no wisdom…we can be pretty certain what is ahead of us. Wars and yet more wars, revolutions and counter-revolutions, Hitlers and super-Hitlers – and so downwards into abysses which are horrible to contemplate.'[6]

Having identified the psychological basis of totalitarianism, Orwell went on to ask why the socialist movement had been so thoroughly and tragically corrupted by totalitarian habits of thought. His startling answer was that socialist doctrine is often peculiarly attractive to people with dictatorial ambitions. By equating social justice with state ownership of the means of production, it naturally appeals to doctrinaire intellectuals who recognise that one of the surest ways of dominating the individual is to establish absolute control of his economic resources. The history of socialism has therefore been characterised by an enormous and conscious fraud practised by an authoritarian leadership on a credulous rank-and-file. While the leading socialists have always paid lip-service to the ideals of equality, democracy and social justice (ideals to which their less sophisticated working-class followers remain loyal), their only real ambition has been to establish a thoroughgoing dictatorship behind a smoke-screen of egalitarian rhetoric: 'Ingsoc, which grew out of the earlier Socialist movement and inherited its phraseology, has in fact carried out the main item in the Socialist programme; with the result, foreseen and intended beforehand, that economic inequality has been made permanent.'[7] It is worth emphasising that these arguments were often strikingly different to those of other left-wing intellectuals who tried to account for the 'degeneration' of the socialist movement, notably Leon Trotsky in works such as *The Revolution Betrayed* (1937). Trotsky's assumption was that the socialist movement had started out in a state of rude political health and only surrendered to authoritarianism at a fairly late stage.[8] The premise of his writings on the USSR was that the Bolshevik Party under Lenin had initially made a sincere attempt to establish a workers' state. The slide towards Stalinism only began when the Bolsheviks responded unwisely (that is, in a manner which Trotsky disapproved of) to a whole range of difficult historical circumstances which imposed immense limitations on their freedom of manoeuvre. The collapse of revolutionary purity had little to do with individual psychology and everything to do with Stalin's inexpert response to foreign aggression, economic backwardness and so on. By contrast, Orwell seemed largely unwilling to divide the history of modern socialism into a prelapsarian Leninist phase and a brutally degraded Stalinist phase. While always recognising the merits of individual socialists (and offering cautious support to small socialist movements which had resisted the Stalinist virus), he took it for granted that the movement had been destabilised from the beginning by the authoritarian thugs who led it. Lenin and Stalin were two sides of the same coin.

It is hardly surprising that Orwell's explanation for totalitarianism should have been ferociously criticised by the left. The accusation that *Nineteen Eighty-Four* is primarily a work of debased Hobbesian pessimism has been a staple of Marxist criticism since the book was published, reaching its apogee in Isaac Deutscher's famous and rather unfair essay '*1984* – The Mysticism of Cruelty' (1954).[9] This makes it all the more ironic that Orwell's theory of totalitarianism owed far more to his reading of Marxist authors than has usually been recognised. More precisely, I would suggest that his psychological explanation of totalitarianism was heavily influenced by communist writings on the rise of fascism, even though he (1) initially attacked the communist theory of fascism, and (2) profoundly misunderstood it. These issues can best be brought into focus by examining Orwell's writings in the few months after he returned from Spain in 1937. As already noted in the Introduction, Orwell had become a hardline opponent of the CPGB's Popular Front strategy after serving with the POUM militia in Catalonia. Having accepted the POUM's line that fascism could only be defeated by socialist revolution, he savaged the communists for their 'blimpish' assumption that the immediate task of the left was to defend 'bourgeois democracy' rather than pushing ahead to abolish capitalism. Since fascism is merely a by-product of capitalism's desperate attempt to save itself from collapse, or so Orwell argued, it follows that the threat of dictatorship will only recede once market society has been destroyed for good: '...a Popular Front (*i.e.*, a line-up of capitalist and proletarian for the ostensible purpose of opposing Fascism) is simply an alliance of enemies and must always, in the long run, have the effect of fixing the capitalist class more firmly in the saddle.'[10] A crucial aspect of Orwell's attack on the Popular Front was his claim that the communists had gone out of their way to obscure the link between fascism and capitalism, simply in order to make their proposed alliance between 'bourgeois and proletarian' seem more plausible. The argument was expressed with particular vigour in the essay 'Spilling the Spanish Beans' (1937), which seems to have been the first thing Orwell wrote after arriving back in Britain:

> Broadly speaking, Communist propaganda depends upon terrifying people with the (quite real) horrors of Fascism. It also involves pretending – not in so many words, but by implication – that Fascism has nothing to do with capitalism. Fascism is just a kind of meaningless wickedness, an aberration, 'mass sadism,' the sort of thing that would happen if you suddenly let loose an asylumful of homicidal maniacs. Present Fascism in this form, and you can mobilise public opinion against it, at any rate for a while, without provoking any revolutionary movement. You can oppose Fascism by bourgeois 'democracy,' meaning capitalism. But meanwhile you have got to get rid of the troublesome person who points out that Fascism and bourgeois 'democracy' are Tweedledum and Tweedledee.[11]

It is surprising that Orwell scholars should have paid so little attention to this passage, since it arguably contains the seeds of much of his later thinking. The theory of fascism which it ascribes to the communists is practically identical to the theory of totalitarianism which later underpinned *Nineteen Eighty-Four.* There is the same attempt to scotch the assumption that modern dictatorships have their roots in politics or economics ('Fascism has nothing to do with capitalism...'), the same emphasis on the role of 'abnormal' psychology and the same insistence that the driving force of totalitarianism is 'mass sadism'. Although Orwell's mature writings on totalitarianism owe a great deal to the theoretical acuity of Bertrand Russell, Franz Borkenau, Arthur Koestler and a host of other thinkers, it is arguable that their essential framework of explanation was suggested to Orwell by the communist propaganda which he encountered as early as 1936. However, this is not a straightforward example of what D.S. Savage has described as Orwell's 'neurotic' capacity to take ideas he had once attacked and bend them to his own purposes.[12] What complicates the issue is that Orwell's interpretation of the communist theory of fascism was almost comically inaccurate. Far from seeking to play down the links between capitalism and fascism, the communists had consistently argued that the rise of Mussolini, Hitler, Franco and their ilk was a direct consequence of capitalism's slide into crisis. The 'official' definition of fascism, spelled out by Georgi Dimitrov at the Seventh Congress of the Comintern in 1935, went so far as to describe the new regimes as 'open, terrorist dictatorship[s] of the most reactionary, most chauvinistic and most imperialist elements of finance capital'.[13] This obviously raises the question of why Orwell should have misunderstood the communists so completely. There is an interesting clue to his uncharacteristic obtuseness in the notes from the *Daily Worker* which he compiled while writing *Homage to Catalonia* in 1937. (The notes have now been reproduced in full in Volume Eleven of the *Complete Works*.) At one point, surveying the *Worker*'s coverage of the early stages of the Spanish Civil War, Orwell noted that the CPGB's General Secretary Harry Pollitt had described fascists as 'gangs of parasites, moral perverts & murderers.' He also recorded Pollitt's opinion that the (pro-Franco) Spanish Foreign Legion was 'composed of murderers, white slavers, dope fiends & the offal of every European country.'[14] Presumably what Orwell found significant about these quotations was that they exemplified the communist habit of equating fascism with organised crime. This habit was especially pronounced in the work of the great radical journalist Claud Cockburn, who reported on the Spanish Civil War for the *Daily Worker* under the pseudonym Frank Pitcairn.[15] (Orwell was bitterly critical of Cockburn/Pitcairn in *Homage to Catalonia.*)[16] In his short book *Reporter in Spain* (1936), written in less than a week as part of the CPGB's pro-intervention propaganda drive, Cockburn consciously employed the conventions of the thriller in order to portray the Civil War as a sort of manichaean struggle between Republican virtue and fascist vice. The Spanish 'rebels' consistently figured as malevolent bullies who had elevated gangsterism to a principle of governance, while their Republican opponents were usually described as instinctive democrats who combined courage, political insight and rude plebeian decency in equal measure. For instance, on the very first page of his book, sitting in a restaurant in Cerbere while rumours of the impending Civil War swirled around him, Cockburn introduced the fascist enemy with the following sub-Greenean vignette:

> Across the restaurant came a pungent smell of violets. A tall fattish man with a waddling gait and expensive clothes walked in and around, and out, and in again to a table.
>
> Two younger men walked beside him. 'Bodyguard' was written all over them. I have seen the same type walking with the big gang-

> sters in Los Angeles back in the prohibition time. They inclined their heads like attaches in expectation of an order.
>
> One, with the customary dress-habits of the gangster, wore an absurdly tight cut Palm beach suit which showed the gun on his hip.
>
> The fat man gently rolled that violet scented handkerchief in his stout hands and kept his eye on the door. The noise of a train rolling through the tunnel under the mountain from the Spanish side brought the fat man to his feet. The trio left.
>
> 'Somebody in particular?', I asked the waiter.
>
> 'They say so,' said he.
>
> 'Well and ?'
>
> 'A Colonel something or other from Madrid. Bigshot. Has an airplane up in Perpignan. Colonel of aviation I think. Lives at the Grand Hotel. Very swell.'[17]

It is easy to see how writing like this might have persuaded Orwell that the communists refused to see the link between fascism and capitalism. In their anxiety to dismiss the Spanish rebels as power-hungry gangsters in the grip of raging personality disorders, writers like Pollitt and Cockburn seemed to be eschewing a political explanation of fascism in favour of a purely psychological one. It is a fascinating example of the way that the excesses of communist rhetoric could often impede the communication of a clear political message. At a more theoretical level, Orwell might also have been misled by the communist emphasis on the *contradictory* nature of fascism. While always portraying fascism as a movement intended to shore up capitalism in its moment of international crisis, many communist writers had emphasised the difficulties it experienced in appealing to a mass constituency. Since ordinary people are instinctively suspicious of big business, or so the argument went, fascist leaders could only attract a mass following by tempering their defence of capitalism with a smattering of populist rhetoric. Hitler, Mussolini and their followers had therefore seasoned their speeches and writings with what John Strachey called propaganda of a 'confusedly anti-capitalist character', implying that one of their purposes was to end the influence of a fundamentally decadent ruling class. Among other things this meant that fascism was a highly unstable method of defending the status quo, since it was always possible that the 'rank and file of the Fascist party' would translate their festering suspicion of the elite into full-scale revolutionary action.[18] Because Orwell took it for granted that communist pronouncements on politics usually contained a hidden agenda, it seems entirely possible that he regarded these arguments as part of a wider but unacknowledged attempt to dissociate fascism from capitalism in the public mind. He was almost certainly wrong.

The 'How' of Totalitarianism

Once he had established that totalitarianism is underpinned by a compulsion to exercise absolute power, Orwell's main objective was to describe how totalitarian governments actually work. Like most other writers on totalitarianism, he recognised that modern dictatorships are ultimately quite different from the authoritarian regimes of the past. He argued that the majority of pre-modern tyrants had tended to rule by force, securing the obedience of their subjects by continuously threatening them with physical violence. By contrast the likes of Stalin, Hitler and Mussolini had somehow managed to reach into the minds of ordinary people and win their unquestioning support. If we had to summarise Orwell's understanding of this process in a single sentence, we could perhaps say that totalitarian goverments achieve the consent of their subjects by creating circumstances in which blatant lies are instantly regarded as pure truth. According to Orwell, who first began to notice this phenomenon during the Spanish Civil War, totalitarian societies have reduced public discourse to an unprecedented level of untruthfulness. The propaganda statements which communist or fascist governments feed continuously into the public mind do not bear 'any relation to the facts, not even the relationship which is implied in an ordinary lie.'[19] Despite living in highly militarised conditions in which poverty is unavoidable and the individual's every move is determined by the state, people are told everyday that theirs is a country of peace, liberty and plenty. Moreover, as Orwell recognised more acutely than anyone else, the mendacity of official ideology extends not simply to the present and the future but also to the past. Because they realise that their errors in the past pose an enormous threat to their air of infallibility, totalitarian governments ascribe immense importance to the rewriting of history. Photographs are retouched; official records are rewritten; school textbooks retail a grossly distorted version of national development. When Winston laboured in the Ministry of Truth to erase all evidence of the Party's fallibility from back issues of the *Times*, he was simply extending a practice which Hitlerism and Stalinism had already brought to a high level of sophistication. The genius of the totalitarian mind is its ability to persuade millions of people that 'pure fantasy' is gospel truth.

Orwell was not suggesting that human beings have a natural disposition to be taken in by lies. If totalitarian states are to make the official ideology seem convincing, they have to create circumstances in which people's minds are almost preternaturally suggestible. As the portrait of Big Brother in *Nineteen Eighty-Four* is intended to show, one of the most powerful ways of doing this is to create a cult of personality around a single individual who personifies the governing class. Although totalitarian governments are always monstrously bureaucratic, Orwell seemed to imply, they invariably appeal to the public by singling out the head of state and endowing him with 'semi-divine' characteristics. Like Stalin or Hitler before him, Big Brother exploited the suppressed religious instincts of a secular age by displaying all the attributes of the Christian God: 'Big Brother is infallible and all-powerful. Every success, every achievement, every victory, every scientific discovery, all knowledge, all wisdom, all happiness, all virtue, are held to issue directly from his leadership and inspiration.'[20] At the same time, as the very name 'Big Brother' implies, personality cults also work by encouraging the individual to draw unconscious parallels between the head of state and the authority figures in his own family. When a brutal dictator is passed off as a substitute father, brother or uncle (think of 'Uncle Joe' Stalin in the USSR), the intention is usually to make his ascribed divinity seem less forbidding and therefore more believable. It is also to ensure that the powerful feelings of loyalty which exist naturally in family life are ultimately directed outwards for the benefit of the state. If millions of people in totalitarian societies are willing to believe everything the government tells them, it is precisely because gods and relatives never lie.

Orwell's portrait of Big Brother is closely related to his terrifying evocation of the role of surveillance in totalitarian societies. The most famous images in *Nineteen Eighty-Four* evoke the capacity of the state to exercise power through what political theorists might now call 'panoptical' means. Each citizen in Oceania has the impression that he is continuously being watched. Armed policemen throng the streets; children are rewarded for spying on their parents; information about the capture and trial of dissidents is given special prominence in the media. Most famously of all, there are 'telescreens' in every room which continuously relay footage of the area in front of them to the Ministry of Love. Although commonsense suggests that it is not possible to monitor the entire population at all times, every citizen proceeds on the assumption that everything he does is known to the authorities:

> There was of course no way of knowing whether you were being watched at any given moment. How often, or on what system, the Thought Police plugged in on any individual wire was guesswork. It was even conceivable that they watched everybody all the time. But at any rate they could plug in your wire whenever they wanted to. You had to live – did live, from habit that became instinct – in the assumption that every sound you made was overheard, and, except in darkness, every movement scrutinised.[21]

Orwell's point was that surveillance is not simply a means of controlling external behaviour. Its main function is to induce ideological conformity by forcing people to behave with extreme caution. Anxious to ensure that his appearance does not betray the presence of improper thoughts, the individual ends up absorbing the dominant ideology simply in order to survive: 'He [Winston] had set his features into the expression of quiet optimism which it was advisable to wear when facing the telescreen.'[22] The government's lies seep into consciousness through the medium of a person's *actions*, rendering themselves immune to criticism in so doing. Moreover, while totalitarian regimes have had undoubted success in telling people what they should think, they have also gone out of their way to transform the very processes of thought. Intent on limiting people's ability to question or challenge the official ideology, they have made concerted efforts to destroy intellectual flexibility by (1) altering the way that the mind processes information, and (2) politicising language to the point where certain styles of thinking become more or less untenable. One of the great virtues of *Nineteen Eighty-Four* is that it clarifies this aspect of totalitarianism by imagining a future in which the techniques of mind control have reached sinister new heights. The novel pays special attention to four of these hypothetical techniques, each of which can be regarded as a nightmarish exaggeration of practices which already existed in the totalitarian countries. The first is that of 'crimestop', which Orwell (in the guise of Emmanuel Goldstein) singled out for analysis in *The Theory and Practice of Oligarchical Collectivism.* Crimestop can best be understood as a method for putting the emotions at the service of the official ideology. Its purpose is to ensure that each individual responds to unorthodox ideas with a sort of visceral disgust, thereby removing them from the field of consciousness without further consideration. It also involves a deliberate coarsening or desubtilisation of the intellectual faculty, so that the weak points of the dominant ideology go wholly unrecognised: 'Crimestop...includes the power of not grasping analogies, of failing to perceive logical errors, of misunderstanding the simplest arguments if they are inimical to Ingsoc'.[23] By contrast, the related techniques of 'blackwhite' and 'doublethink' (also analysed in Goldstein's book) are intended to iron out the potentially calamitous tension between ideology and reality. As we have seen, Orwell regarded totalitarian ideology as the most blatantly untruthful of all forms of discourse. The purpose of blackwhite is to neutralise this element of untruthfulness by inculcating a brazen willingness to deny that it even exists. Confronted by the yawning gap between the official version of reality and reality itself, the person versed in blackwhite will not merely disregard it but automatically presuppose that what he is being told is true: 'it [blackwhite] means...the ability to *believe* that black is white, and more, to *know* that black is white, and to forget that one has ever believed the contrary.'[24] Doublethink is the related ability to manipulate one's conception of the past, so that memories never conflict with the Party's continuous revisions of history. Orwell's definition of doublethink was the single most brilliant piece of writing in the Goldstein book, though at times it seemed general enough to encompass the definition of blackwhite as well:

> *Doublethink* means the power of holding two contradictory beliefs in one's mind simultaneously, and accepting both of them. The Party intellectual knows in which direction his memories must be altered; he therefore knows that he is playing tricks with reality; but by the exercise of *doublethink* he also satisfies himself that reality is not violated. The process has to be conscious, or it would not be carried out with sufficient precision, but it also has to be unconscious, or it would bring with it a feeling of falsity and hence of guilt. *Doublethink* lies at the very heart of Ingsoc, since the essential act of the Party is to use conscious deception while retaining the firmness of purpose that goes with complete honesty. To tell deliberate lies while genuinely believing in them, to forget any fact that has become inconvenient, and then, when it becomes necessary again, to draw it back from oblivion for just so long as it is needed, to deny the existence of objective reality and all the while to take account of the reality which one denies – all this is indispensably necessary.[25]

Words such as 'crimestop', 'blackwhite' and 'doublethink' are all examples of 'Newspeak', the fourth technique of mind control which Orwell analysed in *Nineteen Eighty-Four*. Newspeak is a radically expurgated and abbreviated version of English which has been developed by Party linguists at the behest of the government. Scheduled to become the Party's sole language by 2050 (and already widely used by Oceanian intellectuals), its purpose is to abolish the possibility of heretical thinking by robbing language of its semantic and grammatical complexity. The assumption which underpins it is that language is an indispensable component of thought, in the sense that human beings can only think about things to which they have already attached words. By denuding English of words which correspond to politically dubious concepts or activities (that is, concepts or activities which undermine the power of the state), the Oceanians believe that they can effectively rid their country of all forms of subversion. Moreover, in their efforts to strip away unnecessary words, simplify grammatical structures and eliminate difficult forms of pronunciation, they aspire to create a situation in which the use of language requires as little thought (and therefore offers as little scope for heresy) as any purely reflexive activity.[26]

The concepts of crimestop, blackwhite, doublethink and newspeak are among the most disconcerting in the whole of Orwell's cultural criticism. By emphasising the ability of totalitarian governments to reach into the deepest recesses of the mind, they illustrate with terrible clarity the assumption that totalitarian governments have now achieved absolute power. Yet Orwell was also aware that dictatorships can only survive by greatly exaggerating their vulnerability. One of the Party's main strategies in *Nineteen Eighty-Four* is to create the impression that the state is under imminent threat of being overthrown, either by external conquest or internal uprising. Its propagandists continually assert that Oceania is on the verge of being invaded or that Goldstein's 'Brotherhood' is about to launch an insurrection in all the major cities. Neither of these propositions is true. The Brotherhood does not exist and there is even some doubt as to whether Goldstein himself is still alive. And while Oceania has indeed been at war with either Eastasia or Eurasia for several decades (the enemy changes unpredictably from year to year), the three superstates have long since reached a tacit agreement that all military engagements will be conducted along limited lines. Orwell's point was that the Oceanian government had effectively *invented* the idea of opposition in order to reinforce the status quo. The existence of a siege mentality ensures that Oceanians of all classes tend to rally around their leaders. It also ensures that the people's latent feelings of discontent can be safely directed outwards towards a purely imaginary enemy. (Members of the Party are expected to attend a regular 'Two Minutes Hate' in which they scream abuse at footage of a 'clever' but 'inherently despicable' figure who purports to be Goldstein. The resulting sense of catharsis serves to dissolve any semi-conscious feelings of opposition to Big Brother.) More subtly, the continuous emphasis on opposition provides the government with a powerful means of incriminating potential subversives. When O'Brien invites Winston to join the Brotherhood, he traps him into becoming a fully fledged opponent of the regime by creating the illusion that Oceania is full of like-minded people. This creates the context in which he can be taken to the Ministry of Love and subjected to a brutal process of political re-education. It is also worth emphasising Orwell's startling account of the *economic* reasons behind the government's willingness to fight a permanent war against the other power blocs. Writing in the guise of Emmanuel Goldstein, Orwell argued that political domination can only exist in the midst of widespread poverty. If the majority of people have to work long hours in order to earn a meagre living, they are unlikely to be very concerned with the issue of political freedom. An ingenious totalitarian regime will therefore seek to depress the standard of living while insisting that the existence of hardship is beyond its control. The most effective way of doing this is to keep a country permanently at war, since this allows the government to squander scarce resources while claiming all the while to be protecting the national interest:

> The primary aim of modern warfare (in accordance with the principles of *doublethink*, this aim is simultaneously recognised and not recognised by the directing brains of the Inner Party) is to use up the products of the machine without raising the general standard of living…In a world in which everyone worked short hours, had enough to eat, lived in a house with a bathroom and a refrigerator, and possessed a motor-car or even an aeroplane, the most obvious and perhaps the most important form of inequality would already have disappeared. If it once became general, wealth would confer no distinction…For if leisure and security were enjoyed by all alike, the great mass of human beings who are normally stupefied by poverty would become literate and would learn to think for themselves; and when once they had done this, they

> would sooner or later realise that the privileged minority had no function, and they would sweep it away.[27]

Orwell framed his account of modern dictatorship with a portrait of the role of intellectuals in totalitarian societies. As has often been pointed out, most of the important totalitarian governments of the twentieth century were dominated by people who had at least some claim to be intellectuals: Lenin, Stalin, Hitler, Mussolini and so on. This fact is fully reflected in *Nineteen Eighty-Four.* Party members in Oceania are intellectuals to a man, striving to bend culture to political ends and justifying the actions of the government by invoking a fully integrated 'world view'. Orwell's goal was to explain how this *trahison des clercs* could ever have occurred. Given that modern intellectual culture has been rooted in the existence of free speech, democratic governance and personal autonomy, how could so many intellectuals have thrown in their lot with the idea of dictatorship? His implied answer was that totalitarian movements have corrupted intellectual culture in three main ways. In the first place they have imbued intellectuals with a peculiarly debased form of moral relativism. Whereas the common people retain their belief that moral principles must be observed at all times and in all places, intellectuals on the fascist right and the communist left have long since convinced themselves that any action is justified so long as it advances the interests of their own side: 'A tyrant is all the more admired if he happens to be a bloodstained crook as well, and "the end justifies the means" often becomes, in effect, "the means justify themselves provided they are dirty enough".'[28] One of the most disturbing consequences of this rejection of traditional morality has been a weakening of the belief in objective truth. Since the main role of the totalitarian intellectual is to brainwash the masses with lying propaganda, Orwell argued, it has been necessary for both the communists and the fascists to undermine the assumption that there is a real world 'out there' against which their propaganda can be judged. Modern intellectuals have therefore fallen prey to an extreme form of philosophical idealism which sees the external world as little more than a projection of the Party's collective will. At the same time, in conformity with the idea of doublethink, they have also maintained a purely pragmatic belief in the objectivity of the physical universe when their minds have been turned to scientific activity. The main principles of this terrifying form of intellectual schizophrenia were eloquently summarised by O'Brien while he interrogated Winston in the Ministry of Love:

> ...I tell you, Winston, that reality is not external. Reality exists in the human mind, and nowhere else. Not in the individual mind, which can make mistakes, and in any case soon perishes: only in the mind of the Party, which is collective and immortal. Whatever the Party holds to be truth, *is* truth.[29]

> For certain purposes, of course, that is not true. When we navigate the ocean, or when we predict an eclipse, we often find it convenient to assume that the earth goes round the sun and that the stars are millions upon millions of kilometres away. But what of it?[30]

More prosaically, Orwell also speculated about what Marxists might call the 'cultural relations of production' in totalitarian societies – that is, the specific economic, technological and institutional circumstances in which intellectuals have to do their work. His main argument was that totalitarianism is deeply inimical to the idea of individual authorship. Since genuine creativity can only occur in conditions of relative freedom, it is likely that totalitarian societies will tend to organise cultural production along Fordist lines. Instead of books, scripts, articles and the like being produced by individual authors, they will increasingly be assembled from the work of disparate people who have each been assigned a limited and precisely defined task – planning, writing, editing and so on.[31] This state of affairs is exemplified in the Ministry of Truth, where hundreds of members of the Outer Party collaborate in the production of propaganda. Orwell even predicted that totalitarian societies would one day come close to *automating* the production of texts, not least by inventing machines which would churn out propaganda with a minimum of human intervention. (When Winston gets to know Julia in *Nineteen Eighty-Four*, he learns that 'she worked, as he had guessed, on the novel-writing machines in the Fiction Department.')[32] If the intellectuals of the Outer and Inner Party (as well as their counterparts in Stalin's Russia or Hitler's Germany) are happy to squander their lives in the service of tyranny, it is precisely because their work has been adulterated to the point where its true nature is unclear even to themselves.

British Communism and the Prostitution of the Intellect

Although Orwell was deeply influenced by communist intellectuals, he also regarded them as a baleful portent of what might happen in Britain if the Communist Party ever came to power. His natural assumption was that Strachey, Palme Dutt and their ilk were little better than bloodless egotists with barely concealed dictatorial ambitions, and that their ideas, their attitudes and their *modus operandi* provided a grim blueprint for the intellectual culture of some future Soviet Britain. This perhaps helps to explain why no aspect of his work was more obviously indebted to British communists than his account of the role of the intellectual under totalitarianism. As we have seen, Orwell believed that totalitarian intellectuals tend to practise a bizarre form of philosophical doublethink. Called upon to lie continually in order to win support for their cause, they often fall back on the idea that reality is simply a projection of their particular organisation's collective will. By contrast, when asked to perform tasks which require an accurate knowledge of the world 'out there', they implicitly recognise that the material world exists independently of the mind and obeys its own laws. Although Orwell probably arrived at this view at a fairly early stage (perhaps as early as the Spanish Civil War), it seems to have been powerfully reinforced by his fierce polemical exchange with the communist poet Randall Swingler in 1946.[33] The battle between Orwell and Swingler effectively began when Orwell's essay 'The Prevention of Literature' appeared in the second issue of the journal *Polemic*. As is well known, 'The Prevention of Literature' was a passionate attack on what Orwell regarded as the main threats to freedom of speech in Britain, most of which he ascribed to the excessive prestige of communism. Writing at a time when the British media still laboured under many of the restrictions which had been introduced during the war, Orwell claimed that political journalism was in the process of being corrupted by the 'dangerous proposition that freedom is undesirable and that intellectual honesty is a form of antisocial selfishness.'[34] He was especially concerned that a climate had been created in which it was no longer possible to tell the truth about the USSR. Since the USSR had played such a vital role in the defeat of fascism (and since it could still reasonably be portrayed as a country struggling to establish socialism), British communists had been able to win considerable support for the claim that anyone who disseminated anti-Soviet arguments was simply playing into the hands of the enemy. While Orwell agreed that this point of view was superficially attractive, he also warned that its widespread acceptance would ultimately lead to the wholesale adoption of the totalitarian outlook. As soon as intellectuals took it into their heads that telling lies and suppressing the truth were acceptable means of advancing a political cause, it was only a matter of time until they started rewriting history, denying the existence of objective reality and abolishing the literary imagination.

Swingler's response to Orwell, entitled 'The Right to Free Expression', appeared in the fifth issue of *Polemic* in September–October 1946. At one level it was quite an effective piece of *tu quoque* viciousness, insisting that many of the accusations which Orwell levelled against the communists could equally be levelled against him. Swingler paid special attention to a passage in 'The Prevention of Literature' which claimed that large numbers of Soviet soldiers had defected to Nazi Germany during the War, noting that it was just as vague, tendentious and factually impoverished as the worst pieces of pro-Soviet propaganda. He also expressed his surprise that so widely published an author as Orwell should have claimed that people who wished to expose the 'Russian mythos' were being squeezed out of the British press. However, in spite of its title, the core of 'The Right to Free Expression' was a sinister and unworthy attempt to justify restrictions on free speech. As if to confirm everyone's worst suspicions about the communist attitude towards democracy, Swingler argued that literary culture should be governed by the principle that '…writers must earn the right to intellectual freedom'.[35] What this appeared to mean was that the right to free speech should only be invoked when writers strive to tell the truth. Once they resort to the 'conscious suppression or distortion of the truth in the publication of their findings',[36] they forfeit the right to see their work in print. Swingler tried to justify his argument by sketching a theory of knowledge which clearly derived from the orthodox communist philosophy of the day. (Its ultimate source was probably the sections on epistemology in Lenin's 'Philosophical Notebooks' of 1916.) His main point was that 'absolute truth' is not something which can ever be realistically attained. Since there are strict limits on the amount of data which human beings can register at any one time, or so the argument went, it follows that every statement about external reality will be weighed down by subjective distortions of one sort or another. Moreover, since truth and falsity are so closely intertwined (and since it is desperately difficult to distinguish one from the other), intellectuals must come to recognise that their main social function is not so much to state a particular view but to 'show people how to deal with evidence.'[37] If a writer plays fast and loose with the evidence in order to advance his chosen argument, he can scarcely complain if his work is suppressed. The interesting thing about Orwell's response to Swingler (which took the form of eight ferocious annotations published at the side of the page) was that it clearly anticipated the more philosophical passages in *Nineteen Eighty-Four.* Noting that 'Mr. Swingler would silence me if he could',[38] Orwell argued (or at least implied) that communists have habitually distorted their belief in the 'relativity of truth' in order to justify their attacks on individual liberty. Instead of sticking to the view that all statements contain a mixture of truth and falsity, they have usually behaved as if every observation about the world is either absolutely true or absolutely false. This has enabled them to (1) claim special privileges for their own opinions on the grounds that they contain a perfect reflection of external reality, and (2) suppress non-communist opinions on the grounds that they contain no element of truth whatsoever. What Orwell was effectively claiming was that relativist assumptions are peculiarly vulnerable to totalitarian appropriation, since they can easily be separated out into a form of strict materialism on the one hand ('the world exists independently of the mind and can readily be understood by it') and absolute idealism on the other ('the world is merely a projection of the mind'). There are obvious parallels between the following passage in Orwell's reply to Swingler and the philosophical opinions which were later ascribed to O'Brien:

> I notice with interest that whereas Mr. Swingler attacks me violently for my essay in *Polemic*, he also speaks approvingly of a recent essay of mine in *Horizon*. [Swingler had made a brief and apparently complimentary reference to 'Politics and the English Language', which appeared in *Horizon* in April 1946.] It apparently does not occur to him that the same person, with the same motives, biases, and so forth, was responsible for both articles, and that my title to speak is no higher or lower in one case than in the other. In effect, where he happens to approve of my conclusions, he says to me, '*Go ahead! You are quite right to follow your own judgement*': where he disapproves, he says, '*Do you realise that you are only a single fallible human being and that you have no right to put your own views forward as if they are gospel truth?*' To some extent this happens to the writer everywhere, but above all it happens wherever totalitarian habits of thought prevail. The writer is called a reporter, but is treated as a megaphone. So long as his conclusions are desirable, he is bidden to trust the evidence of his own senses, but as soon as he reveals something that the authorities dislike, he is reminded that all truth is relative, that what appear to be solid objects are merely masses of whirling electrons. etc., etc.[39]

Orwell's implied point in his reply to Swingler was that communist philosophy can easily be distorted to advance totalitarian objectives, regardless of its surface meanings or the intentions with which it was formulated. He made much the same point on the other occasion in 1946 when he used the pages of *Polemic* to respond directly to a communist text. In December 1945, in the first issue of the 'New Series' of *The Modern Quarterly* (a semi-academic journal in which communist intellectuals surveyed the state of contemporary culture), the philosopher John Lewis devoted part of his Editorial to an attack on *Polemic* in general and Orwell in particular. Seeking to identify the 'many and influential sophistries' which had held back the socialist cause in the period since the end of the War, Lewis argued that *Polemic* was symptomatic of a widespread attempt to 'confuse moral issues' by 'break[ing] down the distinction between right and wrong'.[40] He illustrated his point by citing Orwell's essay 'Notes on Nationalism', which had appeared in the first issue of *Polemic* in October 1945. According to Lewis, who expressed himself with uncharacteristic brevity, Orwell had displayed a deplorable lack of moral insight in his essay by '…finding no difference whatever between guilty Germans hanging innocent civilians in 1941 and the victorious allies hanging those same guilty Germans for their crimes in 1945'.[41] Orwell was thus portrayed as a crude exponent of moral absolutism who failed to recognise that the ethical status of similar acts necessarily varies from context to context. A similar accusation was levelled against the popular philosopher C.E.M. Joad (a regular contributor to the BBC's 'Brains Trust' programme whom Orwell had himself criticised sharply),[42] who allegedly exemplified the weakness of *Polemic* by identifying spurious 'Sacred Absolutes' which corresponded to nothing more substantial than his passing states of mind. In the light of these absolutist provocations, Lewis concluded that 'The whole basis of ethics needs re-examination'.[43] He failed to acknowledge that there was *already* an orthodox line on ethics to which communists were expected to adhere.

Orwell defended *Polemic* against Lewis's attacks in an anonymous editorial which appeared in Issue 3 of the magazine in May 1946. His tactic was to focus attention on what he took to be the weaknesses in the communist approach to morality, taking J.D. Bernal's article 'Belief and Action' as his text. (Bernal's article appeared in the same issue of *The Modern Quarterly* which contained Lewis's remarks on *Polemic*. In keeping with its author's famously polymathic tendencies, its purpose was to sketch out the communist approach to metaphysics, science, economics, politics, ethics and the arts. Its opening sentence, which observed that 'This is a time for endings and beginnings', neatly encapsulated the portentous sense of optimism which swept through the world communist movement in the wake of the defeat of fascism.)[44] From the point of view of the reader of *Nineteen Eighty-Four*, the main significance of Orwell's editorial was that it contained a lengthy discussion of his belief that moral relativism can often serve totalitarian ends. Chiding Bernal for his failure to say exactly what he meant (and for the slipshod quality of his prose), Orwell singled out the following passage for analysis:

> A radical change in morality is in any case required by the new social relations which men are already entering into in an organised and planned society. The relative importance of different virtues are bound to be affected. Old virtues may even appear as vices and new virtues instituted. Many of the basic virtues – truthfulness and good fellowship – are, of course, as old as humanity and need no changing, but those based on excessive concern with individual rectitude need reorienting in the direction of social responsibility.[45]

Orwell had no intention of engaging with these 'pompous and slovenly' remarks on their own terms. His argument was that their sole purpose was to provide a collection of euphemisms for political immorality of the worst kind – a characteristic which they shared with most other forms of communist discourse. By emphasising the idea that values change from one period to another, Bernal was effectively expressing the view that (1) 'we must alter our conception of right and wrong from year to year, and if necessary from minute to minute',[46] and (2) 'nearly anything is right if it is politically expedient'.[47] Far from being a central and legitimate component of the doctrine of historical materialism or the Marxist critique of capitalism, moral relativism is simply the means by which the communist movement justifies (or tries to justify) the extreme tactical flexibility for which it is rightly notorious. Insofar as Bernal made a passing reference to universal values such as 'truthfulness and good fellowship', he was motivated by a hypocritical desire to seem respectable: 'The implication of the whole passage is that telling lies might also be a virtue.'[48] Orwell also argued that 'Action and Belief' contained a worrying attempt to emphasise the rights of the community at the expense of the rights of the individual. When Bernal counterposed 'social responsibility' to 'individual rectitude', he seemed to be implying that the only opinion which matters in a socialist society is the opinion of the majority. It follows that there can be no role for the individual conscience in this sort of society, since (or so Bernal allegedly believed) 'right action lies in pushing history in the direction in which it is actually going.'[49]

At first sight, Orwell's attack on Bernal seems deeply unfair. Justified in its assumption that political discourse usually conceals a hidden agenda which needs to be rigorously exposed, it nevertheless comes to the quite unwarranted conclusion that communist philosophy *always* serves as a smokescreen for political self-interest. There is no recognition in the *Polemic* editorial that Bernal's article had been rooted in the insights of historical materialism – a doctrine to which Orwell was himself deeply indebted. When Bernal insisted that certain values are destined to seem less important or even to disappear altogether in the socialist society of the future, he was by no means implying that individuals can drastically alter their ethical outlook from one day to another. He was simply illustrating the fundamental Marxist assumptions that a society's value system is deeply influenced by its prevailing 'mode of production', that certain values are useful in one economic context but not in others (even though they might well linger on into societies in which they are no longer functional) and that any attempt to build socialism will necessarily involve a radical break with the values of capitalism. Nor was his reference to universal values simply a sop to respectable opinion, since British communists (or at least some of them) had always argued that human beings possess a series of basic transhistorical drives which socialist society will bring to fruition. Even more unconscionable were Orwell's distortions of the communist attitude towards the relationship between the individual and society. Although Bernal's apparently dismissive references to 'individual rectitude' were certainly unfortunate (and bore out all Orwell's strictures about the carelessness of his prose), it is clear from his wider remarks that he was not advocating the suppression of the individual conscience or pouring scorn on the idea of individualism. What he was actually implying was that individualism had been grossly corrupted by the rise of capitalism (not least because market competition breeds selfishness in its grossest forms) and that socialist collectivism would go a long way towards harmonising the needs of the individual with the needs of the majority. And yet, in spite of its unscrupulousness and lack of philosophical sophistication, it is hard not to conclude that Orwell's attack on Bernal had a point. As Orwell observed on several occasions in his writings of the 1940s, the history of the CPGB (and of world communism more generally) had indeed been characterised by a tactical flexibility which bordered on outright opportunism. This was especially true of the Party's role in the struggle against fascism. No reader of *Polemic* would have forgotten that the Party vigorously advocated a Popular Front between 1935 and 1939, did its best to hamper the war effort between 1939 and 1941 (solely because of the Hitler–Stalin Pact) and ended up supporting the war after the invasion of the USSR. While the majority of Party members went along with these changes because of loyalty towards the Comintern, it seems entirely possible that the doctrine of moral relativism enabled some of them to do so without outraging their consciences too deeply. If so, Orwell's plain-man Kantianism might not have been as naïve as it seemed. At any rate, his lengthy discussion of moral relativism in *Polemic* directly anticipated O'Brien's terrifying disquisition on the the ethics of totalitarianism in *Nineteen Eighty-Four.*

As we have seen, Orwell was not simply interested in philosophical matters when he wrote about the intellectual culture of totalitarian societies. He was equally interested in the way that intellectual and cultural work is *organised* in these societies. His main assumption was that totalitarianism sounds the death knell on any idea of individual creativity. Since the main function of intellectuals under Hitler, Stalin or Big Brother is to churn out utterly mendacious propaganda (and since genuine creativity presupposes the existence of liberal freedoms), it is more or less inevitable that dictatorships will organise culture around soulless institutions in which texts are produced by committees rather than by individuals. From the point of view of the governments which set them up, the great benefit of these institutions (exemplified by the Ministry of Truth) is that they deprive the individual worker of a clear understanding of his work. No one need feel guilty about producing pap if he is only half aware of what he is doing. What is sometimes overlooked is that Orwell based these arguments not only on his observations of existing dictatorships (important though these were) but also on contemporary developments in the media industries of the democratic nations. He seems to have taken a special interest in the structure of the the film industry, perhaps because he worked as a film critic for *Time and Tide* between 1940 and 1941. In 'The Prevention of Literature' he pointed to the existence of a complex division of labour in Hollywood studios, noting that 'The Disney films…are produced by what is essentially a factory process, the work being done partly mechanically and partly by teams of artists who have to subordinate their individual style.'[50] While Orwell could have derived his understanding of the film industry from a variety of sources, it is worth noting that Hollywood production techniques were rigorously analysed in contemporary Marxist writings on the cinema, meagre though these were. The main communist writer on film at the time was probably Arthur Calder-Marshall, whose essay 'The Film Industry' appeared in C. Day Lewis's famous symposium *The Mind in Chains* in 1937. (Orwell referred to *The Mind in Chains* in a number of his writings, most notably in 'Inside The Whale'.)[51] One of Calder-Marshall's most important themes was the nature of the relationship between creative workers and the studios which employed them. Given that Hollywood is largely in the business of making films for 'nitwits' (Calder-Marshall's vocabulary often belied his anti-elitist posturings), it might have been thought that the studio bosses would face insuperable difficulties in attracting 'people of talent and sincerity' to the industry. In practice there are two good reasons why no such difficulties exist. Whereas the first is purely financial (Hollywood specialises in throwing cash at penurious intellectuals who have been 'struggling along with little money'), the second is largely organisational. In the final analysis, or so Calder-Marshall argued, Hollywood can only retain the loyalty of its artists by rationalising the process of production to the point where the individual artist has no real conception of the film he is working on:

> If the systematic dilution of originality was presented to the artist crudely, he would revolt against it. For this reason the making of a film is put into the hands not of a single artist, but of a number of executives. The scenarist is given full rope: he is encouraged to put all his creative power into his scenario. Then the scenario is handed over to another executive who emasculates it. This happens at every stage in the production: so that the final film represents the resultant of the progressive, creative forces, countered by the forces of reaction. Hence, the paradox arises that under capitalism, which claims to respect individual effort more than mass effort, the individual creator, whether he be scenarist, producer, director, cutter, or actor, is frustrated.[52]

In a dialogue on 'The Proletarian Writer' which Orwell and Desmond Hawkins contributed to BBC radio in December 1940, Calder-Marshall was one of four Marxist writers whom Orwell mentioned by name – the others were Christopher Caudwell, Alec Brown and Edward Upward.[53] Orwell also commissioned Calder-Marshall to contribute a number of talks to the Indian Service of the BBC while working as a producer between 1941 and 1943. Since Calder-Marshall was by no means a communist writer of the first rank, the fact that he stuck in Orwell's mind lends credence to the view that his writings on film were among the sources which Orwell drew on (consciously or otherwise) while sketching his nightmare vision of cultural manipulation in *Nineteen Eighty-Four.*

The Politics of Form

As we have seen, Orwell had a deeply ambivalent attitude towards the influence of communists on the literary culture of his day. Impressed by their critical insight and their use of Marxism as a tool of historical analysis, he nevertheless believed that their demand for politically committed art would ultimately have a ruinous effect on literary standards. My argument in this section is that his concern with these matters is reflected not merely in *Nineteen Eighty-Four*'s content but also in its form. On the one hand, impressed by the chapters on modern literature in John Strachey's *The Coming Struggle for Power*, Orwell forged a new form of dystopian fiction which clearly took account of Strachey's brief remarks about Huxley's *Brave New World.* On the other hand, appalled by the aesthetic of Socialist Realism, he set out to satirise communist literary dogmatism by turning the conventions of the socialist novel on their heads.

John Strachey and the Idea of Dystopia

It has often been pointed out that *Nineteen Eighty-Four* was one of a handful of novels which inaugurated a new form of dystopian fiction. According to critics such as Irving Howe, whose essay 'The Politics of Anti-Utopia' (1962) advances the argument in unusually succinct form, one of the most important features of Orwell's book is that it shows what happens when a believer in Enlightenment principles is obliged to question his beliefs. Grouping *Nineteen Eighty-Four* with Zamiatin's *We* (1922) and Huxley's *Brave New World* (1936), Howe argued that the 'peculiar intensity of such fiction derives not so much from the horror aroused by a possible vision of the future, but from the writer's discovery that in facing the prospect of a future he had been trained to desire, he finds himself struck with horror.'[54] In particular, Zamiatin, Huxley and Orwell expressed their disenchantment with socialist or liberal principles by envisaging a world in which reason has been thoroughly perverted for authoritarian ends. Oceania is a society in which 'functional rationality' takes almost complete precedence over 'substantial rationality' (the terms are Karl Mannheim's). Far from putting their intellectual capacities at the service of genuine scientific, sociological or philosophical inquiry, the rulers of Oceania devote all their energy to devising new techniques which can reinforce their power over society as a whole. One of Howe's crucial insights was that Orwell underscored this point by emphasising the terrifying ability of totalitarian governments to transform human nature. At one level, *Nineteen Eighty-Four* is based on the assumption that human beings possess an instinctive or transhistorical desire for freedom. Instead of portraying the need for personal liberty as something which only arises in certain historical periods, Orwell clearly regarded it as an innate characteristic which has shaped human affairs since the dawn of time. When Winston and Julia defy the government by making love in the countryside, it is precisely the *naturalness* of their rebellion to which Orwell is drawing our attention. The trees and fields of the 'golden country' are an objective correlative for a set of libertarian impulses which have their roots in human biology.[55] However, as Howe went on to point out, none of this means that Orwell regarded the yearning for 'candor, freedom, truth and love' as somehow indestructible. One of the main goals of *Nineteen Eighty-Four* is to dramatise the possibility that totalitarian regimes have discovered techniques for simply expunging the love of freedom from human consciousness, in the process replacing it with an equally powerful hunger for absolute subordination. The point about Winston's 'conversion' to the Party is that it is entirely sincere. The man who announces his love for Big Brother on the final page of the book is in no sense struggling against his better instincts, since the impulses which forced him to rebel have long since been stripped out of his nature:

> When one speaks of the historical determinants of human nature, one tacitly assumes that there is a human nature, and that for all its plasticity it retains some indestructible core. If Zamiatin, Orwell and Huxley wrote simply from the premise of psychological relativism, they would deprive themselves of whatever possibilities for drama their theme allows, for then the very idea of a limit to the malleability of human nature would be hard to maintain. They must assume that there are strivings in men towards candor, freedom, truth and love which cannot be suppressed indefinitely;

> yet they have no choice but to recognize that at any particular historical moment these strivings can be suppressed effectively…[56]

There is an interesting clue to Orwell's preoccupation with the 'plasticity' of human nature in the second part of *The Road to Wigan Pier* (1937), written over ten years before work on *Nineteen Eighty-Four* began. Casting a critical eye over modern dystopian fiction, Orwell invoked an influential work of communist criticism to bolster his account of *Brave New World*: 'It contains its own contradictions (the most important of them is pointed out in Mr John Strachey's *The Coming Struggle for Power*), but it is at least a memorable assault on the more fat-bellied type of perfectionism.'[57] What were the 'contradictions' to which Strachey referred and in what way might they have influenced the writing of *Nineteen Eighty-Four*? Strachey's discussion of Huxley occurred in a section of his book entitled 'The Decay of Capitalist Culture'. Anxious to show that the economic calamities of the post-war years had exerted a devastating influence on all forms of cultural activity (he was writing in 1932 at the height of the 'Class Against Class' period), Strachey argued in one chapter that modern writers such as Proust, Lawrence and Huxley had lost the ability to evoke the 'tragic view of life'. For much of its history, or so the argument went, one of literature's most important functions has been to depict the 'unavoidable tragedies of human existence' in as consoling a way as possible. By portraying characters who were able to confront illness, ageing and death with a measure of courage and realism, the greatest writers had gone some way towards reconciling men and women to their implacable fate. The problem with the leading modernists was that they could no longer distinguish between the corrigible and the incorrigible. While Proust, Lawrence and Huxley had each aspired to express a tragic vision of life, their work was less concerned with ineluctable sources of human misery than with the traumatic but avoidable difficulties which modern society imposes upon us. Proust and Lawrence had attacked the emptiness of upper-class culture in England and France respectively, bemoaning the fact that the aristocracy only seemed distinguished when seen from outside. Huxley's main theme was the spiritual poverty engendered by modern forms of industrial organisation. If *Brave New World* failed to evoke the emboldening sense of cosmic turbulence which characterised the great literature of the past, it was precisely because it tried to attach a tragic ethos to social problems which were (1) of recent historical vintage, and (2) eminently capable of being solved.[58] It is easy to see how Orwell might have been influenced by Strachey's argument. Faced with the claim that Britain's most distinguished dystopian novelist had unwisely focused on the historically specific at the expense of the transhistorical, he perhaps concluded that his own dystopias should aim to break new ground by questioning the very distinction between the two categories. Instead of reverting to the tragedian's classic themes, he therefore tried to show that the real source of tragedy in the modern world is the recognition that humanity's most honourable instincts (the love of freedom among them) are not nearly as permanent as everyone has supposed. When Winston's desire for freedom is stripped out of his system (or when a naturally lascivious woman like Julia is reduced to a neurasthenic prude), we suddenly discover that even our most 'imperishable' and life-affirming characteristics can easily be consigned to history. Insofar as *Nineteen Eighty-Four* indeed attains the status of a genuine tragedy, or so it could be argued, it does so not by affirming the priority of nature over culture but by hinting that the distinction between them no longer applies – or at least not always.

Satirising Socialist Realism

Although *Nineteen Eighty-Four* devotes a lot of space to the specifically cultural aspects of totalitarianism, it says practically nothing about the literary forms which totalitarian states tend to favour. While Orwell makes it clear that Oceanian novels are written on machines in the Ministry of Truth, he does not tell us what forms they employ or what subject matter they address. Nor does he explore the role of poetry and verse in Oceania, save for some scanty remarks about popular songs and their cynical appeal to cheap sentiment. Yet this is not to say that *Nineteen Eighty-Four* is neglectful of literary issues. What I want to argue in this section is that the novel satirises the literature of totalitarianism as surely as it attacks its mode of governance, though *less at the level of content than at the level of form*. More specifically, I argue that its formal characteristics provide an oblique and bitterly hostile commentary on the aesthetic of Socialist Realism – an aesthetic which Orwell had largely encountered in the work of British communists. Having condemned the communists since the mid-1930s for turning literature into a vehicle of propaganda, Orwell's objective in his final book was to satirise their bedrock artistic procedures by inverting, deconstructing or in some other way distorting them. In this sense, *Nineteen Eighty-Four* is not merely Orwell's most accomplished novel but also one of his most stimulating pieces of literary criticism.

The conventions of Socialist Realism were first sketched out at the Soviet Writers' Congress in Moscow in 1934, where keynote speakers such as Andrey Zhdanov, Maxim Gorky and Nikolai Bukharin made it clear that artists throughout the world communist movement were expected to adopt the new form.[59] British Marxists responded to the Soviet challenge with surprising vigour in the two or three decades after the Congress, producing large numbers of novels, poems, paintings and films along the prescribed lines. Among the most important practitioners of the socialist novel in Britain were Alec Brown, Jack Lindsay, Randall Swingler, Lewis Jones and Len Doherty, several of whom had their books reviewed by Orwell.[60] Each of these writers took his lead from Zhdanov's assumption that the purpose of Socialist Realism was to 'depict…[life] truthfully in artistic creations, to depict it neither "scholastically" nor lifelessly, not simply as "objective reality", but rather as reality in its revolutionary development.'[61] At the heart of their writing was an attempt to provide a synoptic or totalising perspective on the existing stage of social development. On the assumption that art can only stimulate political action by fostering a holistic understanding of society's laws of motion, they strove to evoke the economic, political and cultural elements of the prevailing social order in all their 'unity and difference'. These Hegelian ambitions were supplemented by an emphasis on 'revolutionary romanticism', which held that one of the main duties of the socialist writer was to balance the rigorous analysis of the present with a utopian evocation of the communist society of the future. Their narratives were usually focused on a 'positive hero' or 'type' whose promethean qualities exemplified all that was best about the revolutionary working class. The vast majority of their books employed 'traditional' forms and eschewed the technical innovations of modernism, on the grounds that the latter were widely regarded as a symptom of capitalism in decline.

The aspect of Socialist Realism which Orwell most obviously satirises in *Nineteen Eighty-Four* is its emphasis on totality.[62] Where the socialist novel sets out to provide its readers with a synoptic understanding of society, Orwell tries to show why the quest for totality is doomed in advance under totalitarian conditions. Desperate to understand a society he knows he cannot change, Winston spends much of the book struggling to transcend the intellectual barriers which prevent him seeing Oceania in the round. In the period leading up to his arrest he makes an agonising effort to relate each element of the system to all the others, slowly coming to appreciate how telescreens, wars, propaganda and sexual repression all play their part in reinforcing the power of the Party. What holds him back is his failure to grasp why the system exists in the first place: 'I understand HOW: I do not understand WHY.'[63] The terrible irony is that he is only afforded a glimpse of totality as a result of being arrested. When O'Brien tells him that the Party's main objective is to exercise untrammelled power for its own sake ('The object of persecution is persecution'),[64] he finally comes to recognise the motive force on which everything else in his society is centred. Indeed, there is perhaps a sense in which his single biggest defeat is that he is robbed of this insight as soon as it is acquired. By the time he is released from the Ministry of Love, fewer than thirty pages after O'Brien delivers his revelation, everything he once knew has been terrorised out of him. Whereas the hero in a Zhdanovite novel moves inexorably towards a sort of Balzacian omniscience, Winston exchanges absolute knowledge for brainwashed passivity. Like everything else in Oceania, insight into totality is only granted on the Party's own terms.

Winston's failure to comprehend the system does not arise from a lack of cerebral muscle – or at least not entirely. Its main cause is the lack of intellectual flexibility which his position in the system imposes upon him. Especially important here is his experience of working at the Ministry of Truth. In an obvious rebuff to those of his contemporaries who believed that socialism would automatically restore dignity to labour, Orwell portrayed Winston's job as the acme of Fordist tedium. Isolated in a cubicle and condemned to perform the same task all day long, he seems almost physically debarred from transcending the narrow horizons of a middle-ranking Party functionary. A related problem is the way that class distinctions in Oceania are powerfully reinforced by divisions of space. Intent on segregating people from different backgrounds (and thereby disguising the relationship of domination between them), the Party has imposed a radically different character on the areas in which they live. Although Winston moves across London more freely than anyone else in the book, he seems beleaguered at all times by the sort of topographical confusion that Fredric Jameson has famously ascribed to postmodern cultures. To a degree that is unprecedented in Orwell's other novels, the spaces in which the narrative unfolds are heterogeneous in the extreme. The dinginess of the Outer Party's lodgings contrasts sharply with the quiet opulence of the Inner Party's quarters. The various ministries exude an air of high panoptical menace but the proletarian districts teem with rude life. Even the two levels of Mr Charrington's shop seem to exist in different worlds, the ground floor filled with trash and the upper floor radiating domesticity. Insofar as people instinctively shy away from the pursuit of knowledge, it is partly because their rigidly segmented environment imposes insurmountable barriers to sequential thinking.

The snuffing out of Winston's quest for understanding raises important questions about Orwell's approach to characterisation. There is arguably a sense in which Winston is deliberately portrayed as a sort of negative caricature of the 'positive heroes' who throng the Socialist novel. As Zhdanov and his fellow speakers made clear at the 1934 conference, the purpose of a positive hero in socialist fiction is both to reinforce collective identities and to hint at the ways in which human nature might be transformed.[65] On the one hand he embodies all the most obvious characteristics of the particular social group (usually the working class) whose collective power the artist wishes to affirm; yet he also prefigures the well-nigh superhuman level of personal development which the individual might be able to achieve in the communist society of the future. He is someone for whom manual labour and intellectual activity are largely continuous, not the paired terms of an irreconcilable contradiction. With his synoptic or totalising grasp of the various elements in the existing historical conjuncture, he gestures towards an age in which common ownership and material abundance will enable the individual to experiment with a diverse range of economic roles. The outward signs of his distinction are usually a statuesque physique and a permanent expression of serene thoughtfulness, the latter suggesting that his formidable resources of intellect are continuously being applied to the business of creating a better future.

There are two ways in particular in which Winston seems to reverse this formula. The first is that he conspicuously fails to fit in with any of Oceania's established classes or groups. Indeed, one of the most remarkable things about him is what might be called his liminality – that is, the fact that he seems to hover uneasily on the borders between several different groups. Officially a member of the Outer Party, he is strongly drawn towards the Proles but has intellectual gifts which are comparable to those of the Oceanian elite. Neither healthy nor entirely unwell (even if some of his respiratory agonies clearly reflect Orwell's own experience of tuberculosis), he has reached an age at which he is no longer young but only ambiguously middle-aged. He is married but has not seen his wife in many years. More importantly, he is one of the few citizens in Oceania whose sensibility encompasses memories of the pre-revolutionary era as well as a vivid apprehension of the present. (I will return to this point towards the end of the chapter.) Utterly *sui generis* in his way of looking at things, he exemplifies Orwell's insight that men are never lonelier than when being forced to behave like everyone else. Although Orwell specialised in the portrayal of isolated and disaffected individuals, there is no other character in his fiction who is less capable of functioning as the 'type' of a particular social group.

Winston also subverts the formula for the positive hero in his physical being. If the positive hero prefigures the unalienated communist future by achieving a balanced relationship between a healthy mind and a virile body, Winston's body stands as a permanent threat to his intellectual ambitions. Prematurely decrepit and continually suffering from coughing fits, he can only pursue his goal of understanding the Oceanian system by struggling to hold his bodily agonies at bay. It might even be said that his intellectual achievements are inversely proportional to his physical health. By the time O'Brien completes his understanding of the system by revealing the psychological motivations of the elite, he (Winston) has been reduced to a 'bowed, grey-coloured, skeleton-like thing' whose teeth can be prised from his gums with the minimum of effort.[66] Political insight flashes temporarily across the synapses of an agonised brain, then disappears. Even when Winston's body is registering the subversive pleasures of sex, good food and nature, it still threatens to dull his rebellion by sucking him down into a sort of anti-intellectual miasma. The dangers of scorning understanding and surrendering wholly to pleasure are embodied in an extreme form by Julia, who takes no interest in Goldstein's writings and seems to regard the orgasm as an act of rebellion in itself. Not for nothing does Winston describe her as a 'rebel from the waist downwards' – a formulation which delights her.[67]

Orwell's attempt to satirise the positive hero is closely paralleled by his reworking of the socialist novel's affective or emotional structure. The orthodox communist approach to the representation of emotion had first been outlined by Nikolai Bukharin at the Soviet Writers' Congress. Rejecting the Kantian, Hegelian and Schopenhauerian idea that great art is necessarily 'disinterested' (that is, devoid of 'desire and will'), Bukharin described literature as one of the most important means of educating the emotions. Instead of adopting a detached or neutral attitude towards the world around him, or so it was argued, the socialist artist should strive at all times to inculcate a mood of 'active militant force' in his intended audience.[68] The result of this advice was that socialist writers tended to produce work which oscillated fairly predictably between the extremes of class-conscious anger and sub-romantic lyricism. Splenetic descriptions of contemporary capitalism alternated with Parnassian evocations of the socialist future, reflecting and perhaps reinforcing the rather bipolar nature of the communist sensibility. One of the things which *Nineteen Eighty-Four* clearly sets out to do is to subvert this structure of feeling. The novel's dominant tone is one of disinterestedness born of political exhaustion. When Orwell describes the structure of Oceanian society, he does so with a sort of appalled but affectless fascination – an outlook which is also reflected in Winston's curiously deracinated habits of speech. On the rare occasions when the novel splutters into emotional life, it is often to evoke the dark underbelly of the emotional militancy which Bukharin had recommended. There is a particularly memorable example of this when Winston scribbles a furious account of a propaganda newsreel into his diary, excitement swiftly modulating into something approaching sadism:

> April 4th, 1984. Last night to the flicks. All war films. One very good one of a ship full of refugees being bombed somewhere in the Mediterranean. Audience much amused by shots of a great huge fat man trying to swim away with a helicopter after him. first you saw him wallowing along in the water like a porpoise, then you saw him through the helicopters gunsights, then he was full of holes and the sea round him turned pink and he sank as suddenly as though the holes had let in the water. audience shouting with laughter when he sank. then you saw a lifeboat full of children with a helicopter hovering over it…[69]

The political significance of *Nineteen Eighty-Four*'s affective structure is fairly self-evident. Whereas the socialist novel traded on righteous anger as a means of undermining the status quo, Orwell grimly implies that the only rational response to Stalinist tyranny is one of resignation and detachment. Insofar as 'active militant force' plays a role in communist societies, or so he hints, its purpose is not to stimulate change but to reinforce the existing order by whipping up hatred of the regime's real or imagined enemies. Also of relevance in this context is Orwell's handling of the future, which implicitly satirises the element of 'revolutionary romanticism' in the socialist novel. As Bukharin and his colleagues had made clear in their comments on Soviet literature, the purpose of revolutionary romanticism was not to provide a detailed vision of the communist future but to hint at the existential changes which communism might bring about. Implicitly it drew on the venerable Marxist distinction between the sphere of necessity and the sphere of freedom. Quite apart from surveying the struggles of the present, or so the argument went, socialist writers should strive to evoke a future in which the people have been released from meaningless labour, freed from poverty and delivered into a world of substantive liberty. At one level it is fairly obvious that *Nineteen Eighty-Four* seeks to reverse this scheme, portraying the future in terms of the complete disappearance of human freedom. When Winston contemplates his personal future in the period before his arrest, he knows perfectly well that his dalliance with thoughtcrime must inevitably lead to detention, punishment and execution. Government rhetoric is weighed down by the language of necessity, while intellectuals look forward to the day when a behaviourist state manipulates the instinctive responses of every adult. O'Brien famously sums up the Party's ambitions by telling Winston that 'If you want a picture of the future, imagine a boot stamping on a human face – for ever.'[70] What is less noticeable is that Orwell occasionally invokes a much subtler and more metaphysical conception of the rigidly determined nature of the future, not in order to *illustrate* the horrors of totalitarianism but in order to *challenge* them. There are various points in *Nineteen Eighty-Four* at which Orwell endows his characters with the power of precognition. For example, Winston dreams about the Golden Country long before he ever sees it, accurately predicts his incarceration in the 'place where there is no darkness' (the Ministry of Love) and has the distinct feeling that O'Brien can foresee his train of thought. These excursions into Augustinian fatalism stand in stark contrast to the ideology of Party intellectuals. If it is possible to foresee the future, or so Orwell seems to be saying, it follows that at least some events are fixed in advance and cannot be avoided. This idea is wholly at odds with the solipsistic philosophy of Ingsoc, which (as we have seen) seeks to justify the state's continuous lying by portraying history as an infinitely malleable process which is ultimately determined by the collective will of the Party. What Orwell is effectively doing is proposing a startling revision of Engels's observation that freedom entails the recognition of necessity. So long as people realise that certain events are predestined, he implies, they can steel themselves with the recognition that not all aspects of the future are vulnerable to the Party's ceaseless manipulations. No other element in his satire on Socialist Realism is as esoteric as this, nor as little noticed.

Private Rebellions and Public Hopes

Many people have regarded *Nineteen Eighty-Four* as a thoroughly pessimistic capstone to Orwell's career. Ending as it does with the utter defeat of Julia and Winston's mini-rebellion, the novel has often been portrayed as a great socialist's final admission that socialism does not work. Orwell himself resisted this conclusion very strongly. More or less the last thing he wrote for publication was a brief statement in which he stipulated that 'My recent novel is *not* intended as an attack on socialism or on the British Labor [sic] Party (of which I am a supporter)...'[71] He then went on to affirm that the purpose of *Nineteen Eighty-Four* was to expose the totalitarian perversions to which planned economies are susceptible, insisting that the book should be regarded not as a prophecy but as a weapon in the ongoing struggle against tyranny: 'The moral to be drawn from this dangerous nightmare situation is a simple one: *Don't let it happen. It depends on you.*'[72] The fact that Orwell was upset by the misrepresentation of his book (and the fact that it has continued to be read as an anti-socialist tract) makes it all the more important that we should recognise what so many critics have denied – that *Nineteen Eighty-Four*, in spite of its immense air of dystopian gloom, is not without its moments of flickering optimism. At one level, the book is clearly a meditation on the problem of keeping dissent alive in periods of political quiescence. Writing at a time when he believed the international left to be exceptionally weak (and when he took it for granted that totalitarianism was expanding across the whole of the earth), Orwell set out to show how an isolated and eccentric contrarian can quietly subvert the status quo in spite of the absence of organised opposition. The point about Winston Smith is that his everyday life is a continuous challenge to the power of the Party, even though his methods of rebellion at first seem entirely personal. With the possible exceptions of Walter Benjamin, Ernst Bloch and Henri Lefebvre, no other radical writer in the twentieth century had Orwell's ability to reveal the libertarian roots of even the most thoughtless popular habits. His evocation of Winston's chronic taste for nostalgia is a good case in point. As *Nineteen Eighty-Four* makes clear, many totalitarian regimes seek to reinforce their power by drawing an absolute contrast between the past and the present. Their tactic is to portray the period before the birth of the regime as one of unremitting poverty, oppression and misery, while describing the period thereafter as one of immense happiness and progress. When Winston brooded obsessively on his vague memories of childhood, desperate to establish that the feelings of warmth which he associated with his mother were not purely illusory, he was by no means paying a pointless tribute to an irrecoverable past. He was actually trying to skewer the Party's historical myths by proving that pre-revolutionary England was *better* than the age of Big Brother. His fragile impressions of a sort of prelapsarian English decency were subtly reinforced by the cheap antiques which he bought from Charrington's junk shop, notably the Victorian paperweight and the 'peculiarly beautiful' writing book. Like the antiquarian books which Benjamin described in his great essay 'Unpacking my Library' (1931),[73] Winston's illicit possessions were able to resonate with the spirit of the past because their practical purpose had largely been forgotten. In contrast to nearly everything else in a society that was at once brutally utilitarian and deeply inefficient (one thinks of the 'Victory' cigarettes whose tobacco invariably falls out, the comfortless overalls and the ramshackle plumbing sytems), they were objects of pure contemplation and not shoddy bearers of use value. By surrendering his imagination to their rich textures and fine workmanship, Winston conjured an alternative world which threatened the rule of the Party simply by showing that alternatives were possible:

> What appealed to him about it [i.e. the paperweight] was not so much its beauty as the air it seemed to possess of belonging to an age quite different from the present one. The soft, rain-watery glass was not like any glass that he had ever seen. The thing was doubly attractive because of its apparent uselessness...[74]

The other private habit which Orwell invested with high political significance was the act of making love. At least two decades before the idea that the 'personal is the political' became influential on the left, Orwell portrayed the relationship between Winston and Julia as something which struck at the heart of state power.[75] He was not simply implying that the 'sex instinct' engenders a taste for privacy which no totalitarian government can ever tolerate. He was also trying to show that the act of making love goes a long way towards redirecting the energies which are habitually squandered in 'leader worship'. At one point, sharing details of their lives after making love in a disused church tower, Winston and Julia come to the conclusion that dictatorships are necessarily rooted in sexual repression. If the state is to exercise complete control over its subjects, or so they speculate, it has to generate immense reserves of 'hysteria' which can then be sublimated into desperate love of the leader and insensate hatred of his enemies. The best way of doing this is to warp the personality by 'bottling down some powerful instinct [i.e. the sex instinct] and using it as a driving force'.[76] Once the sexual impulse is actually channelled into love-making, it follows that the emotional dispositions which underpin political slavery will begin to dissolve – though perhaps only temporarily. As Julia puts it, employing the terrifically scornful language which marks her out as a less inhibited character than Winston: 'All this marching up and down and cheering and waving flags is simply sex gone sour. If you're happy inside yourself, why should you get excited about Big Brother and the Three-Year Plans and the Two Minutes Hate and all the rest of their bloody rot?'[77] There is also an obvious significance to the fact that Winston and Julia begin their relationship in the depths of the English countryside, hiding out from the Party among the 'rabbit-bitten' pastures, 'ragged' hedges and 'swaying' elms which haunt Winston's dreams. As he made clear throughout his writings, most appealingly in the short essay 'Some Thoughts on the Common Toad' (1946),[78] Orwell always regarded a love of nature as an indispensable component of the libertarian sensibility. Unlike the Tory traditionalists to whom he is often compared, he thought of the English countryside not as a signifier of 'tradition' but as a crucible of indestructible energies where the love of freedom is awoken, nurtured and replenished. To watch a pair of toads mating in the Spring or hares conducting a 'boxing match' in the cornfields is not to be 'sentimental', escapist or unpolitical. It is rather to encounter an annually renewed life-force whose vitality is incompatible with all forms of authoritarianism. It may even be the case that Orwell detected something almost numinous in the British countryside, at least in his later years when tuberculosis perhaps induced a mood of quasi-religious introspection. At any rate, the passages in *Nineteen Eighty-Four* which describe the 'Golden Country' are among the few in his work which attain a sort of visionary intensity.

Wallowing in half-forgotten memories, collecting trinkets, making love and admiring the countryside – Orwell regarded all these things (and several others) as potent specifics against the totalitarian disease. Yet this does not mean that the message of *Nineteen Eighty-Four* was that the impulse to resist has now been irretrievably diverted into the world of private pleasures. Every subversive act which Winston undertakes is set against the background of Oceania's proletarians, whom he sincerely regards (hoping against hope) as the mighty force which will one day bring the system to its knees. While recognising that the Proles are wholly unaware of their potential power, Winston understands in his bones that their way of life is deeply incompatible with the long-term survival of the Party. Like the indomitable English workers whom Orwell eulogised in *The Lion and the Unicorn*, the proles are instinctive liberals. They attach immense importance to their private lives and personal interests and scorn the prevailing forms of collective identity: 'They were not loyal to a party or a country or an idea, they were loyal to one another.'[79] When the Party offends against their taste for privacy once too often (as it surely must), they will rise up and restore the slumbering traditions of English liberty to the heart of national life. If the society they create is likely to be a socialist society (and Orwell strongly implied that it would be), this simply bears out the paradox that the values of classical liberalism can only be realised in a fully democratic, fully post-capitalist order.

Orwell's conflation of the personal and the political is especially vivid in the almost painfully moving passage in which Winston, shortly after making love to Julia for what turns out to be the last time, gazes down at a middle-aged washerwoman putting up laundry in a run-down urban yard. The whole point of the passage is to show that Winston's private acts of rebellion are simply a means of keeping hope alive until the proles finally realise their strength. Noting that the woman has 'no mind…only strong arms, a warm heart and a fertile belly',[80] Winston suddenly realises with a feeling of 'mystical reverence' that the common people extend across the face of the earth. With their instinctive commitment to common decency, their determination to keep their culture alive and their awesome capacity to work unceasingly and still remain cheerful ('At the end of it she was still singing'), they merge seamlessly into an army of 'hundreds of thousands of millions of people' who have 'never learned to think but who [are] storing up in their hearts and bellies and muscles the power that would one day overturn the world.'[81] The world they eventually create will undoubtedly be better than the siege societies they will have to overthrow, since its founding intuition will be that all men and women are equal: '…it would be a world of sanity. Where there is equality there can be sanity.'[82] Anyone who doubts that Orwell retained his belief in socialism until the end of his life would do well to consider these words. Having decided that the proles are a bit like birds, 'stay[ing] alive against all the odds' and 'passing on…[their] vitality' from one generation to the next,[83] Winston reminds Julia of the thrush which had chirped above them during their first meeting in the countryside. And then comes the magnificent conclusion:

> The birds sang, the proles sang, the Party did not sing. All round the world, in London and New York, in Africa and Brazil, and in the mysterious, forbidden lands beyond the frontiers, in the streets of Paris and Berlin, in the villages of the endless Russian plain, in the bazaars of China and Japan – everywhere stood the same solid unconquerable figure, made monstrous by work and childbearing, toiling from birth to death and still singing. Out of those mighty loins a race of conscious beings must one day come. You were the dead; theirs was the future. But you could share in that future if you kept alive the mind as they kept alive the body, and passed on the secret doctrine that two plus two make four.[84]

It is true that this passage can sometimes seem slightly sentimental, especially to the reader who prides himself on his realism. But this can scarcely account for the violent criticism which it has frequently received from members of the Marxist or *Marxisant* left. Typical in this regard is the late Raymond Williams, Orwell's most acute socialist critic, who argued that *Nineteen Eighty-Four*'s vision of the working-class betrayed a 'stale...romanticism' which equated proletarian revolution with 'the rising of the animals'.[85] The point only seems plausible if we overlook one of the novel's most important themes. As we have seen, Orwell's biggest anxiety about totalitarianism was that it had stripped people of their *instinctive* belief in freedom. By counterposing the physicality of the proles against the intellectualism of the Inner and Outer Party, he was not, *pace* Williams, simply engaging in a casual display of old-Etonian snobbery. Instead he was dramatising his view that working people have remained loyal to the libertarian intuitions which they sense on their pulses, whereas their superiors in the middle- and upper-classes, isolated from the wisdom of the body, have long since descended into an arid world of cerebral power worship. Nor was he claiming that working people were incapable of thinking for themselves, since he went out of his way in Winston's eulogy to the washerwoman to affirm that 'Sooner or later...strength would change into consciousness.'[86] Much had happened to Orwell in the fifteen years between *Down and Out in Paris and London* and *Nineteen Eighty-Four*. The (comparatively) vigorous young man who walked the streets with tramps had become an internationally famous author, stricken by tuberculosis and fearful of the spread of Stalinism. Yet there is a sense in which his career ended in the same place where it began, with a sincere, far-sighted and inspiring tribute to the liberal decencies of the common people. The future which

Orwell envisaged was indeed one in which 'hope…lay in the proles'. It is a rich irony that the British communists who influenced him so deeply (but whose influence he never really acknowledged) would probably have hoped for much the same thing.

APPENDIX 1
ORWELL AS HIS OWN CRITIC

One of the charges most frequently levelled against Orwell is that his work is riddled with inconsistencies. Scholars, critics and political activists have accused him of veering wildly between differing perspectives, mixing radicalism and conservatism, patriotism and internationalism and elitism and populism in bizarrely unstable compounds. It has to be admitted that this argument contains more than a grain of truth, not least because of the remarkable tension between Orwell's fiction and his non-fiction. If Orwell's critical project in his essays, articles and reviews is a relatively consistent one (and if his last two novels are clearly of a piece with this project), it sometimes seems as if his first four novels are written by a different person altogether. There is scarcely a single prominent idea in the non-fiction which is not called into question in *Burmese Days*, *A Clergyman's Daughter*, *Keep the Aspidistra Flying* and *Coming Up for Air*, even though important continuities between the two bodies of work can also be identified. One could almost suppose that Orwell's confrontation with literary form precipitated a sort of Machereyan crisis, exposing the 'lacunae' in his own most deeply cherished ideas. The purpose of this brief Appendix is to bring these issues into focus. Section One examines the treatment of cross-class relationships in *Burmese Days* and *A Clergyman's Daughter*, showing how it serves as a counterpoint to the bracing populism of books like *Down and Out in Paris and London*. Section Two interprets *Keep the Aspidistra Flying* as a meditation on aestheticism whose assumptions conflict dramatically with those of Orwell's literary criticism. The Appendix concludes with a survey of *Coming Up for Air*, whose almost Burkean vision of English identity is hardly compatible with the radical patriotism of *The Lion and the Unicorn* or *The English People*.

The Persistence of Hierarchy

Nothing was more important in Orwell's life and work than the idea that meaningful relationships could be established across lines of class. As we have seen, his career as a writer only got underway once his immersion in the underclass gave him something to write about, while his vision of socialism was based on the idea that people like himself would benefit enormously from the inherited decencies of working-class culture. This makes it all the more astonishing that *Burmese Days* and *A Clergyman's Daughter* should have held these ideas up to criticism. *Burmese Days* was written against the backdrop of a tentative attempt by the British to administer parts of their empire along less authoritarian lines. In 1919, responding to the recommendations contained in the Montagu-Chelmsford Report, David Lloyd-George's coalition government attempted to neutralise Indian nationalism by introducing the Government of India Act. The purpose of the Act was to create a 'dyarchic' political system which allowed native Indians to make a limited contribution to the governance of their country. Similar reforms were introduced in Burma in 1923, though only after Burmese nationalists had launched a highly effective boycott of British goods.[1] One way of approaching *Burmese Days* is to see it as an extended commentary on the more fluid relations between the British and their colonial subjects which the new political settlement had opened up. Set in the fictional Burmese outpost of Kyauktada, the novel seeks to dramatise the grave limitations of Montagu-Chelmsford imperialism by displacing its main characteristics onto a purely local drama. Although Orwell makes no attempt to describe the new representative institutions in India and Burma, he explores the problems of sharing power by describing the doomed efforts of his protagonist John Flory to defy the racism of his European colleagues and establish meaningful relationships with native Burmans. In evoking the disastrous consequences of Flory's well-meaning humanitarianism, Orwell is not merely displaying his contempt for ostensibly 'progressive' solutions to the problems of imperialism. As we shall see, he is also calling into question the very idea of a workable alliance between middle-class dissidents and oppressed groups.

The most important relationship in *Burmese Days* is the triangular one between Flory, Dr Veraswami and U Po Kyin. The warm friendship between Flory and Veraswami most obviously symbolises the misplaced idealism of the progressive imperialists. Despite his cynicism about the empire, Flory has no wish to see British rule in Burma brought to an end. While recognising that the purpose of imperialism is not to civilise the colonial peoples but to appropriate their economic resources, his personal mission is simply to put private relations between Europeans and Burmese on a more humane footing. When he befriends the cultivated Veraswami, whose refinement and erudition far exceed those of the imperial class in Kyauktada, he is effectively trying to solve the problems of empire in much the same way that the young Orwell tried to solve the problems of the British class system – that is, by self-consciously reaching out to oppressed groups and relating to them as equals. What Orwell scholars have often failed to point out is that Flory's idealism is stymied more from the Burmese side than from the British. If there is one thing which defines Veraswami's attitude towards Flory (and by extension towards the whole of the imperial class), it is his hair-raising deference. In his early conversations with Flory, even as he strives to emulate the mannerisms of the archetypal English gentleman, he makes it clear that he endorses virtually all the main tenets of imperialist ideology. Faced with Flory's insistence that the British in Burma have no purpose 'except to steal', he argues that the imperial ruling class is bringing modernity to a slothful and inferior people who cannot be trusted to modernise themselves: 'Could the Burmese trade for themselves? Can they make machinery, ships, railways, roads? They are helpless without you.'[2] Invited to comment on the brutal authoritarianism with which the British enforce their rule, he praises the colonisers for bringing law and order to a previously anarchic land. And embarrassed by the argument that the early colonisers had introduced venereal disease into Burma, he groundlessly insists that the whole problem originated with the Indians. It is important to recognise that Veraswami's deference is not merely the antithesis of Flory's egalitarianism but in some ways is actually *produced* by it. In spite of dismissing the idea that someone of his lowly racial origins could ever be the equal of a European, he has evidently been flattered by Flory's friendship and begun to think of himself as a sort of honorary member of the imperial elite. His social ambitions are clearly revealed when he asks Flory to nominate him for membership of Kyauktada's European Club, whose members have been instructed by the regional government to co-opt a single native Burman into their ranks. By refusing to abandon his worshipful attitude towards the British, or so it could be argued, Veraswami is looking forward to the day when his absorption into the ruling class makes him worthy of deference himself.

The obverse side of Veraswami's deference is the seething envy of U Po Kyin, Kyauktada's Sub-divisional Magistrate. The main function of this memorably awful character is to remind us that progressive imperialism invariably sabotages its own mission by driving a deep wedge between different sections of the colonial people. Confronted by the spectacle of Veraswami's friendship with a *pukka sahib*, U Po Kyin responds with fratricidal anger – the anger of a man who has been excluded from elite circles and sees no reason why a fellow Burman should be admitted to them. Just over half-way through the first chapter, at a point when Veraswami and Flory have yet to make an appearance, he declares his intention of destroying both men. It is literally inconceivable that he should regard Flory as a benevolent ruler or Veraswami as the tentative pioneer of a more egalitarian Burma. In order to drive the point home, Orwell makes it clear that U Po Kyin's resentment lies at the heart of everything he does. Although his mind is nimble and shows considerable cunning, it has 'never worked except for some definite end; mere meditation was beyond him.'[3] There is even a sense in which his spiritual corruption is advertised on his body. Porcine, ungainly and waddling, he seems to acquire his enormous weight by feeding off the remains of everyone he destroys. By the time he drives Flory to suicide and leaves Veraswami's reputation in ruins, he has done more than anyone else in *Burmese Days* to expose the terrible illusions of the Montagu-Chelmsford age. When a colonial state seeks to absorb a native elite into the machinery of power, Orwell seems to be saying, those who are chosen will defer and those who are excluded will destroy. There is no middle ground between imperialism and national self-determination.

The circumstances in which Flory commits suicide draw our attention to another weakness of progressive imperialism – one which this time has more to do with the outlook of the colonial class than that of the people they govern. Having fallen in love with Elizabeth Lackersteen and become intent on marrying her, Flory has to make drastic changes to his lifestyle in an effort to shore up his respectability. In particular he has to end his clandestine sexual relationship with Ma Hla May, the young Burmese woman whom he had 'bought…from her parents…for three hundred rupees.'[4] The event which finally tips him into despair occurs when a hysterical Ma Hla May, acting on the instructions of U Po Kyin, turns up at a church service in Kyauktada and publicly accuses him of cruelly abandoning her. The fact that *Burmese Day*'s most sympathetic character is ultimately brought to grief by a sordid affair with a native woman resonates with symbolic importance, since it hints at something deeply disconcerting about the motivation of the progressive enterprise. What Orwell seems to be implying is that the roots of Flory's rebellion lie more in sexual dysfunction than in a principled commitment to equality.[5] Alienated from people of his own kind and incapable of entering into a meaningful relationship with someone he regards as an equal, he seeks consolation of a sort by turning his attention towards a woman of a lower class, a different race and a younger age. The point about Ma Hla May is that her status as a Burmese peasant's daughter makes her childishly easy to objectify. The sense that Flory has stripped her of her autonomy comes across especially strongly in some early descriptive passages, which rely heavily on the iconography of prostitution. Unlike the compassionate, defiant and sweetly practical women whom Orwell's protagonists fall in love with in his other novels, Ma Hla May is a mass of hard lines and angular gestures. Her body is as 'contourless as a bas-relief carved upon a tree', her hair is 'coiled like a tight black cylinder', her skin is the 'colour of new copper'.[6] Her only interests in life seem to be acquiring trinkets and flaunting herself in front of her fellow villagers. Once we have seen what Flory has reduced her to (and once we acknowledge the *appropriateness* of her revenge), it is impossible to be quite so confident about the nobility of his actions. The exemplar of progressive imperialism turns out to be nearly as indifferent to human suffering as any of his more traditional colleagues, even as he beckons the natives to his side and talks warmly about the equality of the races.[7]

If *Burmese Days* is primarily a novel about the relationship between an imperial ruling class and the population it seeks to govern, its relevance to Orwell's wider interest in the relationship between middle-class dissidents and working people is surely clear enough. The exasperating mixture of deference and resentment which Flory encounters in his dealings with Veraswami and U Po Kyin is potentially a feature of any alliance between people of different rank, as Orwell discovered on numerous occasions in the presence of working-class socialists. (He was especially amused by a communist activist who called him 'sir' while selling him the *Daily Worker*!)[8] Orwell's anxiety about cross-class relationships is even more evident in his second novel *A Clergyman's Daughter*, which draws extensively on his experiences of tramping in the early 1930s. Ostensibly a book about the decline of religious faith, it can also be interpreted as a study of how belief of any kind tends to vary from class to class. Tracing the progress of his protagonist Dorothy Hare as she makes the transition from devout stalwart of middle England to anguished atheist, Orwell effectively proposes that the English bourgeoisie are better able than their working-class counterparts to sustain a sense that life is inherently meaningful. When Dorothy abandons her cloistered life in the vicarage and ends up on the streets with tramps, she finds herself immersed in a culture from which all the prerequisites of ideological conviction have been stripped away. Instead of being redeemed by her encounter with the common people, she finds herself facing up to the possibility that life has no meaning at all.

What is it about Dorothy's existence in the fictional village of Knype Hill which allows her to believe that her life is full of significance? Orwell's implied answer to that question is startlingly inconsistent with most of his other writings on middle-class psychology. In *The Road to Wigan Pier* and elsewhere, Orwell makes it clear that one of the greatest miseries of middle-class life is the fear of being declassed. Rarely wealthy and often inclined to overspend massively, nearly everyone in the 'shabby genteel' families worries that a loss of employment, a reduction in salary or some other financial mishap will send them hurtling into the lower orders. The extraordinary thing about Dorothy is that her economic insecurities actually *sustain* her sense that life is worthwhile. Although she spends much of her time trying to eke out an inadequate living, it is precisely the sense that catastrophe could strike at any moment which engenders her almost childish gratitude for her meagre privileges. Her spasms of thankfulness usually take the form of a sudden and overwhelming awareness of the beauty of nature, as when she glances through the church door during a particularly fraught communion:

> Then it happened that she glanced sidelong, through the open south door. A momentary spear of sunlight had pierced the clouds. It struck downwards through the leaves of the limes, and a spray of leaves in the doorway gleamed with a transient, matchless green, greener than jade or emerald or Atlantic waters. It was as though some jewel of unimaginable splendour had flashed for an instant, filling the doorway with green light, and then faded. A flood of joy ran through Dorothy's heart. The flash of living colour had brought back to her, by a process deeper than reason, her peace of mind, her love of God, her power of worship.[9]

If Dorothy's sense of meaning is largely a by-product of her precarious economic circumstances, it is powerfully reinforced by a series of assumptions and habits whose purpose is to smother her anxieties about the prospect of destitution. The most important is a fervent belief in authority (especially divine authority), which imbues her with the comforting illusion that her destiny is being shaped by a benevolent overseer. The authority figures she defers to most readily are God on the one hand and her selfish but seigneurial father on the other, both of whom function in her life like the 'Unique and central Other Subject' of Althusserian lore.[10] Her relationship with God is an extraordinarily visceral one, resting on the assumption that He intervenes in earthly affairs from moment to moment. Whenever she allows an impious thought to flit across her mind (or whenever she fails to live up to the punishingly conscientious standards which she sets for herself), she immediately offers up a prayer of contrition, deprives herself of a pleasure or performs a compensatory ritual. Her rituals are themselves a fertile source of reassurance and meaning, since they allow her to anticipate the plunge into catastrophe on a symbolic level and to exercise a measure of control over it. By inflicting a sharp pain on a small part of her body for a few seconds at a time (her usual practice is to stick a pin into her forearm until she draws blood), she reduces her anxieties to a manageable scale and convinces herself that she can master them. There is also perhaps a sense in which the performance of rituals shores up her imperilled sense of gentility, if only because it defies the grimly utilitarian logic which she associates with the lower orders. To put it another way, her flight into symbolism reminds her that she belongs to a class that has transcended a purely practical approach to life, and in so doing keeps the prospect of poverty and manual labour reassuringly at bay. Even the most florid symptoms of her neurosis are an expression of her class identity.

After losing her memory and finding herself pitched into the world of tramps, gypsies and small-time criminals, Dorothy is deprived of all the things which bring meaning to her life. Although she is not particularly unhappy as she trudges through country lanes or picks hops in the Autumn fields, her sensibility is no longer quickened by the sense of having anything to lose. Lulled into a state of near thoughtlessness by the rigours of her new life, she contemplates her destitution in a spirit of quiet incredulity: 'Was this the life to which she had been bred – this life of wandering empty-bellied all day and shivering at night under dripping trees? Had it been like this even in the blank past? Where had she come from? Who was she?'[11] If the rituals she performed in Knype Hill convinced her that she could hold the material world at arm's length, she now finds herself plunged into a brutally disenchanting confrontation with nature. She discovers that virtually nothing in the life of a tramp is ever done for its own sake. Everything is bound up with the need to find food and shelter, even when this involves a wholesale abandonment of common decency. When she finally gets to work in the fields, spending eight or nine hours a day tearing down hop bines and flinging them into plastic containers, she finds that she can establish a *modus vivendi* with nature but never get the better of it. She does her job efficiently but the skin on her hands is shredded to pieces. In the final analysis, however, the biggest solvent of her sense of meaning is the fact that she no longer has anyone to revere. The streets and fields in which the underclass scrapes a living are scarcely amenable to the influence of God or elderly clergymen. It is not so much that the distinction between the leaders and the led no longer exists, more that anyone who seeks to exercise authority is weighed down by a sense of his own absurdity. The central character in this context is undoubtedly Nobby, the good-natured jailbird who takes charge of Dorothy, Flo and Charlie as they trudge from London into Kent. By undercutting his authority even as he seeks to assert it, Nobby closely resembles the sort of carnivalesque jesters to whom Mikhail Bakhtin and others have ascribed such significance. Described as having a 'coarse, simian face' (and in so doing recalling the 'grotesque realism' which Bakhtin regarded as a staple of carnival), he invariably claims to be acting in the common interest but always reveals his baser motivations in the end. As if to satirise the cultural dimensions of authority, he deploys a colourful but ludicrous rhetoric ('That's the mulligatawny') and strikes up a passable imitation of 'military music' while singing his three favourite songs: 'Sonny Boy', ''Twas Christmas Day in the Workhouse' and '"-----!" was all the band could play'.[12] In the end, in a nightmarish inversion of God's promise of eternal care, he is arrested for thieving and disappears without having the chance to say goodbye. Whereas Orwell's non-fiction writings about the underclass emit a strong whiff of a man being reborn in the midst of great suffering, the enduring impression that one takes away from *A Clergyman's Daughter* is of a life slowly dwindling into nothingness. Even though Dorothy recovers her memory and eventually returns to Knype Hill, her experience of destitution has forced her to recognise 'the deadly emptiness...at the heart of things.'[13] Surveying the world of the lower orders from the perspective of an ordinary member of the shabby-genteel classes, Orwell credits it with a formidable capacity to leech the meaning out of everything.

The Aesthete as Conformist

Whereas *Burmese Days* and *A Clergyman's Daughter* evoke the incapacity of two middle-class misfits to establish meaningful relationships across lines of class and race, *Keep the Aspidistra Flying* provides an even gloomier perspective on a very different type of bourgeois dissidence. Its central theme, which reflects Orwell's lifelong preoccupation with the art-for-art's-sake movement, is the nature of the relationship between aestheticism and social conformity. When its protagonist, the minor poet and aesthete *manqué* Gordon Comstock, throws up his lucrative job at an advertising agency and devotes himself to a life of writing poetry, he believes that he has turned his back completely on a corrupt and spiritually bankrupt civilisation. His ferocious attacks on the 'Money God' mark him out as a sort of poor man's Baudelaire, utterly contemptuous of what might now be called bourgeois 'materialism'. Yet by the end of the novel, haunted by a sense of failure and on the verge of complete destitution, he is happy enough to destroy his poems, marry his pregnant girlfriend and return to his job as a copywriter. His reconciliation with a system he had once sought to oppose is as complete as that of Winston Smith in *Nineteen Eighty-Four*. Far from turning him into an implacable enemy of capitalism, his experiment with bohemianism has forced him to embrace the system with a new enthusiasm. The one-time aesthete stands revealed as the ultimate conformist.

By implying that the aesthete's rebellion against bourgeois society is invariably doomed to failure, Orwell was making a quite different point about aestheticism than the ones he made in his non-fiction. Although he was always highly critical of the art's-for-art's-sake movement, not least because its rejection of politics seemed dangerously quixotic in an age of economic crisis and totalitarian aggression, there was also a sense in which he regarded the aesthete as a sort of fellow traveller of the left (see Chapter Three). His rejection of this perspective in *Keep the Aspidistra Flying* had a lot to do with his understanding of middle-class psychology. Although Comstock believes that he is transcending the world of the 'shabby genteel' when he resigns from his job, Orwell shows that his self-imposed exile is primarily responsible for *enflaming* his bourgeois prejudices. As the only boy in a socially conscious but indigent professional family, Comstock has been brought up to despise the upper classes and the common people in equal measure. While the former are resented for their easy lives and taken-for-granted privileges, the latter serve as a constant terrifying reminder of what might happen if economic misfortune should ever strike. As soon as Comstock is deprived of his professional salary and the respect which goes with it, his class hatreds attain an almost pathological ferocity. For the seasoned reader of Orwell, familiar with the deep strain of populism in the rest of his work, there could scarcely be a more shocking passage than the one in which Comstock surveys the tramps in Westminster and makes no secret of his contempt for them:

> Even now, though it was December, a few poor draggled old wrecks were settling down on the benches, tucking themselves up in sort of parcels of newspaper. Gordon looked at them callously. On the bum, they called it. He would come to it himself some day. Better so, perhaps? He never felt any pity for the genuine poor.[14]

It is not simply that Comstock's intensified class animus prevents him seeing the good in the common people. The more important point is that it *reawakens his sympathy for the class he has tried to abandon.* Weighed down by self-pity, still obsessed with keeping up appearances, he makes no attempt to resist as his bohemian contempt for the philistine middle classes suddenly mutates into a sort of sickly compassion: 'It is the black-coated poor, the middle-middle class, who need pitying.'[15] As such, his reconciliation with the system should ultimately be understood as an expression of class solidarity, not simply as an emergency response to the new responsibilities of fatherhood. There is also a sense in which his descent into poverty renews his respect for the moral acuity of the middle classes, especially their emphasis on the virtues of self-denial. The poorer that Comstock gets, or so Orwell implies, the more vulnerable he becomes to compensatory bursts of outrageous self-indulgence. In the darkly comic pages in which he unexpectedly receives a cheque for fifty dollars, blows it all on drink and prostitutes and ends up in a police cell ('And, by Jove, tomorrow we *were* sober!'),[16] he comes to realise that the immemorial wisdom of his parents' generation just might have something going for it. One of the great paradoxes of *Keep the Aspidistra Flying* is that when Comstock returns to the advertising industry, one of the great motors of consumerist excess, he effectively does so in a spirit of pious asceticism.

If the failure of Comstock's rebellion is ultimately rooted in the tenacity of middle-class ideology (a tenacity symbolised by the aspidistras which are seemingly on display in every room), it is also bound up with a particular set of assumptions about the nature of art. As is well known, one of the main tenets of the art-for-art's sake movement was that aesthetic experience is inherently *subjective*. Rejecting the Kantian (or romantic) assumption that the artist's mode of perceiving reality is somehow of universal significance, aesthetes such as Baudelaire, Pater and Wilde embraced the idea that the aesthetic faculty is intrinsically 'relative' and that each man perceives a work of art in his own way. Summarising his credo in the Preface to *Historical Studies in the Renaissance* (1872), Pater famously observed that the aesthete's first duty when confronted by a work of art is to ask 'What is this song or picture, this engaging personality presented in life or in a book, to *me*?'[17] It seems clear that one of Orwell's more rarefied aims in *Keep the Aspidistra Flying* is to expose this doctrine of the 'relative spirit' to critical analysis. The main vehicle of his critique is Comstock's violently ambivalent relationship towards his own poetry, in particular the brief lyric beginning 'Sharply the menacing wind…' which he begins writing in Chapter One.[18] On the rare occasions when Comstock feels cheerful, his poem strikes him as a solid and eminently publishable piece of work: 'Not bad, not bad at all. Finish it presently. Four or five more stanzas. Ravelston would print it.'[19] By contrast, in his far more frequent periods of disgruntlement, he loathes it with a sort of self-pitying vengeance: 'The octosyllables flicked to and fro. Click-click, click-click! The awful, mechanical emptiness of it appalled him.'[20] Orwell's point is that an immersion in the relativistic world of art provides no foundation on which to construct a sense of moral and cultural continuity, which he clearly regards as the *sine qua non* of psychological health. In a nightmarish parody of Pater's exaltation in the free play of aesthetic subjectivity, Comstock is reduced to a state of neurotic uncertainty by his pitiful failure to establish a settled relationship to a single poem. The full horror of his retreat from objectivity becomes evident about half-way through the book, when Orwell makes it clear that he is deliberately ignoring all evidence from the world 'out there' in order to convince himself that there is a conspiracy against him. By the time he consigns his poems to the London gutters in the penultimate chapter, the only thing that can rescue him from relativism is a return to the middle-class treadmill. The tedious certainties of the white-collar office prove altogether preferable to the gaudy pleasures of the Palace of Art.

The fact that Comstock is so successful in the advertising industry hints at a further reason for the failure of his rebellion. Quite apart from emphasising the relativistic nature of aesthetic response, the art-for-art's sake movement had usually portrayed commercial culture as the degraded antithesis of genuine art. Whereas advertising, cheap novels and other mass-produced entertainments are drably realistic and provide no outlet for the imagination, or so the argument went, genuine works of art turn their back on an uninspiring reality and create new and more compelling worlds. This boldly non-mimetic theory of art was famously summed up by Oscar Wilde when he said that the best artists are basically glorified liars: 'The fact is that we look back on the ages entirely through the medium of art, and Art, very fortunately, has never once told us the truth.'[21] The truly startling point which Orwell seems to be making in his portrait of Comstock is that the antithesis between popular entertainment and art no longer holds, on the grounds that the anti-mimetic impulse has long since migrated from the sphere of serious culture into the sphere of entertainment. On the one hand, Comstock's 'highbrow' poems are oriented towards the least colourful aspects of contemporary reality, mixing grey urban landscapes with anguished protests against the rule of money. On the other hand, the popular forms he pretends to detest are boisterously imaginative and provide much light relief from the pressures of everyday life. The massive posters on the advertising hoardings possess a 'vigorous badness' which speaks powerfully to people's desire for easy solutions ('Just take hot Bovex every night – invigorating – healing!'),[22] while the trashy novels in the commercial libraries take even the most troubled readers out of themselves for hours at a time. When Comstock returns to his job at the New Albion Publicity Company, Orwell implies, it is precisely because the impulse to create alternative realities is now better served by mainstream hacks in high-tech offices than by bohemian aesthetes in garrets. It is almost as if Orwell can be cast as a plain-speaking precursor to Jean Baudrillard, anxious to show how the rise of consumerism has divorced the means of signification from the real world in which they were once anchored. The advertisements which Comstock dreams up with such facility are indeed signs that 'bear no relation to any reality whatever.'[23]

Comstock's refusal to break with the existing order is underscored by his relationship with Philip Ravelston, editor of *Antichrist*, who strives ceaselessly and with precious little success to convert him to socialism. Upper class and effortlessly urbane (and allegedly based on Orwell's friend Richard Rees), Ravelston could almost have been created to illustrate Roger Scruton's acid observation that in 'modern England…the most voluble…radical nuisances of our century have been drawn from the upper echelons, cushioned by privileges which they discreetly enjoy in the very act of denouncing them.'[24] In spite of his sincere desire to see the awful sufferings of the poor brought to an end, he lives in considerable comfort in a well-appointed flat and indulges in bourgeois pleasures with 'all the shameful joy of a dog with a stolen leg of mutton.'[25] If he fails to arouse Comstock's interest in socialism, it is largely for two reasons. The first is that his continuous moralising about poverty serves only to stoke his friend's guilt over his lack of economic success. Once a man has turned his back on a perfectly good living, or so it is implied, the last thing he wants to be reminded of is the iniquities of the capitalist system. More serious still is his failure to dispel Comstock's belief that socialism invariably gives rise to dictatorship. As a dweller in cheap lodging houses and a casual worker in rundown bookshops, Comstock is peculiarly vulnerable to petty displays of authoritarianism. His problems with bad-tempered landladies and censorious employers imbue him with an almost Hayekian sensitivity to the potential dangers of public ownership, which he sums up in his hilarious prediction that socialism will involve

> Some kind of Aldous Huxley *Brave New World*; only not so amusing. Four hours a day in a model factory, tightening up bolt number 6003. Rations served out in greaseproof paper at the communal kitchen. Community-hikes from Marx Hostel to Lenin Hostel and back. Free abortion-clinics on all the corners. All very well in its way, of course. Only we don't want it.[26]

Although Ravelston strives to liberate Comstock from these bohemian prejudices, the unmistakable traces of bourgeois hauteur in his personality make him an unconvincing apostle of freedom. Faced with his wilfully eccentric editorial practices, the alacrity with which he seeks out favours from his many contacts and his secret distaste for beggars and the unemployed, it is difficult to shake the suspicion that socialism is simply the latest means by which the strong assert their will to power. For all his generosity of spirit, Ravelston is the first in a long line of Orwellian characters whose ostensible commitment to social justice is undercut by a definite tendency towards autocracy. Yet he is no match for Comstock's irreverence, which reminds us once again that the aesthete and the socialist make unlikely bedfellows.

In spite of its ingenuity, Orwell's critique of aestheticism in *Keep the Aspidistra Flying* was wholly in keeping with broader trends in the radical culture of the day. The aesthete was vigorously attacked for his lack of social responsibility in a range of communist texts, including Philip

Henderson's *The Novel Today* (1936), Christopher Caudwell's *Illusion and Reality* (1937) and Francis Klingender's *Marxism and Modern Art* (1943). Yet the text to which *Aspidistra* cries out for comparison is surely Oscar Wilde's *The Soul of Man under Socialism* (1891), one of the most sparkling and idiosyncratic products of Victorian radicalism. The implicit purpose of Wilde's essay, which Orwell reviewed flatteringly in the *Observer* in 1948,[27] is to make the case for an alliance of convenience between aesthetes on the one hand and socialists on the other. Starting from the assumption that the highest goal of man is to 'realize the perfection of the soul that is within him',[28] Wilde bases his argument on a typically ingenious paradox. Although capitalism is ostensibly the most individualist of systems, or so he claims, it ends up stunting the growth of the individual by inducing extreme feelings of guilt about the suffering of other people. Confronted by the spectacle of mass poverty, soulless work and industrial ugliness, even the most tenacious individualist feels obliged to abandon his personal ambitions and live a life of selfless altruism. The great virtue of socialism is that it conjures a higher form of individualism on a collectivist base. By substituting common ownership for the anarchy of the marketplace, it creates a world of plenty in which we are at last 'relieve[d] of that sordid necessity of living for others.'[29] Only then does the ideal of ceaseless self-cultivation become a possibility for everyone. Yet if Wilde's socialism was basically libertarian, owing far more to Kropotkin's *Mutual Aid* than to the statist enthusiasms of his friend George Bernard Shaw, it was nevertheless unique in grounding its distrust of authority in aesthetic considerations. Since our inclinations in both art and life are radically subjective, or so the argument went, it is necessary to create a society in which no one feels entitled to impose his preferences on anyone else. A major goal of socialism is thus to do away with the state, the board of management and the patriarchal family, replacing them with a democratic free-for-all which protects the artist in each of us from the critic in everyone else. One of the most intriguing things about *Keep the Aspidistra Flying* is that it seems to take these arguments and stand them on their head. Where Wilde speaks of altruism as a universal duty under capitalism, Orwell evokes a flyblown aesthete whose sympathy lies only with his own class. Where Wilde regards aesthetic relativism as a precondition of personal liberation, Orwell sees it as a nightmarish source of uncertainty. And where Wilde insists that the socialist society of the future must be libertarian or nothing, Orwell sympathises with a character for whom the planned economy is a synonym for tyranny. Given that Orwell had been an avid reader of Wilde since his days at Eton, it seems likely that he was perfectly well aware of the parallels between the two texts.

There is one other place in Orwell's fiction where the relationship between aestheticism and social conformity is briefly examined, though it has rarely been noticed. Among the most important minor characters in *Animal Farm* is Mollie, the 'foolish, pretty white mare who drew Mr Jones's trap'.[30] Vain, narcissistic and deeply devoted to the ribbons which decorate her mane, Mollie exemplifies the aesthete's ambition to turn life itself into a work of art. Her inability to adapt herself to the revolution is evident right from the beginning. As soon as the animals turn Mr Jones and his family out of the farmhouse, she is discovered upstairs holding 'a piece of blue ribbon...against her shoulder and admiring herself in the glass in a very foolish manner.'[31] She makes practically no contribution to the animals' Stakhanovite efforts to sow their first harvest, excusing herself from work on the grounds that she has a stone in her shoe. Finally, several days after Clover spots her talking to a human being over the farm hedge, she runs away from her increasingly suspicious comrades, starts working for a local publican and is immediately written out of history: 'None of the animals ever mentioned Mollie again.'[32] The point which Orwell is making here is very simple but also extremely disconcerting: No matter how lofty their aspirations may be, revolutions invariably give rise to a mood of vulgar utilitarianism which crushes the aesthete underfoot. So it is that a comical white mare evokes the predicament of Vladimir Mayakovsky, Osip Mandelstam and the other sensitive souls who were done to death by the Russian Revolution.

Englishness and Social Order

The tension between the themes of Orwell's novels and those of his non-fiction is arguably at its greatest in *Coming Up for Air*, the last of his novels to be written in the 1930s. Narrated by George Bowling, a fat but good-natured travelling salesman in his mid-forties, the book provides a sketch of the English character which is noticeably different from the ones to be found in *The Lion and the Unicorn* or *The English People*. Whereas Orwell's non-fiction celebrates the radicalism of the English, *Coming Up for Air* unsparingly evokes the darker side of their nature. Its outlook can reasonably be called Burkean or Leavisite, in the sense that its basic themes are the fallen nature of man and the problem of securing social order. Born in the 1890s in the fictional rural village of Lower Binfield, Bowling decides to return there for a short holiday after gambling successfully on a horse. As he thinks back to his childhood and adolescence in the village (an extended act of reminiscence which tells us a great deal about Orwell's early life in rural Oxfordshire), he makes no bones about the fact that the people who surrounded him were perfectly capable of violence, selfishness and brutality. Nevertheless, his implied argument is that small rural communities like Lower Binfield had a genius for containing these anarchic tendencies and implanting a fragile but enduring sense of decency in most of their inhabitants. He goes on to contrast this genius with the culture of the modern city, which he condemns for its licentiousness, vulgarity and incipient disorder. Although Bowling's recollections of Lower Binfield extend over 30,000 words and contain some of the lushest writing in Orwell's novels, anyone who regards them as a sort of masculine variant on *The Country Diaries of an Edwardian Lady* is making a serious mistake.

In spite of his inability to resist nostalgia ('Before the war, and especially before the Boer War, it was summer all the year round'),[33] Bowling takes immediate steps to evoke the crooked timber of Lower Binfield's humanity. The opening pages of his memoir are littered with images of disorder, each of them hinting at the festering passions beneath the quiet rhythms of village life. Market day is disfigured by bitter commercial rivalry and widespread drunkenness; a drunken man falls to the ground and is left there for hours during a General Election; weak parents fail to discipline wilful brats. Especially noticeable is the fact that the characteristics which Orwell most admired about the English are here portrayed as part of the problem. In a stark reversal of the argument of *The Lion and the Unicorn* and *The English People*, Bowling makes no attempt to describe the love of privacy, dislike of militarism or support for the underdog as essential components of an indigenous popular radicalism. Instead he dismisses them as the source of much needless unpleasantness.[34] Nor could the people of Lower Binfield be accused of knowing their own minds. As Bowling wryly points out, nearly all of them held beliefs that were almost comically inconsistent. Lovers of privacy reserved the right to interfere in everyone else's lives; defenders of the underdog condescended to the poor; pacific anti-militarists surrendered to the most abject forms of Jingoism. When Orwell wrote *The Lion and the Unicorn*, less than two years after Bowling's reminiscences came into print, he was confident enough about the underlying consistency of the English character to state that 'England will still be England' when capitalist society has long since been swept away.[35] The message of *Coming Up for Air* is quite different. Far from cleaving to a firm identity shaped over centuries, or so Orwell implies, the English shamelessly alter their values and their beliefs from hour to hour.

If the people of Lower Binfield were so obviously in the grip of antisocial tendencies, how did they manage to form themselves into a relatively stable community? Orwell's answer to that question lies at the heart of *Coming Up for Air*. Although he does not portray the world of Bowling's youth as an especially religious one, he strongly implies that the ultimate guarantor of social order was an unobtrusive but genuine sense of piety. The people of Lower Binfield were scarcely very reverent during their weekly trips to Church (a fact which Bowling's wry description of the informal singing competition between Shooter and Weatherall makes abundantly clear); but most of them took it for granted that their behaviour would one day be judged by a higher power. The quiet, understated but persistent influence of religious assumptions on everyday life is subtly captured in some early topographical imagery, especially Bowling's observation that Lower Binfield was 'shaped roughly like a cross with the market-place in the middle.'[36] Apart from symbolising a sort of Burkean reconciliation between the traditional and the modern, this brilliantly suggestive image also raises the issue of Lower Binfield's economic structure – another benevolent influence on the behaviour of its inhabitants. While Orwell's descriptions of rural labour are not entirely free of sub-romantic flourishes, his basic point is that working on the land is one of the most powerful specifics against human aggression. In their herculean efforts to wrest a living from the countryside, or so he implies, imperfect people can go a long way towards sublimating their least salubrious instincts. The ethical benefits of rural labour are brought home with disconcerting power in the chapters on fishing, especially in the scenes in which the infant Bowling accompanies his brother's gang on a trip to Brewer's stream. As long as the boys are preoccupied with snaring carp, their thuggishness is held at bay and they behave like adults in the making. It is only when Brewer chases them off his land that they revert to barbarous type, amusing themselves with the sort of wanton acts of violence that Orwell could describe with such bracing clarity:

> Then Joe found a late thrush's nest with half-fledged chicks in it in a blackberry bush. After a lot of argument about what to do with them we took the chicks out, had shots at them with stones and finally stamped on them. There were four of them, and we each had one to stamp on.[37]

Orwell is hardly unique in emphasising the capacity of religion and hard work to restrain human folly, but there is another element in his account of Lower Binfields's moral economy which is altogether more surprising. In the passages of *Coming Up for Air* which he devotes to a brief description of Bowling's youthful reading habits, Orwell seems to ascribe enormous moral power to the popular literature of the late-Victorian and Edwardian periods. Surveying Bowling's addiction to comics such as *Gem* and *Magnet* and authors such as Nat Gould, he comes close to reversing the arguments of 'Boys' Weeklies' and his other essays on popular culture. His implied point is that Bowling's immersion in cheap literature plays a central role in shaping his moral character. Its greatest virtue is that it teaches him to rely on his own imaginative resources, opening up a sort of absorbing inner space in which he can distance himself from the real world and all its lurid temptations. Lost in a world of innocent adventure, transported to impossibly exotic places simply by turning the pages of a book, Bowling realises that he need never again suffer from boredom or the potential for moral anarchy which tends to go with it: '…nothing is ever like those first years when you suddenly discover that you can open a penny weekly paper and plunge straight into thieves' kitchens and Chinese opium dens and Polynesian islands and the forests of Brazil.'[38] In stark defiance of the argument of 'Boys' Weeklies' (see Chapter Two), he also benefits greatly from identifying with the heroes in his books and comics. When a young boy is still morally unformed, or so Orwell implies, there is no better way of taming his natural aggression than by holding up a model of principled manliness and encouraging him to aspire to it. Boys who identify with Raffles or Donovan the Dauntless are unlikely to turn out badly, whereas those who eschew the pleasures of literature will probably go the way of Bowling's semi-literate brother Joe, who hates the sight of print and ends up disgracing the family.[39]

Orwell leaves us in no doubt in *Coming Up for Air* that the world of the organic community has disappeared forever. He traces its disappearance to the outbreak of the First World War, which created the circumstances in which Lower Binfield's time-honoured methods of civilising its inhabitants could all be swept away. Once the illusory stability of the Edwardian village had been destroyed by the slaughter in Europe, Orwell implies, nothing on earth could resist the puncturing of religious faith, the massive expansion of industrial production and the corruption of popular culture. Yet unlike a number of other literary exponents of inter-war pessimism, notably Robert Graves in *Goodbye to All That* (1929) and Siegfried Sassoon in *Memoirs of an Infantry Officer* (1930), Orwell is not simply using the War as a convenient symbol of social catastrophe. His broader objective is to advance a subtle (and decidedly Tory) argument about the relationship between morality and politics in the post-war world. Addressing the issue of why thousands of ordinary soldiers uncomplainingly obeyed their orders, Bowling powerfully evokes the capacity of the state to determine everyday behaviour: 'The machine had got hold of you and it could do what it liked with you. It lifted you up and dumped you down among places and things you'd never dreamed of, and if it had dumped you down on the surface of the moon it wouldn't have seemed particularly strange.'[40] What Orwell is effectively doing here is allegorising the moment at which the British state transformed itself into what Michael Oakeshott might have called an 'enterprise association' – that is, a 'purposive association' defined by its pursuit of 'common substantive' goals.[41] As soon as the state begins intervening in all aspects of everyday life, he seems to imply, morality ceases to be a matter for the individual conscience and is instead underwritten by coercive power. The inevitable result is a coarsening of the moral faculty and a dangerous weakening of the democratic impulse, symbolised in Bowling's account of the 1930s by the collapse of mannerliness on the one hand and the menace of fascism on the other. At no point in his early novels does Orwell seem further away from a socialist's belief in the power of the state to create the good society.

The disparity between the themes of Orwell's non-fiction and those of his first four novels should now be clear. There are probably two ways in which it can best be explained, one relating to Orwell's position in the literary culture of the day and the other to the issue of his political psychology. As is well known, Orwell regarded himself as a literary outsider for much of the 1930s. Neither a university graduate nor an habitué of the most fashionable intellectual circles, he felt a deep resentment towards the leading English modernists while admiring some of them greatly. One of the ways in which his resentment expressed itself was in his almost ostentatious embrace of the conventions of the middlebrow novel. As much as he disliked J.B. Priestley and the various other writers who appealed to the semi-educated middle class, nearly all his novels of the 1930s owed a clear and sometimes exaggerated debt to their work.[42] At the level of form this was most obvious in his expansively chatty tone, his use of omniscient narrators and his obsessively detailed rendering of what Roland Barthes might have called the 'proairetic' and 'hermeneutic' dimensions of the narrative. When Orwell set out to tell a story in his early novels, he was rarely content simply to allow the action to unfold in a smoothly linear sequence. His broader concern was to fashion an unusually dense and shapely narrative which served up virtually all the details that the reader might require, advertised its progression from beginning to middle to end with schoolmasterly explicitness and went out of its way to provide a clear resolution to its disparate strands. What I want to suggest here is that Orwell's defiant use of traditional narrative forms, combined with his desire to cock a snook at the modernists, rendered him peculiarly vulnerable to what might be called the ideology of commonsense at the heart of middlebrow culture. One of the most obvious things about the themes of the early novels is that they all betray a sort of no-nonsense suburban brusqueness. Their scepticism about cross-class relationships is entirely consistent with the inherited snobberies of inter-war life, while their critique of aestheticism reflects the severe disapproval of 'fashionable pansies' which had crept into English culture at the time of Oscar Wilde's imprisonment in 1895. Even the sophisticated Toryism of *Coming Up for Air* must have chimed with certain trends in middlebrow culture, not least the taste for rural nostalgia whose most influential contemporary exponent was probably Stanley Baldwin. In seeking to bend the middlebrow novel to his own purposes, or so it could be argued, Orwell surrendered to precisely the sort of commonsensical nostrums which he otherwise opposed.

The more obvious reason for Orwell's ideological inconsistencies is his notoriously fraught relationship with the left. On the one hand, even if we accept that not all the early novels were necessarily anti-socialist, it is tempting to describe their starkly heterodox themes as simply another manifestation of his well-known delight in taunting his own side. Yet the difficulties with this explanation are readily apparent. The fact that Orwell went to such lengths to explore unorthodox ideas (the most recent editions of the first four novels run to well over a thousand pages) suggests that his cussedness answered to an altogether more fundamental need. There is perhaps a sense in which his political eccentricities were actually a *condition* of his commitment to the left. Appalled by the sense of ideological claustrophobia which often existed in radical circles, he could only retain his faith in socialism by periodically luxuriating in the conservative, patriotic and anti-industrial dimensions of his richly contradictory mind. It could even be argued that this made him the most distinguished exemplar of a deeply significant but largely unacknowledged aspect of modern culture. If ours is indeed a world in which 'all that is solid melts into air' (to use Marx's famous metaphor for the rapid rate of change in capitalist societies), it surely follows that thoroughgoing political commitment is one of the most difficult things to achieve. By moving back and forth between radically incommensurable points of view, Orwell exemplified the dilemma of the rootless intellectual as he seeks a fixed ideological point in a society beset by neophilia. As we have seen, his refusal to bow to orthodoxy also allowed him to do his most famous work.

APPENDIX 2
BIOGRAPHICAL DETAILS

This appendix contains brief biographical notes on most of the communist writers whose work I have either discussed or cited in relation to Orwell's ideas about culture. I have not included information on the Soviet critics discussed in the Introduction.[1]

BERNAL, JOHN DESMOND [J.D.] (1901–1971). Physicist and theorist/historian of science. Educated at Stonyhurst College, Bedford School and Emmanuel College, Cambridge. Researcher at the Davy-Faraday Laboratory at the Royal Institution, 1922–1927. Lecturer in Structural Crystallography at the University of Cambridge, 1927–1938. Head of X-Ray Crystallography at the Cavendish Laboratories, 1927–1936. Professor of Physics (later Crystallography) at Birkbeck College, London, 1938–1968. Chief Scientific Advisor to Lord Mountbatten during the Second World War. Author of *The World, the Flesh, and the Devil* (1929), *The Social Function of Science* (1939), *Science in History* (four volumes, 1954), *Marx and Science* (1957) etc.

BROWN, ALEC. Novelist, poet, critic, archaeologist and translator. Educated at Cambridge University. Worked briefly for the *Cambridge Magazine*. Became a Lecturer in English at the University of Belgrade, 1920. Contributor to *The Calendar of Modern Letters*. Earned a brief notoriety in the 1930s for his contributions to *Left Review*, some of which enunciated a theory of literature that owed a great deal to the ideas of the Proletkult movement in the USSR. Made various attempts to introduce Yugoslavian culture to a British audience in the period after 1940. Author of *The Honest Bounder* (1927), *Daughters of Albion* (1935), *The Fate of the Middle Classes* (1936), *Breakfast in Bed* (1937), *Essays on National Art in Yugoslavia* (editor, 1944), *Yugoslav Life and Landscape* (1954) etc. Translator of D.S. Mirsky's *The Intelligentsia of Great Britain* (1935) etc.

CAUDWELL, CHRISTOPHER (pseudonym of CHRISTOPER ST JOHN SPRIGG) (1907–1937). Cultural theorist, novelist, poet and journalist. Educated at the Benedictine Priory School, Ealing. Trained as a journalist on the *Yorkshire Observer*, 1923–1925. Worked as a technical journalist and author for much of the period between 1926 and 1933, specialising in the aeronautics industry. Joint Managing Editor of Airways Publications Ltd until the firm's dissolution in 1933. Converted to Marxism at some point in 1933 or 1934. Joined the Communist Party in 1935 and immediately became politically active in a working-class neighbourhood in Poplar, London. Travelled to Spain in December 1936 to join the British Battalion of the International Brigade. Killed in action near Madrid in February 1937, still eight months short of his thirtieth birthday. The pathbreaking works of Marxist cultural theory which he wrote in the last three years of his life were all published posthumously. Author of *Illusion and Reality: A Study in the Sources of Poetry* (1937), *Studies in a Dying Culture* (1938), *Further Studies in a Dying Culture* (1949), *Romance and Realism: A Study in Bourgeois English Literature* (1970), *Scenes and Actions: Unpublished Manuscripts* (1986) etc.

COCKBURN, (FRANCIS) CLAUD (1904–1981). Journalist, satirist and novelist. Educated at Berkhamsted School and Keble College, Oxford. Worked as a journalist on *The Times* between 1929 and the early 1930s. Joined the Communist Party in response to the Slump and worked for the *Daily Worker* between 1935 and 1946. Began the satirical news-sheet *The Week* in 1933 and rapidly turned it into one of the most scandalous publications in Britain. Moved to Ireland in 1946 and spent most of the rest of his life as a freelance writer. Frequent contributor to *Punch*, the *Sunday Telegraph* and *Private Eye* in the post-war years. Author of *Reporter in Spain* (under the pseudonym Frank Pitcairn, 1936), *In Time of Trouble* (1956), *Aspects of English History* (1957), *Crossing the Line* (1958), *View from the West* (1961), *I, Claud* (1967), *Union Power* (1976) etc.

CORNFORD, (RUPERT) JOHN (1915–1936). Poet and critic. Educated at Stowe School and Trinity College, Cambridge. Joined the Communist Party in 1933 and was widely regarded by his Cambridge contemporaries as one of the most brilliant undergraduates of his day. Became the first person from Britain to fight in the Spanish Civil War. Killed near

Madrid on the day after his 21st birthday. Author of the posthumous collection *Understand the Weapon, Understand the Wound* (1976) etc.

FOX, RALPH (WINSTON) (1900–1936). Literary critic, historian, novelist and journalist. Educated at Heath Grammar School, Halifax, Bradford Grammar School and Magdalen College, Oxford. Participated in the Friends Relief Mission which toured through Central and Southern Russia in 1922. Is thought to have joined the Communist Party in the early 1920s. Worked for the Far East section of the Comintern, 1925–1927. Served as the English Librarian at the Marx-Engels Institute in Moscow, 1930–1933. Wrote prolifically for the *Sunday Worker* in the late 1920s and for the *Daily Worker* from 1930 onwards. Travelled to Spain in the Autumn of 1936 to fight on the Republican side in the Spanish Civil War. Killed in action in Andalusia in December 1936. Author of *The People of the Steppes* (1925), *Storming Heaven* (1928), *Marx, Engels and Lenin on the Irish Revolution* (1932), *The Class Struggle in Britain in the Epoch of Imperialism* (two volumes, 1933), *Lenin: A Biography* (1933), *The Novel and the People* (1937), *This Was Their Youth* (1937) etc.

GARMAN, DOUGLAS (1903–1969). Poet and critic. Educated at Caius College, Cambridge. Assistant editor of *The Calendar of Modern Letters*, 1925–1926 (his association with the magazine came to an end when he embarked on a six-month visit to the Soviet Union in November 1926). Worked as an editor for Wishart and Co. in the early 1930s and as a commissioning editor for Lawrence and Wishart in the late 1930s. Joined the Communist Party of Great Britain in 1934 and subsequently served as its National Education Organiser. Frequent contributor to *Left Review* and the *Modern Quarterly*. Distanced himself from the Party in the early 1950s because of his opposition to the strategy outlined in *The British Road to Socialism*, though it is not clear whether he left the organisation – some say he did, others that he followed the example of his friend Alick West and became a sort of permanently disgruntled internal critic. Took up farming in Dorset towards the end of his life and contributed to various editions of the *Shell Guide to England*. Famously named his pigs after his sisters. Author of *The Jaded Hero* (1927).

HILL, (JOHN EDWARD) CHRISTOPHER (1912–2003). Historian. Educated at St Peter's School, York and Balliol College, Oxford. Fellow of All Souls College, Oxford, 1934–1938. Spent a year in the USSR acquainting himself with Soviet writings on English history, 1935–1936.

Joined the Communist Party of Great Britain in 1936 and remained a member until 1957. Lecturer in History at University College Cardiff, 1936–1938. Served in British Military Intelligence, 1940–1943. Head of the Foreign Office's Russian desk, 1943–1945. Now believed to have acted as a Soviet mole during his years as a civil servant. Fellow and Tutor in Modern History, Balliol College, 1938–1940, 1945–1958. Lecturer in History at Oxford University, 1958–1965. Master of Balliol College, 1965–1978. Subsequently held a number of visiting professorships in Britain, Australia and the USA. Widely regarded as the preeminent post-war historian of the English Revolution. Author of *The English Revolution 1640* (with Edgell Rickword and Margaret James, 1940), *The Soviets and Ourselves: Two Commonwealths* (under the pseudonym K.E. Holme, 1945), *Lenin and The Russian Revolution* (1947), *The Good Old Cause* (edited with Edmund Dell, 1949), *Economic Problems of the Church* (1955), *Puritanism and Revolution* (1958), *Society and Puritanism in Pre-Revolutionary England* (1964), *Intellectual Origins of the English Revolution* (1965), *The Century Of Revolution, 1603–1714* (1961), *Reformation to Industrial Revolution* (1967), *God's Englishman* (1970), *Antichrist in Seventeenth-Century England* (1971), *The World Turned Upside Down* (1972), *Winstanley: The Law of Freedom and Other Writings* (editor, 1973), *Change and Continuity in Seventeenth-Century England* (1974), *Milton and the English Revolution* (1977), *Some Intellectual Consequences of the English Revolution* (1980), *The World of the Muggletonians* (1983), *The Experience of Defeat* (1984), *A Turbulent, Seditious, and Factious People* (1988), *The English Bible In Seventeenth-Century England* (1993), *Liberty Against the Law* (1996) etc.

JACKSON, THOMAS ALFRED [T.A.] (1879–1955). Historian, journalist and critic. Educated at the Duncombe Road School, Holloway. Employed as a compositor at various times in the 1890s and the first decade of the twentieth century. Founder member of the Socialist Party of Great Britain, 1904. Occasionally employed as a political organiser by the Independent Labour Party and as a Tutor at the North-East Labour College in the period between 1909 and 1920. Founder member of the Communist Party of Great Britain in 1920 and a full-time Party worker between 1921 and 1929. Occasionally served as the editor of the Party journals *Communist* and *Workers' Weekly* in the 1920s. Oversaw the arts pages of the *Sunday Worker* with Ralph Fox, 1925–1929. Thereafter scraped a living as a full-time writer. Author of *Dialectics* (1936), *Charles Dickens: The Progress of a Radical* (1937), *Trials of British Freedom* (1940),

Socialism: What? Why? How? (1945), *Ireland Her Own* (1947), *Old Friends to Keep* (1950), *Solo Trumpet* (1953) etc.

LEWIS, JOHN (1889–1976). Philosopher and critic. Educated at University College, London, Cambridge University and the University of Birmingham. Lewis was a committed Christian during the early part of his career, serving as a Pastor at the Unitarian Church in Ipswich. Lectured in Philosophy at the Universities of Cambridge, Birmingham and London. Converted to Marxism in the 1930s and rapidly became one of the most important communist philosophers in Britain after joining the Communist Party. Served on the CPGB's Executive Committee for about a decade after the mid-1940s. Editor of the *Modern Quarterly*, 1945–1956. Famously polemicised against the work of Louis Althusser in *Marxism Today* in the 1960s. Author of *Marxism and Modern Idealism* (1947), *Marxism and the Irrationalists* (1955), *Science, Faith and Scepticism* (1959), *Man and Evolution* (1962), *The Uniqueness of Man* (1974) etc.

LINDSAY, (JOHN) [JACK] (1900–1990). Novelist, historian, critic and cultural theorist. Educated at Brisbane Grammar School and Queensland University. Co-editor of the Australian anti-modernist journal *Vision*, 1923–1924. After moving to England in 1926, served as co-publisher of the Fanfrolico Press until 1930. Co-editor with P.R. Stephensen of *The London Aphrodite*, 1928–1929. Converted to Marxism in the mid-1930s and joined the Communist Party of Great Britain in 1941. Became the key theorist and practitioner of 'mass declamation' during the Popular Front period. Served in the Signal Corps between 1941 and 1943 and as a scriptwriter for the Army Bureau of Current Affairs between 1943 and 1945. Thereafter reverted to full-time writing. Awarded the Order of Znak Pocheta by the Soviet government in 1968 and the Order of Australia in 1981. Author of over 150 books (there is no complete bibliography), including *William Blake* (1927), *Mark Antony* (1936), *Adam of a New World* (1936), *Anatomy of Spirit* (1937), *John Bunyan: Maker of Myths* (1937), *A Short History of Culture* (1938), *England My England* (1939), *Handbook of Freedom* (edited with Edgell Rickword, 1939), *Perspective for Poetry* (1944), *British Achievement in Art and Music* (1945), *Marxism and Contemporary Science* (1949), *Betrayed Spring* (1953), *Rising Tide* (1953), *Moment of Choice* (1955), *After the Thirties* (1956), *Life Rarely Tells* (1958), *Roaring Twenties* (1960), *Fanfrolico and After* (1962), *J.M.W. Turner: His Life and Work* (1966), *Meetings with Poets* (1968), *Origins of Alchemy* (1970), *Origins of Astrology* (1971), *The Normans and their World* (1974), *William Morris*

(1975), *William Blake* (1978), *Hogarth: His Art and his World* (1977), *Monster City: Defoe's London* (1978), *The Crisis in Marxism* (1981).

LLOYD, ALBERT LANCASTER [A.L.] (1908–1972). Journalist, historian, ethnomusicologist and folksinger. Educated at Hornsey Grammar School. Emigrated to Australia in 1934 and worked as an agricultural labourer before returning to Britain in the early 1930s. Joined the Communist Party shortly thereafter and remained a member until his death. Worked as a journalist on the *Picture Post* between 1940 and the early 1950s. Became one of the leading figures in the so-called 'British folk revival' in the 1950s and 1960s. Broadcast regularly for the BBC and pioneered the famous 'Radio Ballads' with his friend Ewan MacColl. Author of *The Singing Englishman* (1944), *Folk Song in England* (1967) etc.

MADGE, CHARLES (HENRY) (1912–1996). Poet, sociologist and co-founder of Mass-Observation. Educated at Winchester College and Magdalene College, Cambridge. Worked as a journalist on the *Daily Mirror*, 1935–1936. Co-founded Mass-Observation with Charles Harrisson in 1937. Joined the Communist Party of Great Britain in 1932 but appears to have moved away from Marxism in the 1940s. Contributor to *Left Review* and C. Day Lewis's symposium *The Mind in Chains*. Worked as a researcher at The National Institute for Economic and Social Research (1940–1942) and at Political and Economic Planning (1943). Served as the Director of the Pilot Press in 1944 and as a Social Development Officer in Stevenage between 1947 and 1950. Professor of Sociology at the University of Birmingham, 1950–1970. Author of *The Disappearing Castle* (1937), *Britain* (with Charles Harrisson, 1939), *The Father Found* (1941), *Industry after the War* (1943), *Society in the Mind* (1964), *Art Students Observed* (with Barbara Weinberger, 1973), *Inner-City Poverty in Paris and London* (with Peter Willmott, 1981) etc.

MARSHALL, ARTHUR CALDER- (1908–1992). Novelist, critic, biographer and documentarist. Educated at St Paul's School, London and Hertford College, Oxford. Befriended Aleister Crowley as a very young man and briefly flirted with occultism. Schoolmaster at Denstone College, 1931–1933. Converted to Marxism in the early 1930s but seems to have become disillusioned by 1941, when he referred to the Thirties as the 'pink decade' in a famous article in the *New Statesman*. Sought in his early novels to forge a totalising style of fiction which made use of what he called the 'composite method'. Began work as a scriptwriter for Metro-

Goldwyn Mayer in 1937 and worked on propaganda films for the Ministry of Information between 1942 and 1945. Collaborated with Paul Rotha on the documentary *The World is Rich* in 1946. Converted to Christianity in the mid-1950s after becoming convinced that Alexander Riall Wadham Woods, the subject of the biography he was researching at the time, was overseeing the project from Heaven. Author of *About Levy* (1933), *Dead Centre* (1935), *Challenge to Schools* (1935), *The Magic of my Youth* (1951), *Havelock Ellis* (1959), *The Scarlet Boy* (1961), *Lone Wolf: The Story of Jack London* (1961), *Wish You Were Here: The Art of Donald McGill* (1966), *Lewd, Blasphemous and Obscene* (1972) etc.

MIRSKY, DMITRY SYVATOPOLK [D.S.] (1890–1939). Literary critic and historian. Educated at St Petersburg University, the Academy of the Imperial General Staff and Kharkov University. The son of an aristocratic family, Mirsky emigrated to the West in 1920 after fighting against the Bolsheviks in the Civil War. Lecturer in Russian at King's College, University of London between 1921 and 1932. Converted to Marxism and joined the Communist Party in 1931. Returned to the USSR in 1932 and rapidly established a reputation as a literary critic. Arrested on suspicion of espionage in 1937 and sentenced to eight years' imprisonment. Died in a labour camp near Magadan in 1939. Author of *Contemporary Russian Literature* (1926), *A History of Russian Literature from the Earliest Times to the Death of Dostoevsky, 1881* (1927), *Russia: A Social History* (1931), *Lenin* (1931), *The Intelligentsia of Great Britain* (1935), *A History of Russian Literature* (1949) etc.

MORTON, ARTHUR LESLIE [A.L.] (1903–1987). Historian and critic. Educated at the King Edward VI Grammar School, Bury St Edmonds, Eastbourne College and Peterhouse, Cambridge. Taught at Steyning Grammar School and at A.S. Neill's progressive school Summerhill in the 1920s. Joined the Communist Party of Great Britain in 1929 and remained a member until the end of his life. Occasional contributor to *Scrutiny* and the *Criterion*. Employed in various capacities by the *Daily Worker*, 1934–1937. Served in the Royal Artillery during the Second World War. Elected to the Urban District Council in Leiston, Suffolk in the late 1940s. Member of the CPGB's East Anglia District Committee until 1974. Active in the Communist Party's Historians' Group from its foundation in 1946. Full-time writer from 1950 onwards. Author of *A People's History of England* (1938), *Language of Men* (1945), *The English*

Utopia (1952), *The Everlasting Gospel* (1958), *The Matter of Britain* (1966), *The World of the Ranters* (1970), *Collected Poems* (1977) etc.

RICKWORD, (JOHN) EDGELL (1898–1982). Poet and critic. Educated at Colchester Royal Grammar School and Pembroke College, Oxford. Served in France in the Artists' Rifles between 1916 and 1918. Subsequently awarded the Military Cross. Contributor to the *New Statesman*, the *Daily Herald* and the *Times Literary Supplement* in the early 1920s. Chief editor of *The Calendar of Modern Letters*, 1925–1927. Converted to Marxism in the early 1930s and joined the Communist Party of Great Britain in 1934. Editor of *Left Review*, 1936–1937. Editor of *Our Time*, 1944–1947. After the War worked as a bookseller and as the Manager of the Hampstead branch of Collett's bookshop in London. Left the CPGB in 1956 but remained a Marxist. Author of *Behind the Eyes* (1921), *Rimbaud* (1924), *Scrutinies* (editor, two volumes, 1928/1931), *Invocations to Angels* (1928), *Twittingpan* (1931), *Essays and Opinions* (1974), *Literature in Society* (1978) etc.

SLATER, (CHARLES) MONTAGU (1902–1956). Novelist, critic, playwright and librettist. Educated at Millom School and as a non-collegiate student at Oxford University. Worked as a journalist on the *Liverpool Post*, the *Morning Post* and *Reynolds News* in the 1920s and early 1930s. Joined the Communist Party of Great Britain in 1927. Co-editor of *Left Review*, 1934–1935. Served as Head of Scripts in the Ministry of Information's Film Division during the Second World War. Collaborated with Benjamin Britten on a number of plays, documentary films, pageants and operas. Wrote the original libretto for Britten's opera *Peter Grimes* (1946), though it was later revised by Ronald Duncan and Eric Crozier. Author of *Second City* (1931), *Haunting Europe* (1934), *Stay Down Miner* (1936), *Once a Jolly Swagman* (1944), *Peter Grimes and other Poems* (1946), *Englishmen with Swords* (1949), *The Trial of Jomo Kenyatta* (1955) etc.

STRACHEY, (EVELYN) JOHN (ST LOE) (1901–1963). Author and politician. Educated at Eton College and Magdalene College, Oxford. Joined the Independent Labour Party in the early 1920s and collaborated with Sir Oswald Mosley on proto-Keynesian proposals for government reflation of the British economy. Labour MP for Aston, 1929–1931. Became a founder member of Mosley's New Party in 1931, leaving once it became clear that Mosley was increasingly attracted to fascism. Converted to Marxism in 1931 and spent much of the next eight years as

Britain's leading populariser of 'official' communist doctrine, though he never became a formal member of the Communist Party. Founded the Left Book Club with Victor Gollancz and Harold Laski in 1936. Broke with the Marxist left in 1940 and later became a key thinker on what became known as the 'revisionist' wing of the Labour Party. Labour MP for Dundee (later Dundee West), 1945–1963. Under-Secretary of State for Air, 1945–1946. Minister of Food, 1946–1950. Secretary of State for War, 1950–1951. Author of *Revolution by Reason* (1925), *The Coming Struggle for Power* (1932), *The Menace of Fascism* (1933), *Literature and Dialectical Materialism* (1934), *The Nature of Capitalist Crisis* (1935), *The Theory and Practice of Socialism* (1936), *Why You Should Be a Socialist* (1938), *What Are We to Do?* (1938), *A Programme for Progress* (1940), *Contemporary Capitalism* (1956), *The End of Empire* (1959), *On the Prevention of War* (1962), *The Strangled Cry* (1963) etc.

SWINGLER, RANDALL (CARLINE) (1909–1967). Poet, novelist and critic. Educated at Winchester College and New College, Oxford. Worked as a schoolmaster in the late 1920s and early 1930s. Joined the Communist Party of Great Britain in 1934 and made a major contribution to the left's theatrical and musical culture. Editor of *Left Review*, 1937–1938. Founder of Fore Publications in 1938. Literary Editor and staff reporter for the *Daily Worker*, 1939–1941. Co-editor of *Our Time* between 1941 and 1942 and editor in 1949. Served in Italy with the 56th Divisional Signals between 1943 and 1945. Broadcast regularly on the BBC and served as a Tutor in adult education for the University of London in the late 1940s. Left the Communist Party in 1956. Helped to establish the *New Reasoner* in 1957. Author of *Poems* (1932), *Crucifixus: A Drama* (1932), *Reconstruction* (1933), *Difficult Morning* (1933), *No Escape* (1937), *Left Song Book* (edited with Alan Bush, 1938), *To Town* (1939), *We're in the Army Now* (1941), *The Years of Anger* (1946), *The God in the Cave* (1950) etc.

UPWARD, EDWARD (FALAISE) (1903-2009). Novelist and critic. Educated at Repton School and Corpus Christi College, Cambridge. An early associate of Christopher Isherwood and W.H. Auden, Upward pioneered a hallucinatory and allegorical style of writing which exercised a profound influence on what became known as the 'Auden Circle'. Invented the imaginary village of Mortmere with Isherwood while both were undergraduates. Served as a schoolmaster in Alleyn's School in Dulwich between 1932 and his retirement in the 1960s. Joined the Communist Party in 1932 but left in 1948 because he felt that its post-war line was 'revisionist'. Upward never renounced his commitment to Marxism and continued to write short fiction of enormous power and wit throughout his old age. Author of *Journey to the Border* (1939), *In the Thirties* (1932), *The Rotten Elements* (1969), *The Railway Accident and Other Stories* (1969), *No Home but the Struggle* (1977), *The Night Walk and Other Stories* (1987), *The Mortmere Stories* (with Christopher Isherwood, 1994), *An Unmentionable Man* (1994), *The Scenic Railway* (1997), *The Coming Day and Other Stories* (2000), *A Renegade in Springtime* (2003) etc.

WARNER, (REGINALD ERNEST) [REX] (1905–1986). Novelist and classicist. Educated at St George's School, Harpenden and Wadham College, Oxford. Began his career as a schoolmaster and held two teaching appointments in Egypt between 1932 and 1934. Leading member of the Auden Circle in the 1930s. Considered himself a Marxist in the 1930s but began to recant after the Nazi–Soviet Pact in 1939. Never joined the Communist Party. Served in Berlin with the Allied Control Commission at the end of the Second World War. Director of the British Institute in Athens, 1945–1947. Held a number of academic posts in the USA in the post-war years, including professorships at Bowdoin College (1962–1963) and the University of Connecticut (1964–1974). Won the Tait Memorial Prize for his book *Imperial Caesar* in 1960. Made an Honorary Fellow of Wadham College, Oxford in 1973. Author of *The Wild Goose Chase* (1937), *The Professor* (1938), *The Aerodrome* (1941) etc.

WEST, (JOHN ALEXANDER) [ALICK] (1895–1972). Literary theorist and critic. Educated at Highgate School, London, Trinity College, Dublin and the University of Berlin. Interned for the entire duration of the First World War in a prison camp at Ruhleben in Germany. Worked as a Lektor in English at Basle University, 1926–1935. Joined the CPGB in 1935 and immediately became active in the Brixton district of London. Co-editor of *Left Review*, 1934–1935. Worked as an English teacher at the Soviet Embassy in London in the post-war years. Author of *Crisis and Criticism* (1937), *A Good Man Fallen Among Fabians: A Study of George Bernard Shaw* (1950), *The Mountain in the Sunlight: Studies in Conflict and Unity* (1958), *One Man in his Time: An Autobiography* (1969) etc.

NOTES

I have tried to use the most accessible authoritative editions of Orwell's work. This means that I have primarily drawn on recent Penguin editions of Orwell's nine full-length books and the paperback editions of Volumes 10–20 of *The Complete Works of George Orwell*, edited by Peter Davison. If a source is cited in more than one chapter, its full details are listed in the relevant first footnote in each of the chapters in which it appears.

Introduction

1 Bernard Crick, 'Introduction' in George Orwell, *The Lion and the Unicorn: Socialism and the English Genius* (London: Penguin, 1982), p. 18.

2 See Raymond Williams, *Orwell* (London: Fontana, 1971). For an acute critique of Williams's book, see Michael Walzer, 'George Orwell's England' in *The Company of Critics: Social Criticism and Political Commitment in the Twentieth Century* (London: Basic Books, 1989). Reprinted in Graham Holderness, Bryan Loughrey and Naham Yousaf (eds.), *George Orwell: Contemporary Critical Essays* (London: Macmillan, 1998). For a more recent attack by a radical academic on Orwell's refusal to observe left-wing orthodoxy, see Scott Lucas, *The Betrayal of Dissent: Beyond Orwell, Hitchens and the New American Century* (London: Pluto Press, 2004).

3 Raymond Williams, *Politics and Letters: Interviews with New Left Review* (London: New Left Books, 1979).

4 For a history of this generation of communist critics, see Philip Bounds, *British Communism and the Politics of Literature, 1928–1939* (London: Merlin Press, 2012). See also Anand Prakash, *Marxism and Literary Theory* (Delhi: Academic Foundation, 1994); Victor N. Paananen, *British Marxist Criticism* (New York: Garland Publishing, 2000); David Margolies, '*Left Review* and Left Literary Culture' in Jon Clark, Margot Heinemann, David Margolies and Carole Snee (eds.), *Culture and Crisis in Britain in the Thirties* (London: Lawrence and Wishart, 1979); Hanna Behrend, 'An Intellectual Irrelevance? Marxist Literary Criticism in the 1930s' in Andy Croft (ed.), *A Weapon in the Struggle: The Cultural History of the Communist Party in Britain* (London: Pluto Press, 1998).

5 The idea that Orwell undertook a dialogue with intellectual or political movements to which he did not strictly belong is not new. Most obviously, John Newsinger has made a powerful case for the claim that Orwell's political outlook was deeply affected by a dialogue with the Trotskyist tradition. See John Newsinger, *Orwell's Politics* (Basingstoke: Palgrave, 2001).

6 For fascinating but not always complementary accounts of Orwell's relationship to Marxism, see Alex Zwerdling, *Orwell and the Left* (London: Yale University Press, 1974); John Rodden, 'Orwell, Marx and the Marxists' in *Scenes from an Afterlife: The Legacy of George Orwell* (Wilmington: ISI Books, 2003); Newsinger, *Orwell's Politics*.

7 The group of writers around the CPGB were not the only Marxists critics who flourished in Britain in the 1930s. There were also the members of the so-called 'Auden Circle' (W.H. Auden, Stephen Spender, C. Day Lewis etc.) as well as a number of contributors to John Middleton Murry's journal *The Adelphi*. If I only mention these other writers in passing in this book, it is because their influence on Orwell's critical writings seems to me to be negligible.

8 George Orwell, 'The Frontiers of Art and Propaganda', *The Listener*, 29 May 1941. Reprinted in *The Complete Works of George Orwell*, Volume 12: *A Patriot After All 1940–1941* (London: Secker and Warburg, 2000) [hereafter CW 12], p. 484.

9 See Jonathan Rose, 'The Invisible Sources of *Nineteen Eighty-Four*', *Journal of Popular Culture*, Vol. 26 No. 1, 1992, pp. 93–107. Reprinted in Jonathan Rose (ed.), *The Revised Orwell* (East Lansing: Michigan State University Press, 1992).

10 Alick West, 'Marxism and Modern Thought', *Left Review*, Vol. 2 No. 1, October 1935, p. 45.

11 Q.D. Leavis, 'The Literary Life Respectable: Mr. George Orwell', *Scrutiny*, September 1940. Reprinted in Jeffrey Meyers (ed.), *George Orwell: The Critical Heritage* (London: Routledge, 1975), p. 189.

12 Philip Mairet, *New English Weekly*, 14 March 1940. Reprinted in Meyers (ed.), *George Orwell: The Critical Heritage*, p. 179. Mairet also said of Orwell that 'It seems to me that he uses a fragment of Marxist ideology now and then, as a substitute for some deeper and more valid criterion which he feels but cannot yet formulate.'

13 Jon Wain, 'George Orwell' in *Essays on Literature and Ideas* (London: Macmillan, 1963), p. 209. Quoted in Alok Rai, *Orwell and the Politics of Despair: A Critical Study of the Writings of George Orwell* (Cambridge: Cambridge University Press, 1990), p. 169n.

14 Alok Rai, *Orwell and the Politics of Despair*, p. 22f.

15 Maurice Cowling, *Religion and Public Doctrine in Modern England*, Volume 3: *Accommodations* (Cambridge: Cambridge University Press, 2001), p. 529.

16 See Newsinger, *Orwell's Politics*, pp. 141–147. I give my own account of Orwell's exchanges with Bernal and Swingler in Chapter 5.

17 See Andy Croft, 'Worlds Without End Foisted Upon the Future – Some Antecedents of *Nineteen Eighty-Four*' in Christopher Norris (ed.), *Inside the Myth. Orwell: Views from the Left* (London: Lawrence and Wishart, 1984).

18 Or next to nothing. Also worth consulting is a brief essay by David B. Epsey which draws some interesting parallels between the work of Orwell and Christopher Caudwell. See David B. Epsey, 'George Orwell vs. Christopher Caudwell – Politics and Literary Criticism', *Illinois Quarterly*, Vol. 36 No. 4, April 1974, pp. 46–60. More recently, Kristin Bluemel traced the influence on Orwell of the radical writings of Stevie Smith, Mulk Raj Anand and Inez Holden. Although Anand was a communist, Bluemel does not focus on this aspect of his literary identity. See Kristin Bluemel, *George Orwell and the Radical Eccentrics: Intermodernism in Literary London* (Basingstoke: Palgrave Macmillan, 2004).

19 The belief that Orwell had nothing in common with the British communists was powerfully reinforced in 1996 by the 'revelation' that he had made a list of communists and fellow-travellers available to the Information Research Department (IRD), a shadowy organisation on the fringes of the Foreign Office whose function was to produce anti-communist propaganda materials. For interesting accounts of Orwell's dealings with the IRD, see Christopher Hitchens, *Orwell's Victory* (London: Penguin, 2002), Chapter 7; Timothy Garton Ash, 'Orwell's List', *New York Review of Books*, Vol. 50 No. 14, September 25 2003.

20 George Orwell, *The Lion and the Unicorn: Socialism and the English Genius* (London: Secker and Warburg, 1941). Reprinted in CW 12, p. 406.

21 Harry Pollitt, 'Mr Orwell Will Have to Try Again', *Daily Worker*, March 17 1937. Reprinted in Mark Howe (ed.), *Is That Damned Paper Still Coming Out? The Very Best of the Daily Worker/Morning Star* (London: People's Press Printing Society, 2001).

22 See James Walsh, 'George Orwell', *Marxist Quarterly*, No. 3, 1956. Reprinted in Irving Howe (ed.), *Orwell's Nineteen Eighty-Four: Text, Sources, Criticism* (New York: Harcourt Brace, 1963); A.L. Morton, *The English Utopia* (London: Lawrence and Wishart, 1978 [1952]), p. 273f; Christopher Norris (ed.), *Inside the Myth*. There is a brief discussion of R. Palme Dutt's letters to the *Guardian* in John Rodden, *George Orwell: The Politics of Literary Reputation* [previously published under the title *The Politics of Literary Reputation: The Making and Claiming of 'Saint George' Orwell*] (London: Transaction, 2003) p. 187.

23 There is now a very substantial body of work on the history of the CPGB. Among the best introductions are the four separate volumes which chart the Party's development from its foundation in 1920 through to its dissolution in 1991. See Francis Beckett, *Enemy Within: The Rise and Fall of the British Communist Party* (London: John Murray, 1995); James Eaden and Dave Renton, *The Communist Party of Great Britain since 1920* (Basingstoke: Palgrave, 2002); Keith Laybourn and Dylan Murphy, *Under the Red Flag: A*

History of Communism in Britain (Stroud: Sutton, 1999); Willie Thompson, *The Good Old Cause: British Communism, 1920–1991* (London: Pluto Press, 1993).

24 Quoted in Andrew Murray, *The Communist Party of Great Britain: A Historical Analysis to 1941* (Liverpool: Communist Liaison, 1995), p. 28.

25 The most important 'revisionist' historians of the CPGB are probably Kevin Morgan, Andrew Thorpe and Matthew Worley. For Andrew Thorpe, see, inter alia, 'Comintern "Control" of the Communist Party of Great Britain', *English Historical Review*, 452, Vol. 112, 1998, pp. 636–662; 'Stalinism and British Politics', *History*, Vol. 83, 1998, pp. 608–627; 'The Communist International and the British Communist Party' in Andrew Thorpe and Tim Rees (eds.), *International Communism and the Communist International, 1919–1943* (Manchester: Manchester University Press, 1993); *The British Communist Party and Moscow, 1920–1943* (Manchester: Manchester University Press, 2000); 'Communist MP: Willie Gallacher and British Communism' in Kevin Morgan, Gidon Cohen and Andrew Flinn (eds.), *Agents of the Revolution: New Biographical Approaches to the History of International Communism in the Age of Lenin and Stalin* (Oxford: Peter Lang, 2005). For Matthew Worley, see, inter alia, 'Reflections on Recent Communist Party History', *Historical Materialism*, No. 4, 1999, pp. 241–261; *Class Against Class: The Communist Party in Britain Between the Wars* (London: I.B.Tauris, 2002). For Kevin Morgan, see, inter alia, *Against Fascism and War: Ruptures and Continuities in British Communist Politics, 1935–1941* (Manchester: Manchester University Press, 1989); *Harry Pollitt* (Manchester: Manchester University Press, 1993); 'Harry Pollitt, the British Communist Party and International Communism' in Tauno Saarela and Kimmo Rentola (eds.), *Communism: National and International* (Helsinki: Finnish Historical Society, 1998). For a Trotskyist critique of the new revisionism, see John McIlroy, 'Rehabilitating Communist History: The Communist International, the Communist Party of Great Britain and Some Historians', *Revolutionary History*, Vol. 8 No. 1, 2001, pp. 195–226.

26 For a useful overview of the CPGB's engagement with cultural issues, see Croft (ed.), *A Weapon in the Struggle*. See also See John Lucas (ed.), *The 1930s: A Challenge to Orthodoxy* (Brighton: Harvester, 1978); Margolies, Heinemann, Clarke and Snee (eds.), *Culture and Crisis in Britain in the Thirties;* Geoff Andrews, Nina Fishman and Kevin Morgan (eds.); *Opening the Books: Essays on the Social and Cultural History of the British Communist Party* (London: Pluto Press, 1995). Apart from editing *A Weapon in the Struggle*, Andy Croft has also done more than anyone else to shape our understanding of the Party's contribution to British literary culture. See, inter alia, '"Extremely Crude Propaganda"? The Historical Novels of Jack Lindsay' in Robert Mackie (ed.). *Jack Lindsay: The Thirties and Forties* (London: University of London Australian Studies Centre, 1984); *Red Letter Days: British Fiction in the 1930s* (London: Lawrence and Wishart, 1990); 'Writers, the Communist

Party and the Battle of Ideas, 1945–1950', *Socialist History*, No. 5, Summer 1994, pp. 2–25; 'Walthamstow, Little Gidding and Middlesbrough: Edward Thompson, Adult Education and Literature', *Socialist History*, No. 8, 1995, pp. 22–48; 'Authors Take Sides: Writers and the Communist Party 1920–1956' in Andrews, Fishman and Morgan (eds.), *Opening the Books*; 'The End of Socialist Realism: Margot Heinemann's *The Adventurers*' in David Margolies and Maroula Joannou (eds.), *Heart of the Heartless World: Essays in Cultural Resistance in Memory of Margot Heinemann* (London: Pluto Press, 1995); 'Culture or Snobology? Writers and the Communist Party' in Socialist History Society, *Getting the Balance Right: An Assessment of the Achievements of the Communist Party of Great Britain* (London: Socialist History Society, n.d.); 'Politics and Beauty: the Poetry of Randall Swingler' in Keith Williams and Steven Matthews (eds.), *Rewriting the Thirties: Modernism and After* (London: Longman, 1997); 'The Boys Round the Corner: the Story of Fore Publications' in Croft (ed.), *A Weapon in the Struggle*; 'The Young Men are Moving Together: The Case of Randall Swingler' in John McIlroy, Kevin Morgan and Alan Campbell (eds.), *Party People, Communist Lives: Explorations in Biography* (London: Lawrence and Wishart, 2001); 'The Ralph Fox (Writers') Group' in Antony Shuttleworth (ed.), *And in Our Time: Vision, Revision, and British Writing of the 1930s* (Lewisburg: Bucknell University Press, 2003); *Comrade Heart: A Life of Randall Swingler* (Manchester: Manchester University Press, 2003).

27 For general histories of the cultural work of the CPGB in the Class Against Class period, see Alun Howkins, 'Class Against Class: The Political Culture of the Communist Party of Great Britain 1930–1935' in Frank Gloversmith (ed.), *Class, Culture and Social Change: A New View of the 1930s* (Brighton: Harvester Press, 1980); Worley, *Class Against Class*, Chapter 6; Bounds, *British Communism and the Politics of Literature*, Chapter 1.

28 Stephensen's most important work in this period was contained in the journal *The London Aphrodite*, which he co-edited with Jack Lindsay. See 'Editorial Manifesto', *The London Aphrodite*, No. 1, August 1928, p. 2.; 'J.C. Squire (Etc.)', *The London Aphrodite*, No. 2, October 1928, pp. 86–92; 'Contrapuntals: An Essay in Amiable Criticism', *The London Aphrodite*, No. 3, December 1928, pp. 228–230; 'Notice to Americans', *The London Aphrodite*, No. 3, December 1928, p. 231; 'The Whirled Around: Reflections upon Methuselah, Icthyphallos, Wheels and Dionysos', *The London Aphrodite*, No. 5, April 1929, pp. 338–341; 'Bakunin', *The London Aphrodite*, No. 6, July 1929, pp. 421–432. For a critical discussion of this body of work, see Bounds, *British Communism and the Politics of Literature*, Chapter 1.

29 See, inter alia, John Cornford, 'The Class Front in Modern Art', *The Student Vanguard*, December 1933. Reprinted in Patrick Deane (ed.), *History in our Hands: A Critical Anthology of Writings on Literature, Culture and Politics from the 1930s* (London: Leicester University Press, 1998).

30 See, inter alia, Montagu Slater, 'The Spirit of the Age in Paint' in Edgell Rickword (ed.), *Scrutinies*, Volume 2 (London: Wishart & Company, 1931).

31 For a discussion of Strachey's critical writings, see Bounds, *British Communism and the Politics of Literature*, Chapter 1.

32 The title of this book was later changed to *Soviet Writers' Congress 1934: The Debate on Socialist Realism and Modernism in the Soviet Union*. Its last printing was in 1977.

33 For an overview of Soviet cultural criticism after 1934, see, inter alia, Dave Laing, *The Marxist Theory of Art: An Introductory Survey* (Brighton: Harvester, 1978), Chapter 2; Bounds, *British Communism and the Politics of Literature*, Chapter 2. There is now a very large body of work on the development of Soviet culture between the October Revolution and the death of Stalin. Among the most useful sources are the following: Régine Robin, *Socialist Realism: An Impossible Aesthetic* (Stanford: Stanford University Press, 1992); C. Vaughan James, *Soviet Socialist Realism: Origins and Theory* (London: Macmillan, 1973); Boris Groys, *The Total Art of Stalinism: Avant-Garde, Aesthetic Dictatorship, and Beyond* (New Jersey: Princeton University Press, 1992); Matthew Cullerne Bown, *Art Under Stalin* (Oxford: Phaidon, 1991); Thomas Lahusen and Evgeny Dobrenko (eds.), *Socialist Realism Without Shores* (London: Yale University Press, 1997); Brandon Taylor and Matthew Cullerne Bown (eds.). *Art of the Soviets: Painting, Sculpture and Architecture in a One-Party State, 1917–1922* (Manchester: Manchester University Press, 1993); Jurgen Rühle, *Literature and Revolution: A Critical Study of the Writer and Communism in the Twentieth Century* (London: Pall Mall Press, 1969); Igor Golomstock, *Totalitarian Art in the Soviet Union, the Third Reich, Fascist Italy and the People's Republic of China* (London: Harper Collins, 1990).

34 A.A. Zhdanov, 'Soviet Literature – The Richest In Ideas. The Most Advanced Literature' in Maxim Gorky, Karl Radek, Nikolai Bukharin, Andrei Zhdanov and others, *Soviet Writers' Congress 1934: The Debate on Socialist Realism and Modernism in the Soviet Union* (London: Lawrence and Wishart, 1977), p. 21.

35 See Nikolai Bukharin, 'Poetry, Poetics And The Problems Of Poetry In The USSR' in Gorky, Radek, Bukharin, Zhdanov et al., *Soviet Writers' Congress 1934*.

36 See Maxim Gorky, 'Soviet Literature' in Gorky, Radek, Bukharin, Zhdanov et al., *Soviet Writers' Congress 1934*.

37 See Karl Radek, 'Contemporary World Literature And The Tasks Of Proletarian Art' in Gorky, Radek, Bukharin, Zhdanov et al., *Soviet Writers' Congress 1934*.

38 The fullest account of Fox's work can be found in Chapter 4 of Bounds, *British Communism and the Politics of Literature*. For briefer surveys of *The Novel and the People*, see Anand Prakash, *Marxism and Literary Theory*; David Margolies, '*Left Review* and Left Literary Theory'; Hanna Behrend, 'An Intellectual Irrelevance? Marxist Literary Criticism in the 1930s'. Several

writers have contributed introductions to the various editions of *The Novel and the People*. By far the most useful is Jeremy Hawthorn's preface to the 1979 Lawrence and Wishart edition. Perhaps the most perceptive brief remarks on *The Novel and the People* are those of the American critic Pamela Fox. See Pamela Fox, *Class Fictions: Shame and Resistance in the British Working-Class Novel, 1890–1945* (Durham: Duke University Press, 1994), p. 55f.

39 For a lengthy survey of West's critical writings, see Bounds, *British Communism and the Politics of Literature*, Chapter 3. Another substantial discussion of West's work can be found in Chapter 6 of Prakash, *Marxism and Literary Theory*. There is an annotated bibliography of West's work in Victor N. Paananen, *British Marxist Criticism*. For an unannotated bibliography, with brief introductory remarks, see Alan Munton and Alan Young (compilers), *Seven Writers of the English Left: A Bibliography of Literature and Politics, 1916–1980* (New York: Garland Publishing, 1981). West's work of the 1930s is briefly surveyed in David Margolies, '*Left Review* and Left Literary Culture' and Hanna Behrend, 'An Intellectual Irrelevance? Marxist Literary Criticism in the 1930s'. The posthumous edition of *Crisis and Criticism* which Lawrence and Wishart brought out in 1974 contains a Foreword by Arnold Kettle and an Introduction by Elisabeth West. For an interesting comparison of West and Caudwell, see Christopher Pawling, 'Revisiting the Thirties in the Twenty-First Century: The Radical Aesthetics of West, Caudwell, and Eagleton' in Shuttleworth (ed.), *And in Our Time*. Also worth consulting are the brief remarks on West in Maynard Solomon (ed.), *Marxism and Art: Essays Classic and Contemporary* (Brighton: Harvester Press, 1979) pp. 492–496; Terry Eagleton, *Marxism and Literary Criticism* (London: Methuen, 1983) p. 56; Terry Eagleton and Drew Milne (eds.), *Marxist Literary Theory: A Reader* (Oxford: Blackwell, 1996) p. 103 and Patrick Deane (ed.), *History in Our Hands: A Critical Anthology of Writings on Literature, Culture and Politics from the 1930s* (London: Leicester University Press) pp. 131–132.

40 Caudwell is the only communist critic from the 1930s whose work has given rise to a substantial secondary literature. See, inter alia, David N. Margolies, *The Function of Literature: A Study of Christopher Caudwell's Aesthetics* (London: Lawrence and Wishart, 1969); Christopher Pawling, *Christopher Caudwell: Towards a Dialectical Theory of Literature* (New York: St Martin's Press, 1989); Robert Sullivan, *Christopher Caudwell* (London: Croom Helm, 1987); Francis Mulhern, 'The Marxist Aesthetics of Christopher Caudwell', *New Left Review*, No. 85, May/June 1974, pp. 37–58; Maurice Cornforth, 'Caudwell and Marxism', *The Modern Quarterly*, Vol. 6 No. 1, Winter 1950–51, pp. 16–33; Bounds, *British Communism and the Politics of Literature*, Chapter 5. For a useful survey of writing on Caudwell, see H. Gustav Klaus, 'Changing Attitudes to Caudwell: A Review of Critical Comments on the

Author, 1937–87' in David Margolies and Linden Peach (eds.), *Christopher Caudwell: Marxism and Culture* (London: Goldsmiths College, 1989).

41 For accounts of *Left Review*, see David Margolies, '*Left Review* and Left Literary Theory'; Craig Werner, '*Left Review*' in Alvin Sullivan (ed.), *British Literary Magazines: The Modern Age, 1914–1984* (London, Greenwood Press, 1986); Margot Heinemann, '*Left Review, New Writing* and the Broad Alliance against Fascism' in Edward Timms and Peter Collier (eds.), *Visions and Blueprints: Avant-Garde Culture and Politics in early Twentieth-Century Europe* (Manchester: Manchester University Press, 1988); E.P. Thompson, '*Left Review*' in *Persons and Polemics: Historical Essays* (London: Merlin Press, 1994); Glenn Jordan and Chris Weedon, *Cultural Politics: Class, Gender, Race and the Postmodern World* (Oxford: Blackwell, 1995) Chapter 3; David Margolies (ed.), *Writing the Revolution: Cultural Criticism from Left Review* (London: Pluto Press, 1998). As Margolies points out, *Left Review* replaced the journal *Viewpoint*, two numbers of which appeared in 1934. British communists also published articles on cultural issues in a range of other journals during the 1930s, including *Labour Monthly*, *Life and Letters Today* and the *Modern Quarterly*.

42 Raphael Samuel, 'The Lost World of British Communism', *New Left Review*, No. 154, November/December 1985, p. 21. The *Daily Worker* had changed its name to the *Morning Star* by the time Samuel was writing.

43 For brief accounts of the cultural dimension of the Popular Front policy in Britain, see, inter alia, James Klugmann, 'The Crisis in the Thirties: A View from the Left' in Clark, Heinemann, Margolies and Snee (eds.), *Culture and Crisis in Britain in the Thirties*; Margot Heinemann, 'The People's Front and the Intellectuals' in Jim Fyrth (ed.), *Britain, Fascism and the Popular Front* (London: Lawrence and Wishart, 1985); Margot Heinemann, '*Left Review, New Writing* and the Broad Alliance against Fascism'; Mick Wallis, 'Heirs to the Pageant: Mass Spectacle and the Popular Front' in Croft (ed.), *A Weapon in the Struggle*.

44 For an overview of this body of work, see Bounds, *British Communism and the Politics of Literature*, Chapter 6.

45 The main articles in *Left Review* on the English radical tradition are as follows: Ajax [Montagu Slater], 'Dick Overton, Leveller', *Left Review*, Vol. 1 No. 1, October 1934, pp. 41–44; Edgell Rickword, Untitled review of Jonathan Swift, *Gulliver's Travels and Selected Writings*, *Left Review*, Vol. 1 No. 6, March 1935, pp. 236–237; F.D. Klingender, 'The Crucifix: A Symbol of Mediaeval Class Struggle', *Left Review*, Vol. 2 No. 4, January 1936, pp. 167–173; Randall Swingler, 'The Imputation of Madness: A Study of William Blake and Literary Tradition', *Left Review*, Vol. 3 No. 1, February 1937, pp. 21–28; T.A. Jackson, 'Dickens, the Radical', *Left Review*, Vol. 3 No. 2, March 1937, pp. 88–95; Alick West, 'The "Poetry" in Poetry' (on Edmund Spenser), *Left Review*, Vol. 3 No. 3, April 1937, pp. 164–168; Samuel Mill, 'The Rebellious Needleman: Tom Paine', *Left Review*, Vol. 3 No. 4, May

1937, pp. 202–207; Rex Warner, 'Jonathan Swift', *Left Review*, Vol. 3 No. 5, June 1937, pp. 266–272; Jack Lindsay, 'William Shakespeare', *Left Review*, Vol. 3 No. 6, July 1937, pp. 333–339; Edgell Rickword, 'John Bunyan', *Left Review*, Vol. 3 No. 12, January 1938, pp. 758–759.

46 For a brief survey of *Our Time*, see Laurence Coupe, 'Our Time' in Sullivan (ed.), *British Literary Magazines*.

47 My account of communist cultural politics in the second half of the 1940s is largely based on Andy Croft, 'Writers, the Communist Party and the Battle of Ideas, 1945–1950'.

48 John Carey, *Original Copy: Selected Reviews and Journalism 1969–1986* (London: Faber, 1987), p. 191.

49 Orwell has probably received more biographical attention than any other modern writer. My brief sketch of his life is based on the following sources, among others: Peter Stansky and William Abrahams, *The Unknown Orwell/Orwell: The Transformation* (Stanford: Stanford University Press, 1994); Peter Lewis, *George Orwell: The Road to 1984* (London: Heinemann, 1981); T.R. Fyvel, *George Orwell: A Personal Memoir* (London: Hutchinson, 1983); Michael Shelden, *Orwell: The Authorised Biography* (London: Heinemann, 1991); Bernard Crick, *George Orwell: A Life*, new edition (Harmondsworth: Penguin, 1992); Stephen Ingle, *George Orwell: A Political Life* (Manchester: Manchester University Press, 1993); Peter Davison, *George Orwell: A Literary Life* (London: Palgrave, 1998); John Newsinger, *Orwell's Politics*; Jeffrey Meyers, *Orwell: Wintry Conscience of a Generation* (New York: W.W. Norton, 2000); D.J. Taylor, *Orwell: The Life* (London: Chatto and Windus, 2003); Gordon Bowker, *George Orwell* (London: Little, Brown, 2003).

50 George Orwell, *The Road to Wigan Pier* (London: Penguin 2001 [1937]), p. 113.

51 George Orwell, 'Such, Such Were the Joys' in *The Complete Works of George Orwell*, Volume 19: *It Is What I Think 1947–1948* (London: Secker and Warburg, 2002) [hereafter CW 19], p. 363.

52 Ibid., p. 383.

53 Ibid., p. 357.

54 Ibid., p. 359.

55 Ibid., p. 359.

56 George Orwell, 'Shooting an Elephant', *New Writing*, No. 2, Autumn 1936. Reprinted in *The Complete Works of George Orwell*, Volume 10: *A Kind of Compulsion 1903–1936* (London: Secker and Warburg, 2000) [hereafter CW 10], p. 504.

57 According to Special Branch papers that were recently deposited in the National Archives in Kew, Orwell approached the CPGB in 1929 and offered to serve as the Paris correspondent for its newspaper *Worker's Life*. His offer was refused. See Stephen Bates, 'Odd Clothes and Unorthodox Views – Why MI5 Spied on Orwell for a Decade', *The Guardian*, September 4 2007.

58 I described Orwell's descent into the underclass as an 'experiment in downward mobility' in the Autumn of 2004. More than three years later I was shocked to discover that Margery Sabin had used exactly the same phrase in an essay on Orwell's non-fiction. Lest I be accused of plagiarism, I had better make it clear that this is a genuine case of Orwellian minds thinking alike. See Margery Sabin, 'The Truths of Experience: Orwell's Nonfiction of the 1930s' in John Rodden (ed.), *The Cambridge Companion to George Orwell* (Cambridge: Cambridge University Press, 2007), p. 46.

59 See Peter Sedgwick, 'George Orwell: International Socialist?', *International Socialism*, No. 37, June–July 1969. Reprinted in Paul Flewers (ed.), *George Orwell: Enigmatic Socialist* (London: Socialist Platform, 2005).

60 Quoted in Sedgwick, 'George Orwell: International Socialist?', p. 14.

61 Orwell, *The Road to Wigan Pier*, p. 108.

62 Ibid., p. 25.

63 Ibid., pp. 30–31.

64 Ibid., p. 161.

65 Ibid., p. 77, p. 80, p. 145. According to Special Branch papers released in 2007, Orwell spoke at communist meetings during his period in the North. These meetings are not recorded in the diary which he kept at the time. See Bates, 'Old Clothes and Unorthodox Views'.

66 Orwell, *The Road to Wigan Pier*, pp. 205–207.

67 There is an especially useful account of Orwell's experiences in Spain in Newsinger, *Orwell's Politics*, Chapter 3.

68 Newsinger, *Orwell's Politics*, p. 50.

69 George Orwell, *Homage to Catalonia* (London: Penguin, 2000) [1938], p. 3.

70 Ibid., p. 3.

71 John Newsinger makes this point in *Orwell's Politics*, p. 64.

72 Bernard Crick, 'George Orwell 1903–1950' in Robert Benewick and Philip Green (eds.), *The Routledge Dictionary of Twentieth-Century Political Thinkers*, second edition (London: Routledge 1998), p. 195.

73 See R.H.S. Crossman, Michael Foot, Ian Mikardo et al., *Keep Left* (London: New Statesman and Nation, 1947), p. 30f. For a brief account of the outlook of the Labour Left in the late 1940s, see Geoffrey Foote, *The Labour Party's Political Thought: A History* (London: Croom Helm, 1985), p. 269f.

74 See Newsinger, *Orwell's Politics*, p. 147f.

75 George Orwell, 'Orwell's Statement on *Nineteen Eighty-Four*' in *The Complete Works of George Orwell*, Volume 20: *Our Job Is To Make Life Worth Living 1949–1950* (London: Secker and Warburg, 2002), p. 134.

76 Saul Bellow, *Mr Sammler's Planet* (New York: Viking Press, 1970). Quoted in Christopher Hitchens, 'George Orwell and the Liberal Experience of Totalitarianism' in Thomas Cushman and John Rodden (eds.), *George Orwell into the Twenty-First Century* (London: Paradigm, 2004), p. 78.

1 The Common People

1 George Orwell, *The Road to Wigan Pier* (London: Penguin, 2001 [1937]), p. 138.
2 Ibid., p. 142.
3 The first writer to draw attention to the element of moral ambiguity in Orwell's outlook was probably Anthony West, who famously argued that Orwell suffered from a 'hidden wound' which caused him to fantasise about the destruction of his own society. See Anthony West, 'Hidden Damage', *New Yorker*, 28 January 1956, pp. 86–92. Reprinted in Jeffrey Meyers (ed.), *George Orwell: The Critical Heritage* (London: Routledge, 1975), pp. 71–79. For a brief summary of West's ideas about Orwell, see John Rodden, *George Orwell: The Politics of Literary Reputation* (London: Transaction, 2003), p. 114. For another unflattering description of Orwell's moral character, see D.S. Savage, 'The Fatalism of George Orwell' in Boris Ford (ed.), *The New Pelican Guide to English Literature*, Volume 8: *From Orwell to Naipaul* (London: Penguin, 1995), pp. 121–137.
4 George Orwell, 'Hop-Picking Diary' in *The Complete Works of George Orwell*, Volume 10: *A Kind of Compulsion 1903–1936*, edited by Peter Davison (London: Secker and Warburg, 2000) [hereafter CW 10], p. 216.
5 Ibid., p. 217.
6 Ibid., p. 226.
7 Ibid., p. 216.
8 George Orwell, 'The Art of Donald McGill', *Horizon*, September 1941. Reprinted in *The Complete Works of George Orwell*, Volume 13: *All Propaganda is Lies 1941–1942*, edited by Peter Davison (London: Secker and Warburg, 2001) [hereafter CW 13], p. 29.
9 George Orwell, *Down and Out in Paris and London* (London: Penguin, 2001 [1933]), p. 202.
10 Ibid., p. 135.
11 Gordon Bowker, *George Orwell* (London: Little, Brown, 2003), p. 2.
12 Orwell, 'Hop-Picking Diary', p. 216. Orwell also described this character in a letter written to Dennis Collings on 27 August 1931. See CW 10, p. 214.
13 Orwell, *Down and Out in Paris and London*, p. 7.
14 Although Orwell portrayed Bozo as a man of unusual spiritual gifts, he clearly felt that many other members of the down-and-out possessed a comparable, though less highly developed, aesthetic sense.
15 Orwell, *Down and Out in Paris and London*, p. 164.
16 Ibid., p. 166.
17 Ibid., p. 167.
18 Keith Alldritt and Patrick Reilly have both made a similar point about the links between Orwell's portrait of Bozo and his later writings on totalitarianism. I had not read their work at the time when I wrote this chapter. See Keith Alldritt, *The Making of George Orwell: An Essay in Literary History* (London: Edward Arnold, 1969), p. 62; Patrick Reilly, '*Nineteen Eighty-Four*:

The Insufficient Self' in Graham Holderness, Bryan Loughrey and Nahem Yousaf (eds.), *George Orwell* (London: Macmillan, 1998), pp. 126–127.

19 The phrase 'the surface of the earth' is taken from George Orwell, 'Why I Write', *Gangrel*, No. 4, Summer 1946. Reprinted in *The Complete Works of George Orwell*, Volume 18: *Smothered Under Journalism 1946* (London: Secker and Warburg, 2001) [hereafter CW 18], pp. 319–320.

20 Orwell, *Down and Out in Paris and London*, p. 191.

21 For the communist contribution to the British Folk Revival, see, inter alia, Gerald Porter, '"The World's Ill-Divided": the Communist Party and Progressive Song' in Andy Croft (ed.), *A Weapon in the Struggle: The Cultural History of the Communist Party in Britain* (London: Pluto, 1998), pp. 171–191.

22 Orwell, *Down and Out in Paris and London*, p. 54.

23 Ibid., pp. 184–185.

24 See Peter Davison's editorial note 'Background to "How the Poor Die"' in CW 18, pp. 455–459.

25 George Orwell, 'How the Poor Die', *Now* [new series], No. 6, November 1946. Reprinted in CW 18, p. 466.

26 Ibid., p. 466.

27 Ibid., p. 466.

28 George Orwell, Review of *Walls Have Mouths* by W.F.R. Macartney, *The Adelphi*, November 1936. Reprinted in CW 10, pp. 514–515. McCartney's book was published by Gollancz in 1936 and issued in a Left-Book-Club edition.

29 H. Gustav Klaus, 'Introduction' in H. Gustav Klaus (ed.), *Tramps, Workmates and Revolutionaries: Working-Class Stories of the 1920s* (London: Journeyman Press, 2003), p. 3. It should be noted that Klaus would *not* include Orwell in the tradition of tramp-writing to which he draws attention, primarily because Orwell was from a different class to the other authors and tended to portray tramps more negatively.

30 Jack Common, 'Jack Common's Recollections' in Audrey Coppard and Bernard Crick (eds.), *Orwell Remembered* (London: Ariel Books, 1984), p. 139.

31 Orwell, *The Road to Wigan Pier*, p. 143.

32 Ibid., p. 144.

33 George Orwell, *Homage to Catalonia* (London: Penguin, 2000 [1938]), p. 2.

34 Orwell described the circumstances in which he changed his mind about the war in 'My Country Right or Left', *Folios of New Writing*, No. 2, Autumn 1940. Reprinted in *The Complete Works of George Orwell*, Volume 12: *A Patriot After All 1940–1941*, edited by Peter Davison (London: Secker and Warburg, 2000) [hereafter CW 12], pp. 269–272.

35 George Orwell, 'Our Opportunity', *The Left News*, No. 55, January 1941. Reprinted in CW 12, p. 346.

36 George Orwell, *The Lion and the Unicorn: Socialism and the English Genius* (London: Secker and Warburg, 1941). Reprinted in CW 12, p. 392.

37 Georgi Dimitrov, *The Working Class Against Fascism* (London: Martin Lawrence, 1935), p. 10.
38 For a brief account of the way that British fascists invoked the Elizabethan age as a means of legitimising their political ambitions, see Richard Thurlow, *Fascism in Britain: From Oswald Mosley's Blackshirts to the National Front*, revised edition (London: I.B.Tauris, 1998), pp. 120–121.
39 Dimitrov, *The Working Class Against Fascism*, p. 70.
40 Edgell Rickword, 'Introduction: On English Freedom' in Edgell Rickword and Jack Lindsay (eds.), *Spokesmen for Liberty: A Record of English Democracy Through Twelve Centuries* (London: Lawrence and Wishart, 1941), p. xi.
41 Ibid., p. viii.
42 Ibid., p. xii.
43 Ibid., p. ix.
44 Ibid., p. ix.
45 See George Orwell, Review *of The Problem of the Distressed Areas* by Wal Hannington; *Grey Children* by James Hanley; *The Fight for the Charter* by Neil Stewart, *Time and Tide*, 27 November 1937. Reprinted in *The Complete Works of George Orwell*, Volume 11: *Facing Unpleasant Facts 1937–1939* (London: Secker and Warburg, 2000) [hereafter CW 11], pp. 98–99; George Orwell, Review of Christopher Hill (ed.), *The English Revolution: 1640*, *The New Statesman and Nation*, 24 August 1940. Reprinted in CW 12, pp. 244–245. It is interesting to note that Orwell reviewed Hill's book just before he began writing *The Lion and the Unicorn.*
46 See, inter alia, Orwell, 'Inside the Whale' in CW 12, p. 108.
47 Orwell, *The Lion and the Unicorn* in CW 12, pp. 394–395.
48 Ibid., p. 392.
49 Ibid., p. 395.
50 Ibid., p. 394.
51 George Orwell, *The English People* (London: Collins, 1947). Reprinted in *The Complete Works of George Orwell*, Volume 16: *I Have Tried to Tell the Truth 1943–1944* (London: Secker and Warburg, 2001) [hereafter CW 16], p. 205.
52 Orwell, *Homage to Catalonia*, p. 187.
53 Orwell, *The Lion and the Unicorn*, p. 396.
54 Ibid., p. 397.
55 Ibid., p. 397.
56 Ibid., p. 432.
57 *The English People* was written in 1943 but not published until 1947.
58 Orwell, 'My Country Right or Left', p. 272.
59 Orwell, *The English People*, p. 210.
60 Ibid., p. 222.
61 George Orwell, 'Introduction' to George Orwell and Reginald Reynolds (eds.), *British Pamphleteers*, Volume 1: *From the Sixteenth Century to the French Revolution* (London: Allan Wingate, 1948). Reprinted in *The Complete Works*

of George Orwell, Volume 19: *It Is What I Think 1947–1948* (London: Secker and Warburg, 2002), p. 109.

62 Ibid., p. 109.

63 Orwell, *The Lion and the Unicorn*, p. 393.

64 It should nevertheless be pointed out that Orwell did not endorse the English suspicion of the intellect without qualification. In *The English People* he argued that '…they [the English] must get rid of their downright contempt for "cleverness"', though even there he acknowledged that 'They will always prefer instinct to logic, and character to intelligence.' See CW 16, p. 227.

65 The phrase 'diagnostician of the left's ills' is taken from Alex Zwerdling, *Orwell and the Left* (London: Yale University Press, 1974), p. 5.

66 For Orwell's attitude towards science and technology, see, inter alia, Steven Edelheit, *Dark Prophecies* (New York: Revisionist Press, 1979); Peter Huber, *Orwell's Revenge: The 1984 Palimpsest* (New York: The Free Press, 1994), pp. 67–75. Huber's account is especially insightful.

67 For the history of the SRS movement, see, inter alia, Gary Werskey, *The Visible College: A Collective Biography of British Scientists and Socialists of the 1930s* (London: Free Association Books, 1988).

68 This paragraph summarises the argument of J.D. Bernal, *The Social Function of Science* (London: Routledge, 1939). Bernal's own summary of the argument is contained in his essay 'Science and Civilisation' in C. Day Lewis (ed.), *The Mind in Chains: Socialism and the Cultural Revolution* (London: Frederick Muller, 1937). For a useful overview of 'Bernalism', see Edwin A. Roberts, *The Anglo-Marxists: A Study in Ideology and Culture* (Oxford: Rowman and Littlefield, 1997), pp. 156–178.

69 Orwell, *The Road to Wigan Pier*, p. 180.

70 Ibid., pp. 185–186.

71 Ibid., p. 107.

72 For Woodcock's account of Orwell's views on education, see George Woodcock, *The Crystal Spirit: A Study of George Orwell* (London: Fourth Estate, 1984), pp. 217–219.

73 Orwell, *The English People*, pp. 224–225.

74 George Orwell, Letter to Ritchie Calder in *The Complete Works of George Orwell*, Volume 14: *Keeping Our Little Corner Clean 1942–1943* (London: Secker and Warburg, 2001), p. 51. Quoted in Huber, *Orwell's Revenge*, p. 72.

75 J. Stewart Cook's letter to *Tribune* is reproduced in *The Complete Works of George Orwell*, Volume 17: *I Belong To The Left 1945* (London: Secker and Warburg, 2001) [hereafter CW 17], pp. 317–318.

76 George Orwell, 'What is Science?', *Tribune*, 26 October 1945. Reprinted in CW 17, p. 324.

77 Orwell, *The Lion and the Unicorn*, p. 427.

78 See George Orwell, Review of *The Fate of the Middle Classes* by Alec Brown, *New English Weekly*, 30 April 1936. Reprinted in CW 10, p. 477; Review of

The Fate of the Middle Classes by Alec Brown, *The Adelphi*, May 1936. Reprinted in CW 10, p. 478.

79 George Orwell, Review of *The Novel To-Day* by Philip Henderson, *New English Weekly*, 31 December 1936. Reprinted in CW 10, p. 534.

80 Alec Brown, Contribution to 'Controversy: Writers' International', *Left Review*, Vol. 1 No. 3, December 1934, p. 77.

81 Alec Brown, *The Fate of the Middle Classes* (London, Gollancz, 1936), p. 99f.

82 Ibid., p. 71.

83 Orwell, *The Lion and the Unicorn*, p. 401.

84 Ibid., p. 402.

85 Ibid., p. 403.

86 Ibid., p. 407.

87 Ibid., p. 407.

88 Ibid., p. 408.

89 H.G. Wells, *Experiment in Autobiography* (London: Gollancz, 1934), p. 17. Quoted in Alec Brown, *The Fate of the Middle Classes*, p. 14.

90 Brown, *The Fate of the Middle Classes*, p. 31.

91 Orwell, CW 10, p. 478.

92 George Orwell, 'Wells, Hitler and the World State', *Horizon*, August 1941. Reprinted in CW 12, p. 538.

93 Ibid., pp. 538–539.

94 Ibid., p. 540.

95 Ibid., p. 540.

96 Ibid., p. 539.

2 The Politics of Mass Communication

1 There has been surprisingly little critical writing on Orwell's ideas about popular culture. See, however, John Coleman, 'The Critic of Popular Culture' in Miriam Gross (ed.), *The World of George Orwell* (London: Weidenfeld and Nicolson, 1971); William T. Ross, 'The Political Basis of Orwell's Criticism of Popular Culture' in Courtney T. Wemyss and Alexej Ugrinsky (eds.), *George Orwell* (New York: Greenwood Press, 1987).

2 See, inter alia, John Strachey, *Literature and Dialectical Materialism* (New York: Covici Friede, 1934); Douglas Garman 'What?...The Devil?', *Left Review*, Vol. 1 No. 1, October 1934, pp. 34–36; Christopher Caudwell, *Studies in a Dying Culture* (London: John Lane The Bodley Head, 1938).

3 For the relationship between British modernism and the politics of the *fascisant* right, see, inter alia, John Harrison, *The Reactionaries* (London: Gollancz, 1967).

4 See, in particular, T.S. Eliot, 'Tradition and the Individual Talent' in *Selected Prose of T.S. Eliot*, edited by Frank Kermode (London: Faber and Faber, 1985).

5 Garman, 'What?...The Devil?', p. 36.

6 George Orwell, 'Boys' Weeklies' in *Inside the Whale and Other Essays* (London: Gollancz, 1940). Reprinted in *The Complete Works of George Orwell*, Volume 12: *A Patriot After All 1940–1941* (London: Secker and Warburg, 2000) [hereafter CW 12], p. 62.
7 Ibid., p. 61.
8 Ibid., p. 65.
9 Ibid., p. 66.
10 Ibid., p. 66.
11 Ibid., p. 67.
12 Ibid., p. 64.
13 Ibid., p. 64.
14 Ibid., p. 60.
15 Ibid., p. 74.
16 Orwell did not make this point explicitly but strongly implied it when he contrasted the main national stereotypes to be found in boys' comics: 'FRENCHMAN: Excitable. Wears beard, gesticulates wildly. SPANIARD, MEXICAN, etc.: Sinister, treacherous. ARAB, AFGHAN, etc.: Sinister, treacherous. CHINESE: Sinister, treacherous. Wears pigtail. ITALIAN: Excitable. Grinds barrel-organ or carries stiletto. SWEDE, DANE, etc.: Kind-hearted, stupid. NEGRO: Comic, very faithful.' (see 'Boys' Weeklies', p. 66). The point of this passage is surely that stereotypes invariably tend to undermine themselves through sheer repetition.
17 For an introduction to the concept of polysemy and its role in British Cultural Studies, see, inter alia, Graeme Turner, *British Cultural Studies: An Introduction* (London: Unwin Hyman, 1990).
18 Jack Lindsay, *England My England: A Pageant of the English People* (London: Fore Publications, n.d. [1939]), p. 64.
19 Orwell appropriated the idea of 'good bad' art from G.K.Chesterton. See, in particular, George Orwell, 'Good Bad Books', *Tribune*, 2 November 1945. Reprinted in *The Complete Works of George Orwell*, Volume 17: *I Belong to the Left 1945* (London: Secker and Warburg, 2001) [hereafter CW 17].
20 Quoted in George Orwell, 'Rudyard Kipling', *Horizon*, February 1942. Reprinted in *The Complete Works of George Orwell*, Volume, 13: *All Propaganda is Lies 1941–1942* (London: Secker and Warburg) [hereafter CW 13], p. 151.
21 Orwell, 'Rudyard Kipling', p. 153.
22 George Orwell, 'In Defence of P.G. Wodehouse', *The Windmill*, No. 2, July 1945. Reprinted in CW 17, p. 59.
23 See, inter alia, 'As I Please [18]', *Tribune*, 31 March 1944. Reprinted in *The Complete Works of George Orwell*, Volume 16: *I Have Tried to Tell the Truth 1943–1944* (London: Secker and Warburg, 2001) [hereafter CW 16]; 'Revenge is Sour', *Tribune*, 9 November 1945. Reprinted in CW 17. Orwell's belief that the allies should resist the temptation to behave vengefully towards the axis powers was powerfully reinforced towards the end of the war, when he toured Europe as a correspondent for the *Observer.* All his

dispatches from Europe are reproduced in CW 17 and in George Orwell, *Orwell: The Observer Years* (London: Atlantic Books, 2003).

24 See Alick West, 'The Detective Story', *Left Review*, Volume 3 No. 12, January 1938, pp. 707–710; 'The Detective Story – 11', *Left Review*, Vol. 3 No. 13, February 1938, pp. 795–798.

25 For a useful overview of left-wing attitudes towards detective fiction in the Britain of the 1930s, see Chris Hopkins, 'Leftists and Thrillers: The Politics of a Thirties Sub-Genre' in Antony Shuttleworth (ed.), *And in Our Time: Vision, Revision, and British Writing of the 1930s* (Lewisburg: Bucknell University Press, 2003).

26 West, 'The Detective Story', p. 707.

27 West, 'The Detective Story – 11', p. 796.

28 Ibid., p. 796.

29 Ibid., p. 797.

30 Ibid., p. 798.

31 Ibid., p. 796.

32 George Orwell, 'The Detective Story' [Grandeur et décadence du roman policier anglais], *Fontaine*, Nos. 37–40, 1944. Reprinted in an English translation in *The Complete Works of George Orwell, Volume 15: Two Wasted Years 1943* (London: Secker and Warburg, 2001) [hereafter CW 15], p. 317.

33 George Orwell, 'Raffles and Miss Blandish', *Horizon*, October 1944/*Politics*, November 1944. Reprinted in CW 16, p. 352.

34 Orwell, 'The Detective Story', p. 317.

35 Orwell, 'Raffles and Miss Blandish', p. 353.

36 Ibid., p. 353.

37 The details of Orwell's semi-rural boyhood in Oxfordshire were vividly and movingly evoked in the 1970s by his childhood friend Jacintha Buddicom. Buddicom's charming descriptions of school holidays devoted to fishing, shooting and rambling in the sun-drenched countryside remind us that Orwell's formative years were not entirely clouded by misery. See Jacintha Buddicom, 'The Young Eric' in Gross (ed.), *The World of George Orwell*; *Eric and Us: A Remembrance of George Orwell* (London: Leslie Unwin, 1974). For a recent account of Orwell's yearning for Edwardian England, see Christine Berberich, 'A Revolutionary in Love with the 1900s: Orwell in Defence of "Old England"' in Alberto Lázaro (ed.), *The Road from George Orwell: His Achievement and Legacy* (Oxford: Peter Lang, 2001).

38 West, 'The Detective Story – 11', p. 797.

39 Orwell, 'Raffles and Miss Blandish', p. 354.

40 Ibid., p. 350.

41 Ibid., p. 350.

42 For Orwell's anti-Americanism and its relation to wider trends among the British intelligentsia of his day, see Dick Hebdige, 'Towards a Cartography of Taste 1935–1962' in Bernard Waites, Tony Bennett and Graham Martin

(eds.), *Popular Culture: Past and Present* (London: Croom Helm in association with the Open University Press, 1982).
43 Orwell, 'Raffles and Miss Blandish', p. 354.
44 See George Orwell, 'Decline of the English Murder', *Tribune*, 15 February 1946. Reprinted in *The Complete Works of George Orwell*, Volume 18: *Smothered Under Journalism 1946* (London: Secker and Warburg, 2001) [hereafter CW 18].
45 The bulk of Orwell's reviews for *Time and Tide* are reproduced in CW 12.
46 George Orwell, 'Pleasure Spots', *Tribune*, 11 January 1946. Reprinted in CW 18, pp. 30–31. For an interesting account of 'Pleasure Spots', see Hebdige, 'Towards a Cartography of Taste', p. 198f.
47 Orwell, 'Boys' Weeklies', p. 76.
48 See, inter alia, Arthur Calder-Marshall, 'The Film Industry' in C. Day Lewis (ed.), *The Mind in Chains: Socialism and the Cultural Revolution* (London: Frederick Muller, 1937). I assess the possible influence of Calder-Marshall's essay on Orwell in Chapter 5.
49 George Orwell, 'Inside the Whale' in *Inside the Whale and Other Essays* (London: Gollancz 1940). Reprinted in CW 12, p. 108.
50 Orwell reviewed two books issued by Mass Observation. See Review of *War Begins at Home*, edited by Tom Harrisson and Charles Madge, *Time and Tide*, 2 March 1940. Reprinted in CW 12; Unsigned Review of *The Pub and the People* by Mass-Observation, *The Listener*, 21 January 1943. Reprinted in *The Complete Works of George Orwell*, Volume 14: *Keeping Our Little Corner Clean 1942–1943* (London: Secker and Warburg, 2001).
51 Charles Madge, 'Press, Radio, and Social Consciousness' in Day Lewis (ed.), *The Mind in Chains*, p. 151.
52 Ibid., p. 152.
53 George Orwell, 'The Art of Donald McGill', *Horizon*, September 1941. Reprinted in CW 13, p. 27.
54 Quoted in ibid., p. 30.
55 Orwell, 'The Art of Donald McGill', p. 27.
56 Richard Rees, *George Orwell: Fugitive from the Camp of Victory* (London: Southern Illinois University Press, 1967 [1962]), p. 7.
57 See V.S. Pritchett, '*The New Statesman & Nation*'s Obituary' in Audrey Coppard and Bernard Crick (eds.), *Orwell Remembered* (London: Ariel Books, 1984).
58 George Orwell, Review of *Byron and the Need of Fatality* by Charles du Bos, translated by Ethel Colburn Mayne, *The Adelphi*, September 1932. Reprinted in *The Complete Works of George Orwell*, Volume 10: *A Kind of Compulsion 1903–1936* (London: Secker and Warburg, 2000), p. 264.
59 George Orwell, *The Lion and the Unicorn: Socialism and the English Genius* (London: Secker and Warburg, 1941). Reprinted in CW 12, p. 404. The italics are Orwell's.

3 Literature and Commitment

1 Edward Upward, 'A Marxist Interpretation of Literature' in C. Day Lewis (ed.), *The Mind in Chains: Socialism and the Cultural Revolution* (London: Frederick Muller, 1937), p. 41.

2 George Orwell, 'Writers and Leviathan', *Politics and Letters*, Summer 1948. Reprinted in *The Complete Works of George Orwell*, Volume 19: *It Is What I Think 1947–1948* (London: Secker and Warburg, 2002) [hereafter CW 19], p. 288.

3 George Orwell, 'Literary Criticism 1: The Frontiers of Art and Propaganda', *The Listener*, 29 May 1941. Reprinted in *The Complete Works of George Orwell*, Volume 12: *A Patriot After All 1940–1941* (London: Secker and Warburg, 2000) [hereafter CW 12), p. 486.

4 George Orwell, Review of *The Development of William Butler Yeats* by V.K. Narayana Menon, *Horizon*, January 1943. Reprinted in *The Complete Works of George Orwell*, Volume 14: *Keeping Our Little Corner Clean 1942–1943* (London: Secker and Warburg, 2001) [hereafter CW 14] p. 279.

5 George Orwell, 'Literary Criticism IV: Literature and Totalitarianism', CW 12. p. 503.

6 Orwell, 'Writers and Leviathan', CW 19, p. 289.

7 George Orwell, 'Authors Deserve a New Deal', *Manchester Evening News*, 5 July 1945. Reprinted in *The Complete Works of George Orwell*, Volume 17: *I Belong To The Left 1945* (London: Secker and Warburg, 2001) [hereafter CW 17], p. 211.

8 Ibid., p. 212. See also Orwell's amusing comparison between the price of books and the price of cigarettes in 'Books *v.* Cigarettes', *Tribune*, 8 February 1946. Reprinted in *The Complete Works of George Orwell*, Volume 18: *Smothered Under Journalism 1946* (London: Secker and Warburg, 2001) [hereafter CW 18], pp. 94–98.

9 I am referring here to the Public Lending Right Bill (1979), which Orwell's friend Michael Foot, in his capacity as Leader of the House of Commons, was partly responsible for guiding onto the statute books. See Michael Foot, *The Uncollected Michael Foot: Essays Old and New 1953–2003* (London: Politico's, 2003), p. 43f.

10 See George Orwell, 'Literary Criticism II: Tolstoy and Shakespeare', *The Listener*, 5 June 1941. Reprinted in CW 12, pp. 491–493.

11 George Orwell, 'Lear, Tolstoy and the Fool', *Polemic*, No. 7, March 1947. Reprinted in CW 19, p. 63.

12 For an insightful account of Orwell's relationship to the art-for-art's-sake movement, see Raymond Williams, *Orwell* (London: Fontana/Collins, 1971), Chapter 3.

13 For Pater's and Wilde's accounts of the nature of art, see, inter alia, Walter Pater, *The Renaissance: Studies in Art and Poetry* (Oxford: Oxford University Press, 1998 [1873]); Oscar Wilde, *Intentions* (London: 1891). Reprinted in *The Complete Works of Oscar Wilde* (Enderby: Blitz Editions, 1990).

14 Oscar Wilde, 'The Decay of Lying' in *The Complete Works of Oscar Wilde*, p. 909.
15 George Orwell, Review of *Personal Record 1928–1939* by Julian Green, *Time and Tide*, 13 April 1940. Reprinted in CW 12, p. 146.
16 George Orwell, *Nineteen Eighty-Four* (London: Penguin, 2000 [1949]), pp. 98–99.
17 Ibid., pp. 153–154.
18 See Edward Aveling and Eleanor Marx Aveling, *Shelley's Socialism* (London: Journeyman Press, 1979 [1888]).
19 For a list of the most important writings from the 1930s on the radical strain in English literature, see the footnotes to the Introduction.
20 George Orwell, 'Charles Dickens' in *Inside the Whale and Other Essays* (London: Gollancz, 1940). Reprinted in CW 12, p. 20.
21 Jackson wrote evocatively about the first half of his life in *Solo Trumpet: Some Memories of Socialist Agitation and Propaganda* (London: Lawrence and Wishart, 1953). For further biographical information, see, inter alia, Stuart Macintyre and Vivien Morton, *T.A. Jackson: A Centenary Appreciation*, Our History pamphlet 73 (London: CPGB History Group, n.d. [1979]); Jonathan Rée, *Proletarian Philosophers: Problems in Socialist Culture in Britain, 1900–1940* (Oxford: Clarendon Press, 1984); Kevin Morgan, 'Jackson, Thomas Alfred (1879–1955)' in *Oxford Dictionary of National Biography* (Oxford: Oxford University Press, 2004) [http://www.oxforddnb.com/view/article/65941].
22 Quoted in T.A. Jackson, *Charles Dickens: The Progress of a Radical* (London: Lawrence and Wishart, 1937), p. 33. For a longer account of Jackson's book, see Philip Bounds, *British Communism and the Politics of Literature, 1928–1939* (London: Merlin Press, 2012), pp. 226–229.
23 For Jackson's account of Dickens's attitude towards children, see *Charles Dickens: The Progress of a Radical*, p. 56f.
24 Orwell, 'Charles Dickens', p. 20.
25 For Jackson's description of Dickens's first period, see *Charles Dickens: The Progress of a Radical*, p. 7f/p. 106f.
26 For Jackson's description of Dickens's second period, see *Charles Dickens: The Progress of a Radical*, p. 7f/p. 111f.
27 For Jackson's description of Dickens's third period, see *Charles Dickens: The Progress of a Radical*, p. 7f/p. 129f.
28 Orwell, 'Charles Dickens', p. 23. It is worth comparing this statement of Orwell's with Jackson's encapsulation of the outlook of Dickens's first period: '...all the preventable ills of the world would be remedied if only men behaved to each other with kindliness, justice, and sympathetic understanding.' (*Charles Dickens: The Progress of a Radical*, p. 109).
29 Orwell, 'Charles Dickens', p. 23.
30 Ibid., p. 23.
31 Ibid., pp. 23–24.

32 Ibid., p. 23.
33 Ibid., p. 23.
34 Ibid., p. 23.
35 See Jackson, *Charles Dickens: The Progress of a Radical*, p. 26f.
36 For Orwell's account of the depiction of revolutionary violence in *A Tale of Two Cities* and *Barnaby Rudge*, see 'Charles Dickens', p. 25f.
37 Orwell, 'Charles Dickens', p. 38.
38 Ibid., p. 30.
39 Ibid., pp. 54–55.
40 See T.A. Jackson, 'The Moscow Trial', *Left Review*, Vol. 3 No. 2, March 1937, pp. 116–118.
41 See Edgell Rickword, Untitled review of Jonathan Swift, *Gulliver's Travels and Selected Writings*, *Left Review*, Vol. 1 No. 6, March 1935, pp. 236–237; Rex Warner, 'Jonathan Swift', *Left Review*, Vol. 3 No. 5, June 1937, pp. 266–272.
42 Rickword, Untitled review of Jonathan Swift, *Gulliver's Travels and Selected Writings*, p. 237.
43 Warner, 'Jonathan Swift', p. 270.
44 George Orwell, 'Politics vs. Literature: An Examination of *Gulliver's Travels*', *Polemic*, No. 5, September–October 1946. Reprinted in CW 18, p. 425.
45 Ibid., p. 422.
46 Ibid., pp. 423–424.
47 Ibid., p. 425.
48 For the anarchist perspective on Orwell, see, inter alia, George Woodcock, 'George Orwell' in *The Writer and Politics* (London: The Porcupine Press, 1948); George Woodcock, *The Crystal Spirit: A Study of George Orwell* (London: Fourth Estate, 1984 [1967]); Nicolas Walter, 'George Orwell: An Accident in Society', *Anarchy: A Journal of Anarchist Ideas*, No. 8, October 1961, pp. 246–255. For a useful overview of anarchist writings on Orwell, see John Rodden, *George Orwell: The Politics of Literary Reputation* (London: Transaction Publishers, 2002), pp. 153–170.
49 Orwell, 'Politics vs. Literature: An Examination of *Gulliver's Travels*', pp. 424–425.
50 George Orwell, 'Imaginary Interview: George Orwell and Jonathan Swift', BBC African Service, 6 November 1942. Published in *The Listener* under the title 'Too Hard on Humanity', 26 November 1942. Reprinted in CW 14, p. 157.
51 Orwell, 'Politics vs. Literature: An Examination of *Gulliver's Travels*', p. 426.
52 Ibid., p. 431.
53 Ibid., p. 430.
54 George Orwell, '*Macbeth* by William Shakespeare, Adapted and Introduced by George Orwell', BBC Eastern Service, 17 October 1943. Reprinted in *The Complete Works of George Orwell*, Volume 15: *Two Wasted Years 1943* (London: Secker and Warburg, 2001) [hereafter CW 15], p. 281.

55 George Orwell, 'Charles Reade', *The New Statesman and Nation*, 17 August 1940. Reprinted in CW 12, p. 232.
56 George Orwell, '"Calling All Students," 5: George Bernard Shaw, *Arms and the Man*', Broadcast on the BBC Asian Service, 22 January 1943. First published in *Books and Authors*, BBC Pamphlet No. 2 (Bombay: Oxford University Press, 1946). Reprinted in CW 14.
57 George Orwell, 'Tobias Smollett: Scotland's Best Novelist', *Tribune*, 22 September 1944. Reprinted in *The Complete Works of George Orwell*, Vol 16: *I Have Tried to Tell the Truth 1943–1944* [hereafter CW 16] (London: Secker and Warburg, 2001), p. 408.
58 George Orwell, 'Talk on *Lady Windermere's Fan* by Oscar Wilde', BBC Eastern Service, 21 November 1943. CW 15.
59 George Orwell, '*The Ways of All Flesh* by Samuel Butler', BBC Home Service, Talk for Schools, 15 June 1945. CW 17. See also '*Erewhon* by Samuel Butler', BBC Home Service, Talk for Schools, 8 June 1945. CW 17.
60 George Orwell, 'Funny, But Not Vulgar', *Leader Magazine*, 28 July 1945. Reprinted in CW 16, p. 484.
61 George Orwell, 'Nonsense Poetry: *The Lear Omnibus* edited by R.L. Megroz', *Tribune*, 21 December 1945. Reprinted in CW 17.
62 Orwell, 'Funny, But Not Vulgar', p. 483.
63 Orwell, 'Nonsense Poetry: *The Lear Omnibus* edited by R.L. Megroz', p. 453.
64 George Orwell, 'Mark Twain – The Licensed Jester', *Tribune*, 26 November 1943. Reprinted in CW 16, p. 5.
65 Ibid., p. 5.
66 Ibid., p. 5.
67 See, inter alia, John Strachey, *The Coming Struggle for Power* (London, Victor Gollancz, 1932); John Strachey, *Literature and Dialectical Materialism* (New York: Covici Friede, 1934); John Cornford, 'The Class Front in Modern Art', *The Student Vanguard*, December 1933. Reprinted in Patrick Deane (ed.), *History in our Hands: A Critical Anthology of Writings on Literature, Culture and Politics from the 1930s* (London: Leicester University Press, 1998); Montagu Slater, 'The Spirit of the Age in Paint' in Edgell Rickword (ed.), *Scrutinies*, Volume 2 (London: Wishart & Company, 1931).
68 Orwell attacked Mirsky's account of the British modernists in *The Road to Wigan Pier* (London: Penguin, 2001 [1937]), p. 168f. For his comments on Henderson, see 'Review of *The Novel To-Day* by Philip Henderson', *New English Weekly*, 31 December 1936. Reprinted in *The Complete Works of George Orwell*, Volume 10: *A Kind of Compulsion 1903–1936* (London: Secker and Warburg, 2000) [hereafter CW 10], pp. 532–534.
69 George Orwell, 'Inside the Whale' in *Inside the Whale and Other Essays*. Reprinted in CW 12, pp. 97–98.
70 Ibid., p. 96. See also Orwell, 'The Re-discovery of Europe', *The Listener*, 19 March 1942. Reprinted in *The Complete Works of George Orwell*, Volume 13: *All Propaganda is Lies 1941–1942*.

71 Orwell, 'Inside the Whale', p. 97.
72 See CW 10, pp. 532–534.
73 See, inter alia, Edgell Rickword, Untitled review of *Literature in a Changing Civilisation* by Philip Henderson, *Left Review*, Vol. 2 No. 1, October 1935, pp. 41–44; Alick West, 'Enthusiastic But Still Lacking Understanding' (review of *Literature in a Changing Civilisation* by Philip Henderson), *Labour Monthly*, Vol. XVII No. 2, November 1935, pp. 708–710; Alick West, '*The Novel To-Day*' (review of *The Novel To-Day* by Philip Henderson), *Labour Monthly*, Vol. XIX No. 7, July 1937, p. 452.
74 Philip Henderson, *The Novel Today: Studies in Contemporary Attitudes* (London: John Lane The Bodley Head, 1936), p. 53f.
75 Ibid., p. 74.
76 Ibid., p. 88.
77 Ibid., p. 82. The phrase 'aesthetic stasis' was quoted by Henderson from Joyce's famous disquisition on the nature of art in *Portrait of the Artist as a Young Man*.
78 Henderson, *The Novel Today*, p. 19.
79 Orwell, 'Inside the Whale', p. 97.
80 Orwell, Review of *The Development of William Butler Yeats* by V.K. Narayana Menon, CW 14, pp. 280–281.
81 Ibid., p. 282.
82 See Gordon Bowker, *George Orwell* (London: Little, Brown, 2003), p. 56.
83 Orwell asked Rayner Heppenstall to draw up a horoscope for his adopted son Richard in a letter written on 21 July 1944. See CW 16, p. 295. His review of Sacheverell Sitwell's book *Poltergeists* appeared in *Horizon* in September 1940. See CW 12, pp. 246–248. He subsequently described some of his own experiences of the paranormal in a letter to Sitwell written on 6 July 1940 (CW 12, pp. 208–209). For his account of the life of Daniel Dunglas Home, see 'Mr Sludge' (review of *Heyday of a Wizard* by Jean Burton), *The Observer*, 6 June 1948. Reprinted in CW 19, pp. 388–390.
84 Orwell, 'Inside the Whale', p. 86.
85 Ibid., p. 89.
86 Ibid., p. 108.
87 Ibid., pp. 110–111.
88 Ibid., p. 87.
89 See, inter alia, Alick West's discussion of Joyce's *Ulysses* in *Crisis and Criticism* (London: Lawrence and Wishart, 1937).
90 Karl Radek, 'Contemporary World Literature And The Tasks Of Proletarian Art' in Maxim Gorky, Karl Radek, Nikolai Bukharin, A.A. Zhdanov et al, *Soviet Writers' Congress 1934: The Debate on Socialist Realism and Modernism in the Soviet Union* (London: Lawrence and Wishart, 1977), p. 153.
91 Ibid., p. 153.
92 Orwell, 'Inside The Whale', p. 103.

93 W.H. Auden, 'Spain' in Valentine Cunningham (ed.), *The Penguin Book of Spanish Civil War Verse* (Harmondsworth: Penguin, 1980), p. 99.
94 Ibid., p. 100. Quoted in Orwell, 'Inside the Whale', p. 103.
95 Orwell, 'Inside the Whale', pp. 103–104.
96 Cyril Connolly, *Enemies of Promise* (London: Routledge, 1938). Quoted in Orwell, 'Inside the Whale', p. 104.
97 Orwell, 'Inside the Whale', p. 100.
98 In the course of his attack on Auden, Orwell wrote 'Take, for instance, a poem like "You're leaving now, and it's up to you boys". It is pure scoutmaster…' As Peter Davison points out in his editorial notes to 'Inside the Whale' in Volume 12 of the *Complete Works*, 'You're leaving now, and it's up to you boys' is actually the first line of C. Day Lewis's 'Poem No. 10' from his collection *The Magnetic Mountain* (1933). See CW 12, p. 113.
99 Edgell Rickword, 'Straws for the Wary: Antecedents to Fascism', *Left Review*, Vol. 1 No. 1, October 1934, p. 20.
100 Ibid., p. 22.
101 Ibid., p. 25.
102 George Orwell, 'Gandhi in Mayfair' (review of *Beggar My Neighbour* by Lionel Fielden), *Horizon*, September 1943. Reprinted in CW 15, p. 209. Fielden's response to Orwell was published in *Horizon* in November 1943. It has now been reprinted in CW 15, pp. 216–221.
103 Orwell, *The Road to Wigan Pier*, p. 167f.
104 See Dmitri Mirsky, *The Intelligentsia of Great Britain*, translated by Alec Brown (London: Gollancz, 1935), Chapter 6.

4 Reforming English Culture

1 See George Orwell and Desmond Hawkins, 'The Proletarian Writer', *The Listener*, 19 December 1940. Reprinted in *The Complete Works of George Orwell*, Volume 12: *A Patriot After All 1940–1941* [hereafter CW 12] (London: Secker and Warburg, 2000).
2 For a useful introduction to Orwell's ideas about language, see Roger Fowler, *The Language of George Orwell* (London: Macmillan, 1995), Chapter 3.
3 See 'Appendix 11: Books Owned by Orwell in 1950' in *The Complete Works of George Orwell*, Volume 20: *Our Job Is To Make Life Worth Living 1949–1950* (London: Secker and Warburg, 2002), p. 289.
4 See Christopher Caudwell, *Illusion and Reality: A Study in the Sources of Poetry* (London: Lawrence and Wishart, 1977 [1937]), Chapter 1.
5 Ibid., p. 153f.
6 George Orwell, 'New Words', CW 12, p. 128.
7 Ibid., p. 130.
8 Ibid., p. 131.
9 Ibid., p. 133.
10 Ibid., pp. 133–134.

11 See Siegfried Kracauer, *Theory of Film: The Redemption of Physical Reality* (Oxford: Oxford University Press, 1960).
12 Fowler, *The Language of George Orwell*, p. 33.
13 Orwell, 'New Words', p. 135.
14 Ibid., pp. 134–135.
15 See Alick West, *Crisis and Criticism and Selected Literary Essays* (London: Lawrence and Wishart, 1975), p. 75f.
16 Ibid., p. 76.
17 Orwell, 'New Words', p. 134.
18 Ibid., p. 129.
19 Ibid., p. 129.
20 Ibid., pp. 132–133.
21 George Orwell, 'Politics and the English Language', *Horizon*, April 1946. Reprinted in *The Complete Works of George Orwell*, Volume 17: *I Belong to the Left 1945* (London: Secker and Warburg, 2001) [hereafter CW 17], p. 428.
22 Ibid., p. 428.
23 Ibid., p. 421.
24 Ibid., pp. 423–425.
25 Ibid., p. 424.
26 For an interesting discussion of the relationship between Orwell's ideas about language and the main theoretical trends in modern linguistics, see John Wesley Young, *Totalitarian Language: Orwell's Newspeak and its Nazi and Communist Antecedents* (London: University of Virginia Press, 1991).
27 Orwell, 'Politics and the English Language', CW 17, p. 430.
28 Ibid., p. 430.
29 George Orwell, *The English People* (London: Collins, 1947). Reprinted in *The Complete Works of George Orwell*, Volume 16: *I Have Tried to Tell the Truth 1943–1944* [hereafter CW 16] (London: Secker and Warburg, 2001), p. 219.
30 Ibid., p. 219.
31 Ibid., p. 220.
32 Ibid., p. 221.
33 See William Wordsworth, 'Preface to the Second Edition of *Lyrical Ballads*' in Hazard Adams (ed.), *Critical Theory Since Plato* (New York: Harcourt Brace, 1971).
34 Alec Brown, Contribution to 'Controversy: Writers' International', *Left Review*, Vol. 1 No. 3, December 1934, p. 76.
35 Ibid., p. 77.
36 Hugh MacDiarmid, Contribution to 'Controversy: Writers' International', *Left Review*, Vol. 1 No. 5, February 1935, p. 182.
37 Montagu Slater, Contribution to 'Controversy: Writers' International', *Left Review*, Vol. 1 No. 4, January 1935, p. 127.
38 Douglas Garman, Contribution to 'Controversy: Writers' International', *Left Review*, Vol. 1 No. 5, February 1935, p. 181.

39 J.M. Hay, Contribution to 'Controversy: Writers' International', *Left Review*, Vol. 1 No. 6, March 1935, p. 222.
40 Ibid., p. 221.
41 Ralph Fox, *The Novel and the People* (London: Cobbett Press, 1948 [1937]), p. 137.
42 Ibid., p. 134.
43 Ibid., pp. 133–134.
44 Fox's actual point was that more research needed to be done to establish whether the King James Bible was indeed indebted to the language of the lower classes; but he strongly implied that a considerable debt existed.
45 Fox, *The Novel and the People*, p. 138.
46 Orwell, *The English People*, p. 221.
47 See George Orwell, 'Propaganda and Demotic Speech', *Persuasion*, Summer Quarter 1944, Vol. 2 No. 2. Reprinted in CW 16, pp. 310–316.
48 George Orwell, '"Voice," 3: A Magazine Programme' in *The Complete Works of George Orwell*, Volume 14: *Keeping Our Little Corner Clean 1942–1943* (London: Secker and Warburg, 2001), p. 77.
49 The typescript for the programme on Oriental influences has been lost. The other five scripts are reproduced in Volumes 13 and 14 of *The Complete Works of George Orwell.*
50 George Orwell, '"Voice," 1: A Magazine Programme' in *The Complete Works of George Orwell, Volume 13: All Propaganda is Lies 1941–1942* (London: Secker and Warburg, 2001) [hereafter CW 13], p. 464.
51 George Orwell, 'Review of *Noblesse Oblige – Another Letter to Another Son* by James Agate; *Perspective for Poetry* by Jack Lindsay', *Manchester Evening News*, 30 November 1944. Reprinted in CW 16, p. 477. For an overview of Lindsay's conception of culture as a form of 'productive activity', see Jack Lindsay, 'Symmetry, Asymmetry, Structure, Dominance' in Victor N. Paananen (ed.), *British Marxist Criticism* (New York, Garland Publishing, 2000). This chapter was originally published in Lindsay's book *The Crisis in Marxism* (1981).
52 Orwell, CW 16, p. 478.
53 Ibid., p. 478.
54 Ibid., p. 478.
55 George Orwell, 'The Prevention of Literature', *Polemic*, January 1946. Reprinted in CW 17, p. 377.
56 Ibid., p. 377.
57 Ibid., p. 377.
58 George Orwell, 'Modern English Verse' in *The Complete Works of George Orwell*, Volume 15: *Two Wasted Years 1943*, p. 134.
59 George Orwell, *Poetry and the Microphone* (London: The New Saxon Pamphlet, 1945). Reprinted in CW 17, p. 76.
60 Ibid., p. 77.
61 Ibid., p. 78.

62 Ibid., p. 79.
63 Ibid., p. 79.
64 Ibid., pp. 79–80.
65 See, inter alia, Raymond Williams, 'Conclusion' in *Culture and Society 1780–1950* (Harmondsworth: Pelican, 1979 [1958]); Hans Magnus Enzensberger, 'Constituents of a Theory of the Media', *New Left Review*, No. 64, November–December 1970, pp. 13–36.
66 Orwell, *Poetry and the Microphone*, p. 80.
67 Ibid., p. 78.

5 The Totalitarian Future

1 Bernard Crick, *George Orwell: A Life*, new edition (London: Penguin, 1992), p. 570. It is only fair to point out that Crick later revised his opinion of *Nineteen Eighty-Four*, insisting that 'it is neither a plausible theoretical model of a totalitarian system, nor intended to be'. See Crick, p. 603.
2 I am not suggesting that *Nineteen Eighty-Four* was *simply* an attack on the USSR. Orwell was clearly seeking to satirise totalitarianism in general, as well as certain emergent features of Western culture (e.g. the rise of a hedonistic popular culture). However, there is no doubt that the book's primary target was Stalinism.
3 There is now a very large secondary literature on Orwell's understanding of totalitarianism. Among the most useful guides to *Nineteen Eighty-Four* are the following: Carl Freedman, 'Antinomies of *Nineteen Eighty-Four*' in Bernard Oldsey and Joseph Browne (eds.), *Critical Essays on George Orwell* (Boston MA: G.K. Hall, 1986); Irving Howe (ed.), *Orwell's Nineteen Eighty-Four: Text, Sources, Criticism* (New York: Harcourt Brace, 1963); Peter Huber, *Orwell's Revenge: The 1984 Palimpsest* (New York: The Free Press, 1994); William Steinhoff, *The Road to 1984* (London: Weidenfeld and Nicolson, 1975); John Wesley Young, *Totalitarian Language: Orwell's Newspeak and its Nazi and Communist Antecedents* (London: University of Virginia Press, 1991); Michael P. Zuckert, 'Orwell's Hopes, Orwell's Fears: *1984* as a Theory of Totalitarianism' in Robert L. Savage, James Combs and Dan Nimmo (eds.), *The Orwellian Moment: Hindsight and Foresight in the Post-1984 World* (Fayetteville: The University of Arkansas Press, 1989).
4 George Orwell, 'As I Please', *Tribune*, 29 November 1946. Reprinted in *The Complete Works of George Orwell*, Volume 18: *Smothered Under Journalism 1946* (London: Secker and Warburg, 2001) [hereafter CW 18], p. 504.
5 George Orwell, 'Notes on the Way', *Time and Tide*, 30 March and 6 April 1940. Reprinted in *The Complete Works of George Orwell*, Volume 12: *A Patriot After All 1940–1941* (London Secker and Warburg, 200) [hereafter CW 12], p. 125.
6 Ibid., p. 125. Although Orwell was ostensibly summarising the argument of Malcolm Muggeridge's book *The Thirties* in this passage, he strongly implied that he agreed with Muggeridge's point.

7 George Orwell, *Nineteen Eighty-Four* (London: Penguin, 2000 [1949]), p. 215.

8 For a fine introduction to Trotsky's account of the degeneration of the world communist movement, see Perry Anderson, 'Trotsky's Interpretation of Stalinism' in Tariq Ali (ed.), *The Stalinist Legacy: Its Impact on Twentieth-Century World Politics* (London: Penguin, 1984).

9 See Isaac Deutscher, '*1984* – The Mysticism of Cruelty' in Howe (ed.), *Orwell's Nineteen Eighty-Four.*

10 George Orwell, Review of *Workers' Front* by Fenner Brockway, *New English Weekly*, 17 February 1938. Reprinted in *The Complete Works of George Orwell*, Volume 11: *Facing Unpleasant Facts 1937–1939* (London: Secker and Warburg, 2000) [hereafter CW 11], pp. 123–124.

11 George Orwell, 'Spilling the Spanish Beans', *New English Weekly*, 29 July and 2 September 1937. Reprinted in CW 11, p. 44.

12 See D.S. Savage, 'The Fatalism of George Orwell' in Boris Ford (ed.), *The New Pelican Guide to English Literature*, Volume 8: *From Orwell to Naipaul* (London: Penguin, 1995), p. 133.

13 Georgi Dimitrov, *The Working Class Against Fascism* (London: Martin Lawrence, 1935) p. 10.

14 George Orwell, 'Abstracts of Reports on the Spanish Civil War from the *Daily Worker* and the *News Chronicle*, 1936–37' in CW 11, p. 291.

15 Cockburn's reports for the *Daily Worker* are collected in Claud Cockburn, *Cockburn in Spain: Despatches from the Spanish Civil War*, edited by James Pettifer (London: Lawrence and Wishart, 1986). For Cockburn's more considered view of the Spanish Civil War, see Claud Cockburn, 'Spanish Tragedy', *Tribune*, 13 July 1956. Reprinted in Elizabeth Thomas (ed.), *Tribune 21* (London: MacGibbon and Kee, 1958); Claud Cockburn, *I, Claud... The Autobiography of Claud Cockburn* (Harmondsworth: Penguin, 1967), p. 161f.

16 George Orwell, *Homage to Catalonia* (London: Penguin, 2000 [1938]), p. 233f.

17 Frank Pitcairn [Claud Cockburn], *Reporter in Spain* (London: Lawrence and Wishart, 1936), pp. 13–14.

18 See John Strachey, *The Coming Struggle for Power* (London: Gollancz, 1932), p. 261f.

19 George Orwell, 'Looking Back on the Spanish War', *New Road*, June 1943 (?). Reprinted in *The Complete Works of George Orwell*, Volume 13: *All Propaganda is Lies 1941–1942* (London: Secker and Warburg, 2001), p. 503.

20 Orwell, *Nineteen Eighty-Four*, p. 216.

21 Ibid., pp. 4–5.

22 Ibid., p. 6.

23 Ibid., pp. 220–221.

24 Ibid., p. 221.

25 Ibid., p. 223.

26 Orwell outlined his conception of Newspeak in an appendix to *Nineteen Eighty-Four* entitled 'The Principles of Newspeak'. See ibid., p. 312f.

27 Orwell, *Nineteen Eighty-Four*, pp. 196–198.
28 George Orwell, 'Raffles and Miss Blandish', *Horizon*, October 1944; *Politics*, November 1944. Reprinted in *The Complete Works of George Orwell*, Volume 16: *I HaveTried to Tell the Truth 1943–1944* (London: Secker and Warburg, 2001) [hereafter CW 16], p. 354.
29 Orwell, *Nineteen Eighty-Four*, p. 261.
30 Ibid., p. 278.
31 See, in particular, George Orwell, 'The Prevention of Literature', *Polemic*, January 1946; *The Atlantic Monthly*, March 1947. Reprinted in *The Complete Works of George Orwell*, Volume 17: *I Belong to the Left 1945* (London: Secker and Warburg, 2001).
32 Orwell, *Nineteen Eighty-Four*, p. 136.
33 For other accounts of the Orwell/Swingler exchange, see Andy Croft, *Comrade Heart: A Life of Randall Swingler* (Manchester: Manchester University Press, 2003) p. 183f; John Newsinger, *Orwell's Politics* (Basingstoke: Palgrave, 2001), p. 144f.
34 Orwell, CW 17, p. 372.
35 Randall Swingler, 'The Right to Free Expression', *Polemic*, No. 5, September–October 1946. Reprinted in George Orwell, CW 18, p. 432. Astonishingly enough, Swingler argued that the belief that 'writers must earn the right to intellectual freedom' was also held by Orwell!
36 Swingler, 'The Right to Free Expression', p. 432.
37 Ibid., p. 433.
38 Orwell, Annotations to Randall Swingler's 'The Right to Free Expression', CW 18, p. 440
39 Ibid., p. 439.
40 Anon [John Lewis], 'Editorial', *The Modern Quarterly*, new series, Vol. 1 No. 1, December 1945, p. 2.
41 Ibid., p. 2.
42 See George Orwell, 'As I Please', *Tribune*, 16 June 1944. Reprinted in CW 16, p. 258f.
43 Anon [John Lewis], 'Editorial', p. 3.
44 See J.D. Bernal, 'Belief and Action', *The Modern Quarterly*, new series, Vol. 1 No. 1, December 1945, pp. 44–59.
45 Ibid., pp. 53–54. Quoted in George Orwell, 'Editorial', *Polemic*, No. 3, May 1946. Reprinted in CW 18, p. 264. Orwell inserted a '(sic)' after the third sentence and italicised the final clause of the last sentence.
46 Orwell, Ibid., p. 264.
47 Ibid., p. 267.
48 Ibid., p. 264.
49 Ibid., p. 264.
50 Orwell, 'The Prevention of Literature', p. 378.
51 See George Orwell, 'Inside the Whale' in *Inside the Whale and Other Essays* (London: Gollancz, 1940). Reprinted in CW 12, p. 108.

52 Arthur Calder-Marshall, 'The Film Industry' in C. Day Lewis (ed.), *The Mind in Chains: Socialism and the Cultural Revolution* (London: Frederick Muller, 1937), p. 64.
53 See George Orwell and Desmond Hawkins, 'The Proletarian Writer', *The Listener*, 19 December 1940. Reprinted in CW 12, p. 297.
54 Irving Howe, 'The Fiction of Anti-Utopia' in Howe (ed.), Orwell's *Nineteen Eighty-Four*, p. 176.
55 This example is mine, not Howe's.
56 Howe, 'The Fiction of Anti-Utopia', p. 178.
57 George Orwell, *The Road to Wigan Pier* (London: Penguin, 2001 [1937]), p. 189.
58 See John Strachey, *The Coming Struggle for Power*, p. 206f.
59 See Maxim Gorky, Karl Radek, Nikolai Bukharin, A.A. Zhdanov et al, *Soviet Writers' Congress 1934: The Debate on Socialist Realism and Modernism in the Soviet Union* (London: Lawrence and Wishart, 1977).
60 For the history of the socialist novel in Britain, see, inter alia, David Smith, *Socialist Propaganda in the Twentieth-Century British Novel* (London: Macmillan, 1978); H. Gustav Klaus 'Socialist Fiction in the 1930s: Some Preliminary Observations' in John Lucas (ed.), *The 1930s: A Challenge to Orthodoxy*; H. Gustav Klaus (ed.), *The Socialist Novel in Britain: Towards the Recovery of a Tradition* (Sussex: Harvester Press, 1982); Andy Croft, *Red Letter Days: British Fiction in the 1930s* (London: Lawrence and Wishart, 1990).
61 A.A. Zhdanov, 'Soviet Literature – The Richest In Ideas. The Most Advanced Literature' in Gorky, Radek, Bukharin et al, *Soviet Writers' Congress 1934*, p. 21.
62 As is well known, the most distinguished analysis of the role of totalising thought in the socialist novel has been advanced by the Hungarian critic Georg Lukács. See, inter alia, *Writer and Critic and Other Essays* (London: Merlin Press, 1970).
63 Orwell, *Nineteen Eighty-Four*, p. 83.
64 Ibid., p. 276.
65 See, inter alia, Nikolai Bukharin, 'Poetry, Poetics And The Problems Of Poetry In The USSR' in Gorky, Radek, Bukharin et al, *Soviet Writers' Congress 1934*, p. 253f.
66 Orwell, *Nineteen Eighty-Four*, p. 284.
67 Ibid., p. 163.
68 See Bukharin, 'Poetry, Poetics And The Problems Of Poetry In The USSR', p. 196f.
69 Orwell, *Nineteen Eighty-Four*, p. 10. The intensity of Winston's sadistic response is captured not merely by the staccato rhythms of his prose but also by his sudden abandonment of capital letters and his irregular punctuation.
70 Orwell, *Nineteen Eighty-Four*, p. 280.

71 George Orwell, 'Orwell's Statement on *Nineteen Eighty-Four*' in *The Complete Works of George Orwell*, Volume 20: *Our Job Is To Make Life Worth Living 1949–1950* (London: Secker and Warburg, 2002), p. 135.
72 Ibid., p. 134.
73 See Walter Benjamin, 'Unpacking my Library' in *Illuminations* (London: Jonathan Cape, 1970).
74 Orwell, *Nineteen Eighty-Four*, p. 99.
75 Orwell's ideas about the relationship between sexuality and political power were perhaps influenced by the writings of the English anarchist Alex Comfort, whose pioneering book *Barbarism and Sexual Freedom* (1948) appeared while *Nineteen Eighty-Four* was being written. The influence of the English anarchists on Orwell's political thinking, especially his understanding of totalitarianism, needs to be investigated more fully than it has been so far. For an interesting preliminary survey of the matter, see David Goodway, *Anarchist Seeds Beneath the Snow: Left-Libertarian Thought and British Writers from William Morris to Colin Ward* (Liverpool: Liverpool University Press, 2006), Chapter 6.
76 Ibid., p. 140.
77 Ibid., p. 139.
78 See George Orwell, 'Some Thoughts on the Common Toad', *Tribune*, 12 April 1946. Reprinted in CW 12.
79 Orwell, *Nineteen Eighty-Four*, p. 172.
80 Ibid., p. 228.
81 Ibid., p. 229.
82 Ibid., p. 229.
83 Ibid., p. 229.
84 Ibid., p. 230.
85 Raymond Williams, *Orwell* (London: Fontana, 1971), p. 78.
86 Orwell, *Nineteen Eighty-Four*, p. 229.

Appendix 1

1 Jeffrey Meyers assesses the relevance of the Montagu-Chelmsford Report to Orwell's career in Burma in *Orwell: Wintry Conscience of a Generation* (New York: W.W. Norton, 2000) p. 55f.
2 George Orwell, *Burmese Days* (London: Penguin, 2001 [1934]), p. 39.
3 Ibid., p. 4.
4 Ibid., p. 52.
5 There is a growing body of work which critically examines the representation of women in Orwell's writings. See, inter alia, Daphne Patai, *The Orwell Mystique: A Study in Male Ideology* (Amherst: University of Massachusetts Press, 1984); Beatrix Campbell, 'Orwell – Paterfamilias or Big Brother' in Christopher Norris (ed.), *Inside the Myth: Orwell: Views from the Left* (London: Lawrence and Wishart, 1984); Deirdre Beddoe, 'Hindrances and Help-Meets: Women in the Writings of George Orwell' in Norris (ed.), *Inside the*

Myth. For a spirited defence of Orwell against the charge of misogyny, see Christopher Hitchens, *Orwell's Victory* (London: Penguin, 2002), Chapter 6.

6 Orwell, *Burmese Days*, p. 51.

7 There is also a sense in which Orwell's critique of progressive imperialism addresses itself to the structural constraints of the imperial system. When the villagers in Kyauktada attack their imperial overseers after Ellis strikes a young boy across the face with a cane, Flory naturally sides with his own people, even though he defuses the crisis by resorting to comparatively restrained methods of crowd control. Orwell's point is that the division between oppressor and oppressed groups is determined at some deep structural level and cannot be overcome by good intentions alone. See *Burmese Days*, p. 252f.

8 See George Orwell, 'Letter to Eleanor Jacques, 19 October 1932' in *The Complete Works of George Orwell*, Volume 10: *A Kind of Compulsion 1903–1936* (London: Secker and Warburg, 2000), p. 271.

9 George Orwell, *A Clergyman's Daughter* (London: Penguin, 2000 [1935]), p. 11.

10 See Louis Althusser, *Lenin and Philosophy and other Essays* (New York: Monthly Review Press, 1971), p. 178.

11 Orwell, *A Clergyman's Daughter*, p. 106.

12 Ibid., p. 100. The first word of the third title is excised in the original.

13 Orwell, *A Clergyman's Daughter*, p. 292.

14 George Orwell, *Keep the Aspidistra Flying* (London: Penguin, 2000 [1936]), p. 77.

15 Ibid., p. 77.

16 Ibid., p. 198.

17 Walter Pater, *The Renaissance* (Oxford: Oxford University Press, 1998 [1872]), p. xxix.

18 Somewhat improbably, Orwell published the poem under his own name in *The Adelphi* in November 1935. Its title, not reproduced in *Keep the Aspidistra Flying*, is 'St Andrew's Day, 1935'. See CW 10, pp. 402–403.

19 Orwell, *Keep the Aspidistra Flying*, p. 71.

20 Ibid., p. 38.

21 Oscar Wilde, 'The Decay of Lying' in *The Soul of Man under Socialism and Selected Critical Prose* (London: Penguin, 2001), p. 188.

22 Orwell, *Keep the Aspidistra Flying*, p. 257.

23 Jean Baudrillard, 'The Precession of Simulacra' in John Storey (ed.), *Cultural Theory and Popular Culture: A Reader* (Hemel Hempstead: Harvester Wheatsheaf, 1994), p. 365.

24 Roger Scruton, *Thinkers of the New Left* (Harlow: Longman, 1985), p. 129. Rather unfairly, Scruton singles out Beatrice Webb and Tony Benn as his two examples of the upper-class 'radical nuisance'.

25 Orwell, *Keep the Aspidistra Flying*, p. 110.

26 Ibid., p. 97.

27 George Orwell, Review of *The Soul of Man Under Socialism* by Oscar Wilde, *The Observer*, 9 May 1948. Reprinted in *The Complete Works of George Orwell*, Volume 19: *It Is What I Think 1947–1948* (London: Secker and Warburg, 2002), p. 333.
28 Wilde, *The Soul of Man under Socialism and Selected Critical Prose*, p. 137.
29 Ibid., p. 127.
30 George Orwell, *Animal Farm* (London: Penguin, 2000 [1945]), p. 2.
31 Ibid., p. 14.
32 Ibid., p. 31.
33 George Orwell, *Coming Up for Air* (London: Penguin, 2000 [1939]), p. 37.
34 For example, he implies that the English love of privacy was often simply an elaborate cover for domestic inequality, noting how his own mother had been more or less excluded from areas of the house associated with the family business. He also shows that the suspicion of militarism rarely gave rise to anything more substantial than a sullen hostility towards soldiers.
35 George Orwell, *The Lion and the Unicorn: Socialism and the English Genius* (London: Secker and Warburg, 1941). Reprinted in *The Complete Works of George Orwell*, Volume 12: *A Patriot After All 1940–1941*, edited by Peter Davison (London: Secker and Warburg, 2000), p. 409.
36 Orwell, *Coming Up for Air*, p. 37.
37 Ibid., p. 65.
38 Ibid., p. 90.
39 Orwell also touches on the role of popular literature in the lives of Lower Binfield's adults. Describing the reading habits of Bowling's parents, he notes that they both favour newspapers which portray the world in highly sensational terms. For example, Bowling's mother is especially fond of the *News of the World*, on the slightly macabre grounds that it 'had more murders in it' (p. 46). Orwell's point appears to be that material of this sort tends to reinforce the moral sense by inducing a mild form of siege mentality. In creating the impression that the world 'out there' is infinitely wicked, it encourages the inhabitants of villages like Lower Binfield to think of their own locales as havens of moral wisdom which need to be defended. See *Coming Up for Air*, p. 46 and pp. 53–54.
40 Orwell, *Coming Up for Air*, p. 116.
41 Oakeshott famously explored the distinction between 'enterprise associations' and 'civil associations' in *On Human Conduct* (1975). For a useful introduction to this aspect of his work, see Robert Grant, *Oakeshott* (London: The Claridge Press, 1990), Chapter 6.
42 The fact that Orwell generally employed traditional forms did not make him averse to the occasional bout of modernist experimentation. The obvious example is the chapter of *A Clergyman's Daughter* set in Trafalgar Square, which famously pastiches Joyce's *Ulysses*.

Appendix 2

1 Much of the biographical information in this appendix is derived from the following sources:

Phil Baker, 'Marshall, Arthur Calder- (1908–1992)' in *Oxford Dictionary of National Biography* [http://www.oxforddnb.com/view/article/50937].

James M. Borg, 'Lindsay, John (1900–1990)' in *Oxford Dictionary of National Biography* (Oxford: Oxford University Press, 2004) [http://www.oxforddnb.com/view/article/54683].

Ann Brett-Jones, 'Ralph Fox: A Man in His Time', *Bulletin of the Marx Memorial Library*, No. 137, Spring 2003, pp. 27–41.

Alec Brown, *The Fate of the Middle Classes* (London: Gollancz, 1936).

Robert Brown, 'Slater, (Charles) Montagu (1902–1956)' in *Oxford Dictionary of National Biography* [http://www.oxforddnb.com/view/article/74935].

Cressida Connolly, *The Rare and the Beautiful: The Lives of the Garmans* (London: Fourth Estate, 2004).

Andy Croft, 'The Young Men are Moving Together: The Case of Randall Swingler' in John McIlroy, Kevin Morgan and Alan Campbell (eds.), *Party People, Communist Lives: Explorations in Biography* (London: Lawrence and Wishart, 2001).

Andy Croft, *Comrade Heart: A Life of Randall Swingler* (Manchester: Manchester University Press, 2003).

Andy Croft, 'Swingler, Randall Carline (1909–1967)' in *Oxford Dictionary of National Biography* [http://www.oxforddnb.com/view/article/62375].

Maurice Cornforth (ed.), 'A.L. Morton – Portrait of a Marxist Historian' in Maurice Cornforth (ed.), *Rebels and Their Causes: Essays in Honour of A.L. Morton* (London: Lawrence and Wishart, 1978).

Vic Gammon, 'Lloyd, Albert Lancaster (1908–1982)' in *Oxford Dictionary of National Biography* [http://www.oxforddnb.com/view/article/50988].

A.H. Halsey, 'Madge, Charles Henry (1912–1996)' in *Oxford Dictionary of National Biography* [http://www.oxforddnb.com/view/article/57883].

Jeremy Hawthorn, 'Preface' in Ralph Fox, *The Novel and the People* (London: Lawrence and Wishart, 1979).

Charles Hobday, *Edgell Rickword: A Poet at War* (Manchester, Carcanet, 1989).

Claire Harman, 'Rickword, (John) Edgell (1898–1982)' in *Oxford Dictionary of National Biography* [http://www.oxforddnb.com/view/article/40704].

Richard Ingrams, 'Cockburn, (Francis) Claud (1904–1981)' in *Oxford Dictionary of National Biography* [http://www.oxforddnb.com/view/article/30946].

Harvey J. Kaye, *The British Marxist Historians: An Introductory Analysis* (Oxford: Polity, 1984).

Martin Kettle, 'Obituary: Christopher Hill', *The Guardian*, 26 February 2003.

Kevin Morgan, 'Jackson, Thomas Alfred (1879–1955)' in *Oxford Dictionary of National Biography* [http://www.oxforddnb.com/view/article/65941].

Alan Munton and Alan Young, *Seven Writers of the English Left: A Bibliography of Literature and Politics, 1916–1980* (London: Garland Publishing, 1981).
Michael Newman, 'Strachey, (Evelyn) John St Loe (1901–1963)' in *Oxford Dictionary of National Biography* [http://www.oxforddnb.com/view/article/36337].
Robert Olby, 'Bernal, (John) Desmond (1901–1971)' in *Oxford Dictionary of National Biography* [http://www.oxforddnb.com/view/article/30813].
Christopher Pawling, *Christopher Caudwell: Towards a Dialectical Theory of Literature* (New York: St Martin's Press, 1989).
Edwin A. Roberts, *The Anglo-Marxists: A Study in Ideology and Culture* (Oxford: Rowman and Littlefield, 1997).
G.S. Smith, 'Mirsky, Dmitry Svyatopolk (1890–1939)' in *Oxford Dictionary of National Biography* [http://www.oxforddnb.com/view/article/62697].
Robert Sullivan, *Christopher Caudwell* (London: Croom Helm, 1987).
Hugh Thomas, *John Strachey* (London: Eyre Methuen, 1973).
G.J. Warnock, 'Warner, Reginald Ernest [Rex] (1905–1986)' in *Oxford Dictionary of National Biography* [http://www.oxforddnb.com/view/article/39846].
Alick West, *One Man in his Time: An Autobiography* (London: George Allen and Unwin, 1969).

INDEX